The Medieval Hero on Screen

The Medieval Hero on Screen

Representations from Beowulf to Buffy

Edited by MARTHA W. DRIVER
and SID RAY

with a foreword by
Jonathan Rosenbaum

McFarland & Company, Inc., Publishers
Jefferson, North Carolina, and London

LIBRARY OF CONGRESS CATALOGUING-IN-PUBLICATION DATA

The medieval hero on screen : representations from Beowulf to
   Buffy / edited by Martha W. Driver and Sid Ray ; with a
   foreword by Jonathan Rosenbaum.
       p.   cm.
   Includes bibliographical references and index.

   ISBN-13: 978-0-7864-1926-5
   softcover : 50# alkaline paper ∞

   1. Heroes in motion pictures.   2. Middle Ages in motion
pictures.   3. Literature, Medieval—History and criticism.
I. Driver, Martha W. II. Ray, Sid, 1966–
PN1995.9.H44M44   2004
791.43'652—dc22   2004014708

British Library cataloguing data are available

Cover image: Viggo Mortensen in *The Two Towers* (2002)

Manufactured in the United States of America

McFarland & Company, Inc., Publishers
   Box 611, Jefferson, North Carolina 28640
   www.mcfarlandpub.com

Acknowledgments

This collection of essays, as any, is indebted to the hard work of its contributors. We would like to thank the authors featured here, all of whom were a joy to work with. We are especially grateful to Kevin J. Harty and Jonathan Rosenbaum whose advice, insight, and generosity went beyond what we asked of them. Others who contributed to the completion of the book are Gill Kent, our copy-editor, and our student assistants at Pace University, Elona Pira who helped with the initial research, and Eileen Brumitt who helped with the proofreading. Peter Rollins first encouraged Martha's interest in films on medieval themes and remains an inspiration. We thank Pace University for providing released time for each of us to focus on this project and the Faculty Resource Network sponsored by New York University which enabled Sid to complete her part of the research. Most important, we thank our families for their unstinting love and support.

M.W.D
S.R.

Table of Contents

Foreword

Jonathan Rosenbaum

It is a curious fact, at least to me, that I am writing a foreword to this book, even a short one. I'm neither a medievalist nor a historian; I have not seen many of the films discussed, and, perhaps because I spend much of my time reviewing films for a weekly newspaper, the *Chicago Reader*, I *have* seen but have mainly forgotten some of the others. As a professional film critic who occasionally gets invited to speak and teach at college campuses, I have the benefit of both close and long-range views of film history, and try to create some two-way traffic between these positions in my writing.

It has always been a handicap for film scholars that one cannot necessarily count on all the important works being accessible or even widely known. In the essays that follow, some of my favorite films with medieval themes and settings have been only briefly touched upon—I am thinking especially of Carl Dreyer's *The Passion of Joan of Arc* and Eric Rohmer's *Perceval*—while others, including Fritz Lang's magnificent two-part, five-hour *Die Nibelungen* (1924), and *Les visiteurs du soir* (1942), a haunting fantasy written by Jacques Prévert and Pierre Laroche and directed by Marcel Carné during the French Occupation, are not mentioned. (I realize that *Les visiteurs du soir* has been relatively scarce in the United States in recent years—unlike *Die Nibelungen*, a beautiful restoration of which is now available on DVD from Kino Video).

I am, however, grateful to Martha Driver, one of this book's coeditors, for giving some respectable attention to Robert Bresson's remarkable (if eccentric) *Lancelot of the Lake* even if I disagree with her translation of "écriture"—an admittedly difficult and ambiguous term to render in English—in her introduction to the first section. When Bresson declared, "Le cinéma n'est pas un spectacle, c'est un écriture," I believe he meant something close to "The cinema is not a spectacle, it is a form of writing"—meaning, in effect, a form of expression that is as personal as a signature yet also as objectively material as a block of text (which may or may not be a document).

This is not to say that the cinema is not a document, regardless of what Bresson meant or did not mean; all the essays in this book testify to the fact that it is. But cinema is also an art, and the fact that it traces something (and is therefore an artistic act) and also leaves a trace (which makes it a historical artefact) helps to explain why writing about it becomes such a complicated business. Most complicated of all is the fact that the historical trace left by a film has an artistic inflection—which doesn't necessarily mean that its makers have artistic sensibilities (personally, I entertain some doubts about Luc Besson, based on past experience, which is one reason why I have avoided seeing his *The Messenger: The Story of Joan of Arc*), only that its effects on viewers always have an artistic dimension.

In one way or another, I would contend that all the contributors to this volume are grappling with this complexity in different ways, even if the art that they have in mind is more often the art of history than it is the art of cinema. And some of the most interesting essays here are historical even when they take up medievalism to speak about the present rather than the past. I am thinking especially of Anke Bernau's revealing observations on the subject of medieval virginity, Tom Henthorne on *Star Wars* and *E.T.: The Extra-Terrestrial*, and Carl Grindley's reflections on medieval weaponry, all of which have many pertinent and timely things to say about the world we are living in. And other pieces here, including Kevin J. Harty's analysis of the various film versions of a Damon Runyon's "Little Miss Marker," are surely swimming in the same water. This makes them political and aesthetic acts in which medievalism becomes a way of decoding both the present and the recent past, much as Orientalism was for the late Edward Said.

The passages in this collection that I am more prone to differ with are those that strike me as insufficiently attuned to film history, despite their fidelity to other kinds of history. Henthorne is astute when he details all the popular boys' adventure stories that got worked into *Star Wars*, but he leaves out the imitations of specific shots from Leni Riefenstahl's epic Nazi spectacle *The Triumph of the Will* and diverse World War II air battles from Hollywood features of the early 40s, both of which were used by George Lucas in creating his own storyboards. I am even more bothered by Edward Benson's allusion to "the surviving print of Dreyer's *Passion*"—which implies that the film's original version is lost (in fact, it was rediscovered in a Norwegian mental asylum in the 1980s, and is currently available in excellent editions on video and DVD) simply because it differs from the published screenplay—and to his supposition in the same essay that Jacques Rivette would have let an interest in "luring adolescent male viewers to repeat showings" of his Joan the Maid determine the nature of Sandrine Bonnaire's haircut in that two-part film. Neither of these objections, however, invalidates or even challenges Benson's important understanding of the Maid—a valuable interpretation of the historical record which also affects my readings of the Dreyer and Rivette films—but in both cases I think the artists have perhaps been undervalued, at least where their art is concerned.

I should finally add that the subject of the medieval in film is so immense that even a comprehensive collection like this one cannot expect to do much more than broach some of the more pertinent topics and approaches. If I were to make a list of all the films that taught me something about medievalism, I would undoubtedly have to include even John Ford's classic 1956 Western *The Searchers*—not so much for its sexual politics (though these are surely relevant) as for its handling of narrative time and duration, in particular the change of seasons, in relation to its epic quest. But, then again, it is an important part of the value of a book of this kind to expand and deepen our grasp of the subject from the anecdotal to the cosmic, broadening our horizons in the process, and this is a task that the editors and their contributors have accomplished with imagination, scholarship, and discernment.

Preface: Hollywood Knights

MARTHA W. DRIVER *and* SID RAY

"I'll never get a chance to meet Robin Hood again."
"Oh stop moaning. He's obviously a dangerous man. Unbalanced,
if you ask me, giving away what isn't even his."
"That's what Robin Hood always did. Even I know that."
"Oh, of course. You know it all."
"He was one of my heroes."
"Heroes? Heroes? What do they know about a day's work?"
—Time Bandits

The Middle Ages has always been a "site of heroic fantasy," producing a wide range of heroic character types who quest and battle for various causes.[1] Many of these types have been reproduced, augmented, and subverted in medieval film, a genre comprised of films with medieval themes, stories, or characters that can include, besides films set in the Middle Ages, spaghetti westerns, science fiction movies, neogothic films, and even Hong Kong action cinema. The rich variety of films falling into the medieval category suggests that the films' heroes, like those from medieval literature, present a dynamic and valuable field of study.

The anachronism of medieval film alone has much to teach us about how we see the Middle Ages and how our understanding of it is mediated by the culture we inhabit. As Terry Gilliam implies in his medieval film, *Time Bandits* (1981), the medieval hero is a romantic construct that is often at odds with the beliefs and values of mass audiences in late twentieth-century America.[2] The hero as conceived in postmodern America usually bears little resemblance to a medieval knight with his storied *nobilitas, genealogie,* or *gentilesse.* In medieval film, we are more

5

likely to encounter a medievalized Marlboro Man than a faithful representation of the Pearl Poet's Sir Gawain, for example, whose idea of a day's work is vastly different from the work ethic promoted in modern-day America. Gilliam's film about time travel from the twentieth century to the classical and medieval worlds is a fitting allegory for the creation of the medieval film genre itself, which allows people to travel back in time to a distant and fantastic world that, for reasons we theorize in this collection, is attractive, comforting, even seductive to modern mass audiences. For, in order to appeal to a contemporary audience, film must reinvent the Middle Ages and create in the medieval hero a hodgepodge of traits derived from a mixed understanding of what is medieval and of traits we value in the heroes of postmillennial Western culture.

The idea of the hero in Western culture has been shaped by many forces: by characters of classical, medieval, and modern literature; by personality types categorized by psychoanalysts Otto Rank and Carl Jung; by the thousand faces identified by Joseph Campbell; by female heroics brought to light by the women's movement; by images of soldiers in battle; and even by firefighters at the collapsing World Trade Towers. These types and images overlap, creating layer upon layer of heroic identities for filmmakers to present.

The essays in this book explore the ways in which filmic representations of medieval heroes differ from historical and literary ones and theorize the reasons for and meaning of those differences. They address the value of teaching such films and of studying enduring symbols of the heroic as represented in these films not only as a way of getting the attention of students who might not immediately be drawn to medieval subjects but also as a way of learning how our culture perceives and pays homage to cultures of the past.

By addressing a range of filmic texts—not simply films about King Arthur, for example, or Joan of Arc or Robin Hood—this collection discusses films that explore the Middle Ages from a number of directions, including those with medieval settings derived from medieval intertexts, or those that are simply based on medieval themes or even on false assumptions about medieval history, costume, character, and narrative. The book's aim, however, is not to define one representative or monolithic medieval film hero, who does not of course exist, but to examine the nuances of the hero's various images—chivalric knight, swashbuckling bandit, martyred saint, benevolent sorcerer, colonial Celtic rebel, the fastest sword in the West (or East), horseless Grail-seeker, warrior princess, alpha male in tights, to name just a few popular representations. We further explore whether the ideologies informing these characters are serious or parodic, realistic or surrealistic, drawn from history or the imagination, a process of unmasking that will further reveal our own interest in the heroic and how to define it.

The essays in this collection suggest that medieval film is unique as a storytelling medium in that it can simultaneously tell us about people and culture in the past, in the present, and in the future though of course depicting no era with absolute precision. Medieval film is, after all, a product of medievalism, which, as Kevin J. Harty has noted, "is a continuing process of creating and recreating ideas of the medieval that began almost as soon as the Middle Ages had come to an end." The genre itself is like a crystal ball or magical mirror, Harty adds, "in which the present and the future can be studied in light of the past and the past can be reimagined in light of the present and the future."[3] Film brings to its representation of the hero postmodern concepts and contexts and tends to impose those ideas onto the medieval world.

In the stories composed and written down in the Middle Ages, there is no fixed or representative medieval hero either: the characters in the Arthurian legend have their problems; Joan has been variously interpreted; and Robin Hood has his dark side. In the medieval hero on film, scholars, students, and critics, however knowledgeable about medieval literature and history and their intertwined narratives, confront a character who is even more dynamic and shape-shifting than his or her medieval prototype. As this volume suggests, the study of medieval film, which reflects multiple eras and societies at once—the culture of the Middle Ages in Europe, the development (or rise) of medievalism in the nineteenth century, and the culture of consumerist, millennial Europe and America—has its own intellectual rewards. It deepens our understanding of storytelling and the creation of myth; it reveals history's indeterminacy, the importance of informed and nuanced interpretation, and shows film's power to reimagine an era.

The essays in this volume suggest that medieval film is a site where ideology is created. Many medieval films encourage a cult following; hence films as diverse as *Monty Python and the Holy Grail, Conan the Barbarian*, and *The Princess Bride* are viewed over and over again, until the ability to quote them becomes second nature and a means of recognizing a cohort. Epics informed by medieval literature (or its criticism) such as films from the *Star Wars* series and *The Lord of the Rings* trilogy have been among the most lucrative and thus broadly influential of any films. And if *Gone with the Wind* is a medieval film, as Rosemary Welsh has persuasively argued, then medieval film's influence extends very far indeed.[4] Because of its extensive influence and authority, medieval film requires that we read against the grain to identify the sites in which a particular ideology is at work.

The gendering of the medieval hero on film is one of those sites,

Buttercup (Robin Wright) and Westley (Cary Elwes) from *The Princess Bride* (1987).

and the depiction of women has not necessarily become more enlightened since the medieval period. Heroes may be women as well as men, a fact recognized in the Middle Ages; the heroic qualities in women such as Joan of Arc and Christine de Pizan are noted in medieval texts, and the heroic aspects of classical and fictional women have been extolled by authors such as Giovanni Boccaccio and Geoffrey Chaucer. Moreover, while, as Mary Beth Rose writes, "The stress on movement and adventure, on rescue, rule, exploration, and conquest, points to a tradition of heroism as distinctly masculine," there has always been a category for female heroics, which Rose characterizes as "that which privileges not the active confrontation with danger, but the capacity to endure it, to resist and suffer with patience and fortitude, rather than to confront and conquer with strength and wit."[5] Films have depicted female characters as both more heroic and less heroic than the literature and history of the Middle Ages warrant. Nevertheless, female characters are often relegated to the margins in medieval film and in medieval film criticism to date. Through its gendering of heroes, film can reveal just how willing a mass audience is to accept nontraditional gender categories and roles. Further, because medieval film and medieval film criticism tend to privilege the masculine experience, some of the essays in this volume intervene in the masculinist process both by recognizing and reading female heroes and by interpreting the ways in which various forms of femininity and masculinity are encoded as appropriate or inappropriate models of behavior.

Medieval films more often than not feature a male hero and present a range of masculine behaviors. Jacqueline Jenkins claims, in what appears to be an understatement, that "Medieval romances ... have consistently been the site for the working through of contemporary concerns with masculinity."[6] Indeed, reference to the Middle Ages seems to grant films license to present extreme forms of masculinity and to justify, even celebrate, war (which was also, to judge from history, the centerpiece of medieval culture). As Jonathan M. Elukin notes in a 1994 essay, "The recent military action against Iraq was a bonanza for medievalists" as American politicians depicted nations in the Middle East as fiefdoms of the Middle Ages and cast themselves as the crusading agents of democracy.[7] Transported thus from his era, the male medieval hero brings traits to the cinema that reflect the values and behaviors of the times in which he is filmed. *Braveheart* might not have won the Academy award for Best Picture if Mel Gibson's William Wallace had suckled milk from the breasts of a strange woman in order to revive himself as he does in the source text, Blind Harry's *The Wallace*.[8] Then again, Gibson does present Princess Isabella (played by Sophie Marceau) as a hero, albeit a passive one, by making her the vessel for Wallace's future offspring; to do so, Gibson advances her age considerably given that the historical Isabella was only nine years old when Wallace died. Medieval film's appropriation of the Middle Ages to impose what is often a conservative ideology on the present is easily accomplished in depictions of ideal masculinity where whiteness, heterosexuality, youth, strength, and entitlement rule. Nevertheless, the medieval hero, both literary and filmic, has many facets that are sometimes contradictory—nobility, piety, and strength, but also rebelliousness, outlawry, and rakishness.

Issues of gender, periodicity, and appropriation are endemic and central to medieval film. Behavior is codified and ways of thinking are imposed, not only by the films themselves but also by critics of those films. The distance between the medieval period and the cinematic era is vast, allowing ample space for distortion about the medieval idea of history and the classical past. Umberto Eco has written, "The Middle Ages preserved in its way the heritage of the past but not through hibernation, rather through a constant retranslation and reuse; it was an immense work of bricolage, balanced among nostalgia, hope, and despair."[9] Eco's words might apply to "medieval film," a term that in itself sounds like an oxymoron. Medieval film is certainly anachronistic, but we should not dismiss it for being so. As David Williams remarks, "Not only are many medieval stories themselves set in the past, and a past not defined with the archaeological precision of circumstance we now seem to require, but they tend to be non-realistic, to be set in worlds of the mind more often than in muddy streets."[10] Medieval film is a genre that often looks to the future and at the past as we see, for example, in *Star Wars*, a futuristic adventure that is set "a long time ago in a galaxy far away." Ironically, the version of history employed in much of medieval film resembles in many ways the version of history employed in the Middle Ages, before histor*icism* had been invented, when, as Glenn Burgess says, "The study of history was not so much the need to seek the truth about the past as the need to seek truths that would be valid in the present." The study of history, of the past, in the Middle Ages was "to provide moral lessons for the present, and that was its basic function." Historicism began to develop in the mid-eighteenth century, and with it came our present-day understanding of historical inquiry—that history should be considered in its own context by a disinterested eye.[11]

Because medieval film tends to adopt an interpretive and often moralistic approach to telling stories about the past, creating a "Mickey Mouse history" as Mike Wallace calls it, medieval film has, understandably, more difficulty achieving authenticity than medieval literature, which is, after all, a product of its own time.[12] Twice as many filters come between the medieval film narrative and medieval story. Medieval film narrative is not only colored by the context, biases, fantasies, projections and lacunae of the medieval storyteller but also by those of the modern filmmaker and the actors' performances. Added to these mediating factors are those that audience members themselves bring to the cinema. The analyst of medieval film has many levels of mediation to decode.

Fredric Jameson theorizes that the only realism in the postmodern world is our "realizing that, for whatever peculiar reasons, we seem condemned to seek the historical past through our own pop images and stereotypes about that past, which itself remains forever out of reach."[13] Medieval heroes are easily translated into the pop images through which we seek the past, which, in turn, can exert a tyrannical hold over our understanding of the Middle Ages. Because the male hero of medieval film is a role model in a more Manichaean world than that which today's cinematic audiences inhabit, he has the power, for example, to define ideal masculinity and set limits on female agency. He reinforces ideas that the filmmaker feels are worth upholding—class distinctions, heterosexuality, patriarchy, imperialism, eurocentrism, free trade, globalization, nationalism—or, more rarely, alternatives to them.

The essays in this volume begin with the central question of authenticity. Part I, "What's Accuracy Got to Do with It? Historicity and Authenticity in Medieval Film," demonstrates the tendency to bend history to fit a political agenda in medieval film: upholding, for example, a Protestant work ethic and nationalist and corporate interests (an irony

William Wallace (Mel Gibson) defies the English in *Braveheart* (1995).

given the feudal economy and Roman Catholicism of the medieval period), reinforcing traditional hierarchies and gender roles. Put bluntly, the filmmaker's agenda more often than not supports white male heterosexual hegemony. David Salo, an expert in Quenya and Sindarin, languages created by J.R.R. Tolkien, and a language advisor on the set of

The Lord of the Rings, addresses some of these issues. His essay, "Heroism and Alienation through Language in *The Lord of the Rings*," examines the paradox medieval film negotiates as it authenticates fantasy and imposes realism on an invented world. Salo argues that Tolkien's (and director Peter Jackson's) "medievalism" with its illusions of authenticity is in fact strikingly modern; it idealizes not the medieval period but the late nineteenth century when the technological age and its accompanying globalization were about to begin. The created languages spoken by the characters, he argues, set boundaries and create otherness, marking the familiar from the strange, imagining a false past in which there are clear distinctions between good and evil. Here, Salo suggests, medieval film can take us out of our own era and place us in a false but comforting fantasy setting.

William F. Woods explores a very different contextualization of the medieval period in film in his essay "Authenticating Realism in Medieval Film." Examining medieval films that are geared toward "high brow" audiences, Williams posits the existence of a "vital immediacy" that makes certain medieval films feel authentic. Woods argues that medieval films such as *The Return of Martin Guerre*, *The Advocate*, and *Henry V*, which were less lucrative than blockbusters such as *The Fellowship of the Ring* and *The Two Towers*, force audiences to confront their own problems instead of providing relief from them.

Part II, "Kid Crusaders: Heroic Children on Film," explores the ways in which medieval films directed at youthful audiences can impose beliefs on children by offering particular heroes as role models. Medieval films, especially those about knights, dragons, and heroes, are often adopted into children's culture but are not always harmlessly amusing. Henry A. Giroux writes that children's films "possess at least as much cultural authority and legitimacy for teaching specific roles, values, and ideals as more traditional sites of learning such as the public schools, religious institutions, and the family."[14] Kevin J. Harty's essay, "Shirley Temple and the Guys and Dolls of the Round Table," addresses some of these issues. Harty focuses on "medievalized" film versions of Damon Runyon's story "Little Miss Marker" to show how heroic Arthurian tropes help to determine what is suitable conduct for children.

Examining films of the seventies and eighties, Tom Henthorne is concerned about the promotion of reactionary values in medieval films for children. His essay, "Boys to Men: Medievalism and Masculinity in *Star Wars* and *E.T.: The Extra-Terrestrial*," shows how the reading of the chivalric tradition at the end of the nineteenth century provides a basis for a masculine ideal characteristic of the Reagan era. Henthorne argues that the neomedieval science fiction films *Star Wars* and *E.T.* were reactions to the women's liberation movement. The essay further discusses the attempts to appropriate the sense of community idealized in stories of King Arthur by Americans in the latter half of the twentieth century.

Part III, "Iron Maidens: Medieval Female Heroes on Film," focuses on the ways in which medieval film not only prescribes what is the proper, even ideal, femininity for modern mass audiences but also, conversely, how medieval film provides images of women that clash with the history or literature it draws from. Though the medieval woman on film is not usually fierce or warlike, unlike actual medieval women who defended the gates when their husbands were at war or sometimes rode into battle alongside men, she does wield power for what she believes are just causes. The stereotypes imposed from modern cultural ideas are certainly shown on film—a female character might be portrayed as loving and nurturing if she is good, for example, or as predictably deceitful and promiscuous if bad, but she also takes action. Whether there is a medieval context or not, movie audiences have come to expect more from the female characters than utter passivity. Indeed, Peter Jackson's *The Fellowship of the Rings* (2001) has an eye for disrupting gender bias that is lacking in the source written by Tolkien (1954). In the film, Aragorn's female love interest, Arwen, replaces Tolkien's male character, Glorfindel, as the hero of the horse chase that saves Frodo's life. Though women's roles in medieval film remain, for the most part, limited, history provides us with many heroic medieval women. Most notably, Joan of Arc led the troops on the French battlefield; she also fiercely and heroically maintained her faith, virginity, and male attire.

Anke Bernau's essay, "Girls on Film: Medieval Virginity in the Cinema," explores how one of the most central and complex gender identities of the medieval period is treated in modern cinematic representations of Joan of Arc and considers the wider ideological implications of those representations for a twenty-first-century audience. Bernau focuses on how virginity, which is indeterminate, can be perceived as heroic. She examines presentations of powerful virgins on film in the context of the renewed interest in sexual abstinence that has arisen during the last decade.

Examining a different subgenre of medieval film entirely, Diana E. Slampyak's essay, "Chivalric Virtues in Female Form: *Crouching Tiger, Hidden Dragon*'s Wudan Warrior Princess as Medieval Hero," makes a compelling case for reading the heroic women of Ang Lee's *Crouching Tiger, Hidden Dragon* as derived in part from medieval romance. Slampyak's analysis illustrates the intrinsic reciprocity between the English and Chinese battle traditions but suggests that the blending of Western and Eastern narratives allows the film to transcend the rigid conventions of the genres. While English medieval ideas encroach on, even colonize, this Chinese film, the Chinese "woman warrior" inversion of gender roles also subverts the European patriarchal tradition.

Arwen (Liv Tyler) rescues Frodo in *The Fellowship of the Ring* (2001).

Unexpected medieval film heroes are also the topic of Susan Butvin Sainato's essay, "Not Your Typical Knight: The Emerging On-Screen Defender." Tracing a trajectory of characters in medieval films from *Excalibur* to *Shrek*, Sainato focuses on Buffy of *Buffy the Vampire Slayer* as representative of the hero that has emerged from the medieval film tradition. This hero can fight evil, save friends in distress, be an effective leader, and look fashionable and beautiful at the same time. Moreover this hero does her homework, diligently spending time at the library researching the most effective methods to combat her foes.

Part IV, "Time Bandits: Contemporary Appropriations," describes the ways in which medieval film appropriates aspects of the medieval world to create nostalgia for a time when values were perceived to be clear and distinct—when men were men and women were women, when a caste system separated the elite from the masses, when homosexuality was unimaginable as a category, and "when white men ruled."[15]

Carl James Grindley's essay, "The Hagiography of Steel: The Hero's Weapon and Its Place in Pop Culture," focuses on the hero's weaponry, characterizing the relationship between arms and the man and demonstrating how, on film as in literature, fetishization of weaponry validates the hero who wields those weapons. Using the example of Dirty Harry whom he regards as similar to Anglo-Saxon characters such as the

Wanderer, the Seafarer, and Beowulf, Grindley suggests that weaponry is a vehicle for refiguring medieval tropes to accommodate modern ideology.

Also considering the issue of appropriation is Michael A. Torre-grossa's essay, "The Way of the Wizard: Reflections of Merlin on Film," which explores how the figure of Merlin from the Arthurian legend has been adopted by filmmakers depicting wizards from a variety of traditions, an appropriation that suggests Merlin's archetypal quality and the privileging of the wizened, male teacher-guide in European and American culture.

Culminating this section is Caroline Jewers' essay, "Hard Day's Knights: *First Knight, A Knight's Tale,* and *Black Knight,*" which considers the political aspects of three Knight's Tales on film and the nature of their dialogue with the literary past and, more specifically, how these recent films become vehicles for scripting contemporary values about race, gender, class, global expansionism, and democracy.

Cultural critic bell hooks believes that "even though most folks will say that they go to the movies to be entertained, if the truth be told lots of us ... go to the movies to learn stuff."[16] With this in mind, the collection concludes with Part V, "'Stond and Delyver': Teaching the Medieval Movie," a pedagogical primer on medieval film and its uses in the classroom not only to help students visualize a medieval narrative, but also, perversely, to illustrate the medieval world by showing what it is not. Film has become an indispensable classroom tool partly because, as Giroux puts it, film is "useful as a resource to offset dominant textbook ideologies and invaluable as a pedagogical tool to challenge officially sanctioned knowledge and modes of learning."[17] Yet film obviously brings its own ideological contents to the classroom.

Edward Benson's essay, "Oh, What a Lovely War! Joan of Arc on Screen," reviews the four most well-known films about Joan of Arc to illustrate the anomalies and contradictions enacted in her story and to instruct us on the ways in which filmmakers encode their cultural/historical fears and fantasies within feature films.

In his essay, "The Hero in the Classroom," John M. Ganim reports from his own teaching experiences. Ganim assesses how the self-conscious interpretation and reformulation of medieval themes in film results in a sometimes self-deluding and sometimes revelatory dialogue with modernity. Benson's and Ganim's essays on teaching medieval film remind us that using film in the classroom has obvious benefits but also hidden dangers. To paraphrase Laurie E. Osborne, we must be careful "to address film form and convey how it enables analyses of contemporary film ideologies as well as the uses to which [the Middle Ages] has been put."[18] In short, we need to attend to the culture of filmmaking as much as to the medieval culture or ideologies the film depicts.

Collectively, these essays present medieval film as both a comple-ment to the study of the medieval period and as a field worth studying on its own. Moreover, they demonstrate that medieval film is fertile ground for a range of critical approaches—from formalism and histori-cism to feminism, post-structuralism and cultural studies. Indeed, medieval film allows us to apply our ways of reading to extraliterary ele-ments—not only to the sound, color, angle, acting, spectatorship, and editing of cinema but also to the subject of historical revisionism. Most importantly, perhaps, in considering such "high" art films as *The Return of Martin Guerre,* which garner an abundance of intellectual capital, and those created to appeal to a mass audience, mostly children, such as *Harry Potter and the Sorcerer's Stone,* which are sometimes vehicles for the promotion of conservative ideology, the essays in this volume under-score the importance and value of studying a rich variety of cultural rep-resentations, which can reveal much about earlier cultures and more about perceptions of our own.

Notes

1. Susan Aronstein and Nancy Coiner, "Twice-Knightly: Democratizing the Middle Ages for Middle-Class America." *Medievalism in North America,* ed. Kath-leen Verduin (Cambridge: D.S. Brewer, 1994), p. 213.

2. *Time Bandits,* directed by Terry Gilliam (Great Britain: Handmade Films, 1981), looks at the idea of the hero in history from a nihilist perspective and makes fun of everyone from Alexander the Great (played by Sean Connery) to Robin Hood (John Cleese).

3. Kevin Harty, "Introduction," *The Reel Middle Ages: American, Western and Eastern European, Middle Eastern, and Asian Films about Medieval Europe* (Jefferson, NC: McFarland, 1999), p. 3.

4. See Rosemary Welsh, "Theorizing Medievalism: The Case of *Gone with the Wind," Medievalism in the Modern World: Essays in Honour of Leslie J. Work-man,* ed. Richard Utz and Tom Shippey (Turnhout: Brepols, 1998).

5. Mary Beth Rose, *Gender and Heroism in Early Modern English Literature* (Chicago: The University of Chicago Press, 2002), pp. xi–xii.

6. Jacqueline Jenkins, "First Knights and Common Men: Masculinity in American Arthurian Film," *King Arthur on Film: New Essays on Arthurian Cin-ema,* ed. Kevin Harty (Jefferson, NC: McFarland, 1999), p. 81.

7. Jonathan M. Elukin, "Medieval Language and Politics: Making the World Safe for Feudalism," *Medievalism in North America,* ed. Kathleen Verduin (Cam-bridge: D.S. Brewer, 1994), p. 232.

8. See Blind Harry, *The Wallace,* in *Scottish Literature: An Anthology,* Vol. 1, ed. David McCordick (New York: Peter Lang, 1996), p. 154.

9. Umberto Eco, "The Return of the Middle Ages," *Travels in Hyperreality,* tr. William Weaver (San Diego: Harcourt Brace Jovanovich, 1986), pp. 84–85.

10. David J. Williams, "Medieval Movies," *Yearbook of English Studies* 20 (1990): 19.

11. Glenn Burgess, *The Politics of the Ancient Constitution: An Introduction to English Political Thought, 1603–1642* (Philadelphia: University of Pennsylvania Press, 1992), pp. 8–9.

12. Mike Wallace, "Mickey Mouse History: Portraying the Past at Disney World," *Radical History Review* 32 (1985).

13. Fredric Jameson, "Postmodernism and Consumer Society." *Movies and Mass Culture*, ed. John Belton (New Brunswick, NJ: Rutgers University Press, 1996), p. 194.

14. Henry A. Giroux, *Breaking in to the Movies: Film and the Culture of Politics* (Malden, MA: Blackwell Publishers, 2002), p. 100.

15. Bruce Smith writes that "to distinguish 'homosexual' men from 'heterosexual' men is, then, a distinctively twentieth-century way of constructing sexuality.... Homosexual behavior may be a cross-cultural phenomenon; homosexuality is specific to our own culture and to our own moment in history," *Homosexual Desire in Shakespeare's England: A Cultural Poetics* (Chicago: University of Chicago Press, 1991), p. 12.

16. bell hooks, *Reel to Real: Race, Sex, and Class at the Movies* (New York: Routledge, 1996), p. 2.

17. Giroux, p. 4.

18. Laurie E. Osborne, "Clip Art: Theorizing the Shakespeare Film Clip." *Shakespeare Quarterly* 53.2 (2002): 240.

Works Cited

Aronstein, Susan, and Nancy Coiner. "Twice-Knightly: Democratizing the Middle Ages for Middle-Class America." In *Medievalism in North America*, ed. Kathleen Verduin. Cambridge, U.K.: D.S. Brewer, 1994.

Blind Harry. *The Wallace*. In *Scottish Literature: An Anthology*, Vol. 1, ed. David McCordick. New York: Peter Lang, 1996.

Burgess, Glenn. *The Politics of the Ancient Constitution: An Introduction to English Political Thought, 1603–1642*. Philadelphia: University of Pennsylvania Press, 1992.

Eco, Umberto. *Travels in Hyperreality*, tr. William Weaver. San Diego, CA: Harcourt Brace Jovanovich, 1986.

Elukin, Jonathan M. "Medieval Language and Politics: Making the World Safe for Feudalism." In *Medievalism in North America*, ed. Kathleen Verduin. Cambridge, U.K.: D.S. Brewer, 1994.

Giroux, Henry A. *Breaking in to the Movies: Film and the Culture of Politics*. Maldon, MA: Blackwell, 2002.

Harty, Kevin J. "Introduction." In *The Reel Middle Ages: American, Western and Eastern European, Middle Eastern, and Asian Films about Medieval Europe*, ed. Kevin J. Harty. Jefferson, NC: McFarland, 1999.

hooks, bell. *Reel to Real: Race, Sex, and Class at the Movies*. New York: Routledge, 1996.

Jameson, Fredric. "Postmodernism and Consumer Society." In *Movies and Mass Culture*, ed. John Belton. New Brunswick, NJ: Rutgers University Press, 1996.

Jenkins, Jacqueline. "First Knights and Common Men: Masculinity in American Arthurian Film." In *King Arthur on Film: New Essays on Arthurian Cinema*, ed. Kevin J. Harty. Jefferson, NC: McFarland, 1999.

Osborne, Laurie E. "Clip Art: Theorizing the Shakespeare Film Clip." *Shakespeare Quarterly* 53.2 (2002).

Rose, Mary Beth. *Gender and Heroism in Early Modern English Literature*. Chicago: The University of Chicago Press, 2002.

Smith, Bruce. *Homosexual Desire in Shakespeare's England: A Cultural Poetics*. Chicago: University of Chicago Press, 1991.

Wallace, Mike. "Mickey Mouse History: Portraying the Past at Disney World." *Radical History Review* 32 (1985).

Welsh, Rosemary. "Theorizing Medievalism: The Case of *Gone with the Wind*." In *Medievalism in the Modern World: Essays in Honour of Leslie J. Workman*, ed. Richard Utz and Tom Shippey. Turnhout: Brepols, 1998.

Williams, David J. "Medieval Movies." *Yearbook of English Studies* 20 (1990).

Filmography

1939 *Gone with the Wind*, d. Victor Fleming, with Clark Gable, Vivien Leigh. U.S.: Warner Studios.

1975 *Monty Python and the Holy Grail*, d. Terry Jones and Terry Gilliam, with Terry Jones, Terry Gilliam, Graham Chapman, John Cleese, Eric Idle, Michael Palin. U.K.: Python (Monty) Pictures.

1977 *Star Wars*, d. George Lucas, with Mark Hamill, Harrison Ford, Carrie Fisher. U.S.: Twentieth Century–Fox.

1981 *Time Bandits*, d. Terry Gilliam, with Sean Connery, Shelley Duvall, Ralph Richardson. U.K.: Handmade Films.

1982 *Conan the Barbarian*, d. John Milius, with Arnold Schwarzenegger. U.S.: Universal.

1987 *The Princess Bride*, d. Rob Reiner, with Cary Elwes, Robin Wright, Mandy Patinkin. U.S.: MGM/United Artists.

1995 *Braveheart*, d. Mel Gibson, with Mel Gibson. U.S.: Icon Productions, Ladd, Twentieth Century–Fox.

2001 *Harry Potter and the Sorcerer's Stone*, d. Chris Columbus, with Daniel Radcliffe. U.S.: Warner Bros.

2001 *The Lord of the Rings: The Fellowship of the Ring*, d. Peter Jackson, with Elijah Wood, Ian McKellen, Viggo Mortensen, Cate Blanchett. U.S.: New Line Productions.

2002 *The Lord of the Rings: The Two Towers*, d. Peter Jackson, with Elijah Wood, Ian McKellen, Viggo Mortensen, Cate Blanchett. U.S.: New Line Productions.

I

What's Accuracy Got to Do with It?

Historicity and Authenticity in Medieval Film

Martha W. Driver

"Le cinéma n'est pas un spectacle, c'est une écriture."[1]

Writing about historical film in his 1987 essay on Abel Gance's *Napoleon*, Marc Ferro asks the compelling question: "Where does the truth lie in all this history?" Ferro provides this provocative answer:

> With distance, one version of history replaces another but the work of art remains. And so, with the passage of time, our memory winds up by not distinguishing between, on the one hand, the imaginative memory of Eisenstein or Gance, and on the other, history such as it really happened, even though historians seek to make us understand and artists seek to make us participate.[2]

As Ferro suggests and we know from our own experience, film provides immediacy and simultaneously appeals to the imagination, engaging the viewer in the past and involving him emotionally and imaginatively in the action on screen. Film is a central part of our entertainment culture that involves a range of people, often including our students, in formal and informal dialogues about moral and social issues. With film in particular, one is generally conscious (if one is watching consciously) of intentional and unintentional anachronism, and the imposing of contemporary social or political values on the past. This might disturb the teacher of history or literature who hopes for more realistic or truer representation, for documentary rather than fantasy. Openness to a variety of representations, however, whether of medieval works of art or of moments in medieval history or of stories popular in the Middle Ages, can freshen our historical perspectives, awakening us as well to the cultural attitudes and agendas underpinning those interpretations. In other words, movies are multivalenced, telling us simultaneously about the distant past and about more recent events and social attitudes.

To characterize the fluid content of medieval texts, the critic Paul Zumthor uses the term "mouvance." The term means alive, "moving," unfixed. Zumthor has described medieval literature as "a sequence of productions."[3] Like the retellings of the Robin Hood legend or the King Arthur stories on film, medieval texts are multivalenced and often open-ended, the same stories told and retold across time, in many cultures and in many languages. Medieval literature, chronicles, and art can further be said, again like film, to be collaboratively produced. Medieval authors like Geoffrey of Monmouth, Chaucer, and Giovanni Boccaccio draw on rich sources of folktale and earlier narrative to tell their stories. The expertise revealed in the telling of old tales, technical acumen, and the display of rhetorical skill were more valued in medieval culture than originality.

The tendency to recast an older story in light of current tastes or to address contemporary issues under the guise of historical representation is not, in fact, new. When examining the illuminated pages of a medieval Book of Hours, for example, de luxe manuscripts produced for wealthy patrons, we notice both realistic details and idealized elements. Buildings and implements, for instance, are often realistically rendered while in the farming scenes that illustrate the calendar portions of these texts, the costumes of the peasants are brightly colored, the women's aprons crisply white and clean. Their hands and faces, no matter the task at hand, whether slaughtering or grape-picking, appear freshly washed. Such pictures were, of course, painted for the pleasure of the books' aristocratic owners. The images are charming and sanitized, similar to the scrubbed version of historical films produced in Hollywood in the 1940s and 1950s. Conventions of representation, readily recognizable iconography, and reaffirmations of social stereotypes were apparently as popular in the calendar pages of Books of Hours as they are later on film, types of visual shorthand promoting idealized scenes of daily life.

Compare, for example, the sweeping (and immaculate) stage sets of Sir Laurence Olivier's 1944 film of *Henry V* with the muddy outdoor footage of Kenneth Branagh's 1989 version. Olivier's film gives an idealized heroic account of the Battle of Agincourt, while Branagh's vision is more gruesome, violent, and to us, realistic, reflecting another stereotype that the Middle Ages were "dark, dirty, violent ... unstable or threatening."[4] Just as our perceptions of realism, of history, in medieval art are shaped by visual conventions, so too with films. As film critic Jonathan Rosenbaum commented to me some years ago, "It doesn't matter if the historical details of the film are authentic. They just have to look authentic to the audience."[5] Authenticity is a convention of costume drama, part of the visual language in the re-creation of history on screen, and a starting point for the recovery of the true historical elements underlying the fiction, if one wishes to explore them. Discussing film, the director Robert Bresson rather enigmatically suggested that "Le cinéma n'est pas un spectacle, c'est une écriture" (Cinema is not a spectacle, it is a document). His *Lancelot du Lac* (1974) creates a powerful modern version of the Arthur story, the timely emphasis on warfare and bloodshed presenting "war as anonymous and indifferent slaughter, with faceless phantoms in the darkness battling and perishing beneath heavy armor that instantly turns into scrap metal as soon as the bodies become mute."[6] As Bresson suggests, film can stand as a kind of history alongside the writing of professional historians, giving us glimpses into the past, which is otherwise only available through texts, documents, and artifacts. Film provides an imaginative immediacy and reality, a luminous world we physically enter by watching and listening. Film, in fact, is an important scholarly medium, revealing not only historical aspects of the Middle Ages but perceptions of the Middle Ages in various times and places, and also in popular culture, a theme that will reappear in some form in all of the essays in this volume.

David John Williams has further pointed out, "The cinematic Middle Ages represents the way many people really think of that part of their history,"[7] an idea that may be reassuring to some though alarming to others. The greatest films with medieval themes may draw effectively from the historical record, *The Return of Martin Guerre* (1982), for example, or from a classic work of literature as is the case with Eric Rohmer's *Perceval le Gallois* (1978).[8] The two essays in this opening section discuss the ways in which a range of medieval story elements have found their way into twentieth-century film. In an important and persuasive essay, "Heroism and Alienation through Language in *The Lord of the Rings*," David Salo, linguistic advisor to the recent *Lord of the Rings* film trilogy directed by Peter Jackson, looks at the careful reconstruction of J.R.R. Tolkien's medieval fantasy world, even to the making and speaking of Tolkien's several invented languages as markers of gender, race, and class. William F. Woods further examines questions of authenticity and history in his essay "Authenticating Realism in Medieval Film," drawing his examples from a range of films including *The Seventh Seal* (1957), *Excalibur* (1981), *The Return of Martin Guerre*, *The Name of the Rose* (1986), *Braveheart* (1995), and *The Advocate* (*L'Heure de Cochon*, 1994). Both essays demonstrate that appearances of authenticity draw audiences into film and that film itself is interpretative, just as scholarship, history, and primary sources themselves are interpretative.

Notes

1. Robert Bresson, quoted by Jonathan Rosenbaum, "The Battle of Armor, the Softness of Flesh: Bresson's *Lancelot du Lac*," *Movies as Politics* (Berkeley: University of California Press, 1997), p. 202.

2. Marc Ferro, *Cinema and History*, tr. Naomi Green (Detroit: Wayne State University Press, 1988), p. 73.

3. Paul Zumthor, *Essai de Poétique médiévale* (Paris: Editions du Seuil, 1972), pp. 74–81.

4. David John Williams, "Medieval Movies," *Yearbook of English Studies* 20 (1990): 10. For more on the Olivier version, made during World War II and "dedicated to the commando and airborne troops of Great Britain," see Sue Harper, *Picturing the Past: The Rise and Fall of British Costume Film* (London: British Film Institute, 1994), p. 86ff.

5. Conversation with Jonathan Rosenbaum, author, film critic and reviewer for the *Chicago Reader*, also cited in my introduction to *Film & History. Special Focus: Medieval Period on Film*, vol. 29, 1–2 (1999): 7.

6. Rosenbaum, "The Battle of Armor, the Softness of Flesh: Bresson's *Lancelot du Lac*," pp. 204–205.

7. David John Williams, "Looking at the Middle Ages in the Cinema: an Overview," *Film & History. Special Focus: Medieval Period on Film*, vol. 29, 1–2 (1999): 9.

8. Rohmer's *Perceval* shares a painterly sensibility with *The Lady and the Duke*, directed by Rohmer in 2002. The latter is set during the French Revolution and drawn directly from the diary of an aristocratic eyewitness, Grace Elliott, the mistress and later the friend of the Duke of Orleans. Though realism of staging is not central to either effort—*Perceval* was shot entirely on a sound stage, and the *Lady and the Duke* utilizes sets painted on canvas—both films give the viewer the sense of being a fly on the wall, present at each crucial scene.

Heroism and Alienation through Language in *The Lord of the Rings*

DAVID SALO

In December 2001 the first installment of director Peter Jackson's film adaptation of J.R.R. Tolkien's *The Lord of the Rings* was released. The film prompted a blizzard of critiques by fans of and (self-proclaimed) experts on Tolkien's writings. Much of their critique does not concern itself with the film's acting, direction, or plot but rather with the appearance of *authenticity* and what one can only call, for lack of a better term, *historicity*. Many fans of Tolkien's works possess a sense of some authentic essence in Tolkien's works, one tangible enough that they can sense deviations from this authenticity.

Tolkien has created so effective a simulacrum of a historic era that readers of the book and watchers of the film can believe themselves able to picture the correct costume, armor and weaponry, architecture, social customs, and languages of the various tribes and cultures of his Middle-earth. The verisimilitude of the effect becomes more comprehensible when it is seen that Tolkien's Middle-earth is firmly rooted in the history of our own world through countless allusions, both overt and covert.

The notion of a recreation of a fantasy world having historical authenticity poses a paradox. That which is "fantastic" may be considered to be in itself imaginary, unreal, pretended, false—in a word, *inauthentic*, implying valuelessness and fraud. To be truly inauthentic there must be a betrayal of an original authenticity, and such betrayal cannot exist where no authenticity is found; a forgery cannot itself be forged.

The word *historical* also seems like the antithesis of fantasy; although fantasy books and films can be set, like other works of fiction, in credible facsimiles of what we call "the real world," those characteristics that set fantasy apart are just those things that make it fundamentally ahistorical. The actual manifestation in our world of fantastic elements such as magic, nonhuman intelligences, and power on a superhuman scale would reshape history in such a way as to make it unrecognizable, marking the end of history as we know it. Recognizing this, most creators of fantasy take their works completely out of history, setting them in the unknowably distant (and therefore mythical) past, the unimaginably strange and unpredictable future, or an entirely other universe.

A fantasist is therefore obliged to create a credible simulacrum of a real history so consistent in itself that anomalous details can be detected and deemed *inauthentic*. Such simulacra, with a wealth of consistent detail, are found in the works of Tolkien as well as in their representation on film by Peter Jackson. Tolkien has invented an imaginary prehistoric time period with so little connection to our own world that it effectively becomes a parallel universe.[1] This universe, recreated with much additional detail in the film adaptation, has—within certain spatial and temporal bounds—a uniquely conceived geography, history, chronography, mythical literature, and of course languages. It remains incomplete, as it is hardly possible for a single author or filmmaker to supply all of the convincing detail of a real world; yet both book and film continue to create the effect of a slice of authentic history recorded long ago and now retold.

Tolkien always stated that *The Lord of the Rings* took place in our own world, not on some distant planet; but to explain the differences in geography and language, he suggested that it was set several thousand years BC, before the dawn of recorded history.[2] This is, however, only a convenient fiction that can be disposed of on the basis of our current knowledge of Earth's geological and archaeological prehistory. What we actually perceive in Tolkien's writing is not an attempt to recreate a prehistoric world (of, for instance, the last Ice Age) but rather a mixture—though not a haphazard one—of elements from the ancient, medieval, and early modern worlds. This mixture is faithfully reproduced in Jackson's work: we see on the screen Hobbits in near-modern dress, Riders of Rohan in early medieval armor, cities of Gondor with Byzantine architecture, as well as purely fantastic elements such as the forests of the Elves and caverns of the Orcs.

Though Tolkien was a scholar and student of medieval languages and cultures, his work reflects a thoroughly modern understanding of the past as a fundamentally alien place. Modern historians have stressed the ways in which ancient cultures differed from our own, in dress, language, custom and ways of thought. In Tolkien's work, the alienness of our own past is transformed into the alienness of the strange countries of Middle-earth. Both the alienness and its links to the antecedents of modern culture have now been made visible—and also audible, through language and music—in Jackson's film.

Tolkien called his work a "heroic romance,"[3] comparable perhaps to works like *Beowulf* or Malory's *Le Morte Darthur*, both of which deal with imaginary and mythicized pasts. But the authors of both the Old English epic and the Middle English romance had a "flatter" view of history; the warriors of Heorot and the knights of Camelot are fanciful or idealized portrayals of the authors' contemporaries, using customs, tools, and diction of the same period as their authors. For the medieval author, only the names of people differentiated the ancient world from his own, and distant lands were just slight variations on one's own country.

Tolkien, however, did not attempt to make his invented world seem *immediately* familiar to his twentieth-century readers. He repeatedly uses the device of alienation, that is, the distancing of the subject matter from the commonplace and the familiar, or the construction of the exotic and strange. This can involve, for instance, the depiction or description of unusual incidents; the introduction of novel geography or characters; and the use of exotic language or nomenclature. At every step Tolkien, followed closely by Jackson, has taken pains to distance Middle-earth from his own century: clothing, customs, weapons, language are all as different as he could make them without completely losing intelligibility.

And yet, since Tolkien is dealing with an entirely created world, in order to develop the sense of alienation he must supply readers with a baseline "reality" that has some aspects of familiarity, so that all his world will not appear equally exotic (and therefore equally banal). Tolkien's technique is to wrap familiarity within exoticism, so that the familiar may be rediscovered and appear newly strange against the background of the alien.

Tolkien's "familiar world" is the Shire of the Hobbits. This Shire is an idealized and archaized version of the late-nineteenth-century rural Warwickshire of Tolkien's boyhood.[4] The Hobbits themselves are miniature reflections of the eighteenth-to-nineteenth-century English farmer, but their world has been stripped of all of the more advanced technology of those centuries. There is no electricity and no telegraph; there are no railroads and no guns in the Shire. On the other hand, there are still paper, umbrellas, pony-drawn carriages, a post office, and periodic elections; the Hobbits are not really supposed to live in an ancient or medieval world. Though the contrasts have been somewhat reduced, the Hobbit is still an anachronism dropped into a much more archaic milieu; and as such, he serves as a mediator, facing a strange outside world with much the same sense of alienation as the reader.

This contrast is faithfully reproduced in Jackson's version of the story.

The Hobbits of the movie wear costumes that might be from the rural England of the late nineteenth to early twentieth century. They live in holes and houses that—except for the characteristically Hobbitish features of round windows, doors, and hallways—could easily be English country cottages, while their standard gathering place is that most typical of modern English institutions, the pub. Given the immense changes in the Western world over the past century, these features in the film now appear even more archaic than Tolkien intended them; but the viewer can still feel the sense of alienation of the Hobbits from their surroundings as they travel ever farther from the safe green world of their countryside.

Many aspects of the world beyond the Shire have been borrowed generously from European history. Despite its supposed prehistoric setting, the story takes place in an advanced Iron Age with the weapons and armor of late antiquity or the Middle Ages. The Kingdom of Gondor—the faded remnant of part of a much mightier realm of the earlier Third Age—suggests a kind of decaying Byzantium, weak and threatened but still heir to the civilization of Rome, a suggestion that the film's design team, in creating the architecture of the Gondorian capital city of Minas Tirith, has clearly taken to heart. Reading Tolkien's Appendices confirms this impression; between Gondor and Rome/Byzantium we observe a similar pattern of rise and fall, with a Carthage-like seagoing enemy in the pirate realm of Umbar, Arab-like "Southron" enemies, and repeated waves of "Easterling" invaders suggesting Sarmatians, Huns and Avars.

Peter Jackson has given his films a slightly different focus, perhaps a wise choice given the difficult nature of questions of nationalism and the "clash of civilizations" at the beginning of the twenty-first century. In the film treatments, the human enemies of the kingdoms of Gondor and Rohan have taken second place to the monstrous Orcs and Uruk-hai, creations of the Dark Lord Sauron and the fallen wizard Saruman. Emphasizing the Orcs allows Jackson to portray the struggle in the book as primarily an attack by inhuman forces upon "The World of Men" (a repeated motif in Jackson's *The Two Towers*) rather than one that also involves war and diplomacy between human countries and armies. By doing so, Jackson avoids too-direct parallels between the situation shown in the film and the present-day world, though perhaps at the cost of a subtlety present in Tolkien's work; Tolkien recognizes that even in wars with a "good side" and a "bad side," the deeds of the good will not necessarily be above reproach and even enemies are to be pitied.

Tolkien's awareness of the historic and prehistoric memories of the landscape are reflected in a visit by his protagonists to the ancient Barrow-downs (modelled upon grave-mounds of Bronze Age Britain) as well as the ruins they frequently come across, memories of an older world. Much of the atmosphere of *The Lord of the Rings* (the movie, with its emphasis on visuals, even more than the book) comes from the presence of icons of age. The period of "the end of the Third Age" is not a prefabricated medieval set piece like the nineteenth-century castle of Neuschwanstein but shows evidence of having succeeded a long, if mostly undetailed, past whose scars and remains are everywhere to be seen. The eye rests during its travels upon such memorials of (fictitious) antiquity as the remnants of the watchtower of Amon Sûl or the monumental statue-pillars of Argonath (built as enormous "miniatures" by the film's design team). These memorials are either fallen and ruinous or bear witness to a style and grandeur of architecture that is no longer contemporary with the action of the main story.

The most thoroughgoing and overwhelming effect of an alien world and culture arises, however, from Tolkien's use of language and its effect in Jackson's film. Three different types of innovative language use stand out: Tolkien's manipulation of the English language of the characters to achieve different speech styles that represent the different backgrounds and preoccupations of the characters; the use of names of persons and places to evoke different cultures; and the insertion of particular phrases in Tolkien's invented languages. All three have their counterparts in the film version, some of which cannot be represented well in a book: the use of different accents and intonations by the characters and the insertion of a considerable quantity of subtitled Elvish dialogue.

The first of these requires the least comment, as it is a fairly common device of authors who want to portray characters of different backgrounds. For Tolkien it primarily serves to distinguish the Hobbits from others, with the Hobbits speaking in a colloquial and occasionally "rustic" style, laced with homely proverbs and a familiarity of manner, while the Elves, Dwarves, and men of Gondor and Rohan speak in an elevated, ceremonial style marked by slightly archaic vocabulary or phrasing.[5] The speech of the Orcs (rarely heard) is also different, marked by contempt, anger, and the frequent use of rather tame epithets such as "filth" or "dunghill rat."

In Jackson's film, the writers (Jackson, Fran Walsh, and Philippa Boyens) have largely followed Tolkien in terms of the stylistic differences between the speech of the characters. But language coaches Andrew Jack and Roisín Carty have also been able to distinguish the Hobbits both from each other and from their companions, with the Hobbits speaking a variety of British dialects (Billy Boyd, playing Peregrin Took, using his native Scottish accent), and important figures such as Ian McKellen (Gandalf) and Christopher Lee (Saruman) speaking the best King's English. Cate Blanchett (Galadriel) speaks with an almost excessively perfect and precise pronunciation, which is very appropriate for an Elf who knows the "Common Speech" (represented by English) very well but has little opportunity to use it. Some Orcs have been given an artificial dialect that strikes many viewers as "Cockney."

The use of invented names and phrases in the book is, however, much more pervasive than stylistic differences, and more precise in its delineation of different cultures and stages of development. We start with the familiar: the Shire hosts names of impeccable English origins, many quite intelligible in their meanings, such as Bywater, Whitwell, Overhill, and Rushey; these are, Tolkien says, "devised according to the style, origins, and mode of formation of English (especially Midland) place-names."[6] Tolkien was, of course, writing for an English-speaking audience, and as the associations he evokes are based on speech, not nationality, they remain equally intelligible to English speakers from America, Australia, Canada, or New Zealand. The effect is probably somewhat different on people whose linguistic background is not English.

As the Hobbits travel outside the Shire, in both book and film, the names they encounter grow stranger and the feeling of crossing boundaries increases. In their first stop outside the Shire, the Hobbits come to Bree, a place marked by its use of Anglicized Welsh names such as Bree, Chetwood, and Combe, reflecting Welsh *bre*, "hill," *coed*, "wood," and *cwm*, "valley." Yet these names, while not immediately intelligible, still have a ring of familiarity; the Hobbits have not yet crossed into the true unknown.

As the Hobbits leave Bree with their guide Strider, they come to an area where familiar and strange names are mingled; the transition into the alien has begun. Strider himself is revealed to have the foreign name of Aragorn; the hill of Weathertop is named as Amon Sûl; and the rivers Hoarwell and Loudwater turn into the mysterious Mitheithel and Bruinen.[7] Further travel introduces utterly foreign names like Gwathló, Moria, Lothlórien, Anduin, and Emyn Muil. These mark the boundary between the familiar, or at least recognizable, and the strange, pictorially reinforced in the films by the transition from agricultural or pastoral scenery to barren lands and wilderness. Even without knowing that these names are *called* "Elvish," the names themselves introduce us into a strange land where even the commonplace, by virtue of its new name, has become exotic and alien. There is a quality in these names that rises above the mere otherness of strange costume or customs; the words themselves impart an enchantment of beauty or of terror. To achieve authenticity in that realm requires an insight not only into the specific details of Tolkien's languages but into language itself and the ways it can be used to effect certain responses in the reader or listener.

Languages were particularly important to Tolkien; he was by training a historical linguist who specialized in early Germanic languages such as Old English, Old Norse, and Gothic. These, and other languages with which Tolkien was acquainted, were the inspiration for the languages that Tolkien invented and described, writing dictionaries and lengthy grammatical notes; languages of a style that can be tantalizingly familiar in sounds and grammar but whose details are almost entirely invented. These languages include the Elvish languages Quenya and Sindarin, the Dwarvish language Khuzdul, the ancient human language Adûnaic, the debased language of the Orcs, and fragments of many other tongues.

Frodo with his sword, Sting, in *The Fellowship of the Ring* (2001).

Unlike many languages (such as Esperanto) that have been invented for purely utilitarian reasons, or even science-fictional languages such as Klingon, Tolkien's invented languages are imagined in historical detail. Each language has its own detailed pseudohistory: a fictional though highly plausible pedigree that explains what they look and sound like and by whom they are used. Within Tolkien's world, however, each language characterizes its speakers, identifying their allegiances and history. No Orc will pronounce the Sindarin Elvish name of the angelic figure "Elbereth"; Sindarin, especially in the film, is reserved for characters of heroic stature, the Elves and Elf-allied Dúnedain (such as Aragorn).

Though none of these languages is a copy of a real-world language, most are intentionally reminiscent, in sound and structure, of languages that educated European readers might be familiar with. These items of linguistic reference serve as an index (though admittedly a rather esoteric one) to the associations that Tolkien intended to make by using languages of a specific style, associations which he hoped at least some readers would sense, even if only subconsciously. In a sense, these invented languages stand in for particular languages of the ancient and medieval world and are therefore intentionally made to resemble them.

The most ancient (in terms of Tolkien's pseudohistory) of the languages seen in *The Lord of the Rings* is the Elvish language Quenya. Tolkien called it an "Elven-Latin" and worked to reinforce the image of Quenya as Latin by altering its spelling; for instance, he used the letters *c* and *qu* where he might have used *k* or *kw*, simply because Latin commonly uses those letters for the sounds of *k* and *kw*. In Middle-earth, Quenya stands in for Latin, in the sense that it is an archaic tongue no longer spoken as a native language but still used to record anything of importance; it is to be seen as a throwback to an earlier and perhaps nobler time.

In structure Quenya is also designed to be like Latin: both languages have complex inflectional systems for both nouns and verbs, though in this respect Quenya is even more archaic than Latin and might be compared to a very archaic Indo-European language such as Sanskrit. In other respects Tolkien simply pleased himself in designing Quenya, sometimes drawing upon languages such as Finnish,[8] sometimes just picking out constructions from various European languages that he found aesthetically attractive.

Above all, Tolkien tried to create a language that suited his preferences for what a language *should* sound like; he liked words ending in vowels, dental sounds such as *t, l, r, n*, and *s*, resonant sounds such as *m, n, l, r, w, y*, open syllables (consisting of just a consonant and a vowel, or a vowel alone), and a simple set of five vowels with long and short variants. He disliked sounds that broke the flow of air in speech, particularly voiced stops (*b, d,* and *g*) except in certain combinations; he avoided complex clusters of consonants, forbidding them at the beginning and end of words and allowing only a very limited set of sequences in the middle of a word. Most people will not recognize these techniques but they will get the sense of a very mellifluous, sonorous language that can be spoken with great clarity and elegance, just from looking at a phrase such as *Ai laurië lantar lassi súrinen*.[9]

Quenya's younger cousin among the Elvish languages is Sindarin, which is still a "living language" among Elves and some humans at the time of *The Lord of the Rings*. Unlike Quenya, Sindarin has a single clear source that it imitates, namely Welsh. Tolkien had been fascinated by the small amount of Welsh he had heard as a child, though he studied it only later in life; nonetheless, he "found in it an abiding linguistic-aesthetic satisfaction,"[10] and his early invented languages began to acquire a Celtic cast that only became stronger with each revision. By 1950 Tolkien's design for Sindarin was heavily Welsh-inspired in pronunciation (though not in orthography) and in grammatical features, such as complex plurals that involve vowel changes and a series of initial consonant mutations.[11] In doing so, Tolkien was consciously evoking a sense of mingled familiarity and otherness; Welsh is, after all, native to the British Isles and a language of which most Britons are aware but ignorant.

Sindarin possesses some but not all of the qualities that Tolkien found appealing structurally and phonetically. But insofar as it is less perfect, it is perhaps more realistic and appealing as a language that appears "lived in," a language that one can make daily use of. It is also notable as the language where Tolkien most frequently and obviously used his skills as a historical linguist, deriving a language far removed from the common template used for all of Tolkien's Elvish languages.

Sindarin is supposed to be a close relative of Quenya, but Quenya is more archaic, and much closer to the imaginary "proto–Elvish" that was the common ancestor of both languages. To produce Sindarin, Tolkien unleashed upon proto–Elvish a vast array of sequential changes, all well within the realm of historical probability for human languages. The resulting Sindarin words are often hardly recognizable as cognates of the Quenya words to which they are related. The Quenya word *alda*, "tree," is exactly cognate to, though it little resembles, Sindarin *galadh*; almost as difficult to see is the relationship between Quenya *quetta*, "word" and Sindarin *peth*, or Quenya *telpe*, "silver" and Sindarin *celeb*. This is a display of linguistic virtuosity that may not be fully appreciated by most people, but the attentive reader will at least perceive such repeated roots as *mir*, "jewel," *el*, "star," *sil*, "shine white," *nen*, "water," *(g)ond*, "stone," and so see something of the underlying linguistic unity of the two languages. A reader seeing *silivren penna miriel o menel aglar elenath*[12] will probably note both the similarity to Quenya and the greater complexity of sound in words like *silivren* and *aglar*. The viewer in a movie theater has less opportunity to make such comparisons, but can probably get an even clearer idea of the differences in style through hearing the languages spoken.

The languages are therefore treated much like the scenery. They are not ideal and ageless specimens of what a language ought to be, but have been aged, encrusted with "flaws" such as redundancies, homonyms, and irregular inflections that are reminiscent of natural languages. In this way they can become part of the aged landscape in which they are set, present memories of a distant past, contributing to a sense of alienation in time. They are evocative in the same way as the film sets of Amon Hen or Helm's Deep, constructions evidently built long ago but battered over the centuries by the forces of time and war.

In Peter Jackson's film, Sindarin provides a mode for marking the strangeness of the Elves. Portraying Elves convincingly is perhaps the most difficult task for any movie adaptation of Tolkien—they must be played by humans, and yet they must not seem human. Dwarves and Hobbits may be distinguished by height, but Elves—even with pointed ears—require something more. Distinctive costuming and hairstyling (not to mention an apparently magical inability to get dirty) are significant, but the use of Elvish language, subtitled where appropriate, provides further support to the viewer's impression of the Elves as an alien people.

The language of the Dwarves, Khuzdul, is rather different from the Elvish tongues and was intended to be perceived as alien in all ways: the Hobbit Sam Gamgee calls it "a fair jaw-cracker"[13] (though only in the book). It is also intended to be perceived as mysterious, "the secret dwarf-tongue that they teach to none."[14] In fact it is modelled upon the Semitic languages, with their triconsonantal root systems; examples are the words *khazâd*, "dwarves," *Khazad-dûm*, "dwarf-delving," *Khuzdul*, "Dwarvish," where the sounds *kh-z-d* refer to the people of the Dwarves. Tolkien on more than one occasion compared the Dwarves to Jews, "at once native and alien in their habitations, speaking the languages of the country, but with an accent due to their own private tongue."[15] The Dwarvish language is therefore intended to be reminiscent of Hebrew in construction and in sociolinguistic function. It is an ancient language, treasured but not much used as a common speech, spoken by a wandering people long ago expelled from their original home. It is also a language with many rough edges, spoken with a greater regard for consistency and utility rather than phonetic beauty. A line such as *Baruk Khazâd! Khazâd ai-mênu!*[16] reflects the pragmatic concerns of Dwarvish miners and warriors, not the artistic concerns of Elvish poets.

In the movie, the primary examples of the Dwarvish language occur either in inscriptions (which are not read aloud) or in the sound track (in a very evocative choral piece composed by Howard Shore). It is less clearly associated with the sole Dwarf character, Gimli, whose actor (John Rhys-Davies) has opted for a somewhat Welsh-sounding accent. The connection between Dwarvish and Hebrew is not reinforced in any way by the costumes, art, or architecture associated with the Dwarves, which are largely based on pure fantasy motifs.

Another ancient language of a similar type that takes a prominent place in Tolkien's history is Adûnaic, the language of the kingdom of Númenor, Tolkien's version of Atlantis. Adûnaic, like Khuzdul, has a recognizably Semitic-style structure; however, its phonology is rather more simplified and consistent than that of Hebrew and suggests a much more archaic Semitic language. It can be compared to the ancient language of Assyria and Babylon, suggesting that Númenor, as the parent culture of the civilized realms of Middle-earth, stands in much the same relation to them as those ancient Semitic kingdoms stood to the later civilizations of Greece, Rome, and medieval Europe. When Tolkien uses

Queen of the Elves Galadriel (Cate Blanchett) bids farewell to the questing Frodo (Elijah Wood).

Adûnaic in sentences such as *Adûn izindi batân tâidô ayadda: îdô kâtha batîna lôkhî*,[17] he is trying to evoke an impression of an ancient and solidly built civilization long since dead but with an enduring legacy.

By covert historical allusions such as these, Tolkien has built up a world that seems to have great depth and reality. The degree of reality imparted to Tolkien's languages through the sheer process of invention cannot be understated; some of them have sufficient vocabulary and details of grammar to allow them to be used for communication, and a significant number of fans make convincing attempts to do so. The languages therefore can be considered *real* in a much more vivid way than the Shire or Gondor are real, belonging to that class of things which, by virtue of being described, come into existence. The particular emotional response these languages call forth is due not merely to the completeness of their invention but to the degree to which they remind us of languages, societies, and histories that we already know of.

At the polar opposite from Quenya are the languages of the Orcs and of Sauron, of which only small samples are given. These languages do not stand in for any particular languages of the real world; rather, they represent all those aspects of language which Tolkien disliked, particularly in sound. Unlike the Elvish languages, the Orkish languages prefer back vowels (particularly *a* and *u*), velar sounds (*k, g, kh*) and many complex consonant clusters in the middle of words: *Nazgûl, Grishnákh, Radbug, Lugbúrz.* By means such as these, Tolkien evokes a sensation of chaos and conflict, creating languages full of harsh contrasts. A character uttering the phrase *Uglúk u bagronk sha pushdug Saruman-glob búbhosh skal*[18] can be assumed not to mean well. In the film, the occasional Orkish lines are not very distinct from the other nonlinguistic vocalizations of the Orcs, but they certainly sound cacophonous enough. More audible examples of the speech of Sauron occur in the dialogues between Sauron and Saruman and in voiceovers associated with the Ring, and are suitably unpleasant in sound.

There are two other languages that play prominent roles in *The Lord of the Rings* but which have not been invented by Tolkien. The most obvious is Westron, which is simply English. Obviously, the English language cannot have had the same history in Tolkien's world as it has had in ours; Tolkien affirms that the English of Middle-earth is actually a translation from another language, which is not represented in the story; but he also provides "archaic" words that look like earlier forms of English, for instance *Sterrendei*, which is supposed to be the name of the first day of the week ("Starday") in the Hobbits' calendar. In the film, of course, English is used by tacit convention as the common language of communication; no explanation is given for the use of English by all the main characters, any more than most films set in historical epochs explain their use of modern languages.

The other prominent language is that of the horse-breeding people of Rohan, which is a dialect of Old English. Little of it is actually reproduced in the book, but there are enough names of people, places, and isolated words to leave no doubt about its identity, along with short phrases such as *ferthu Théoden hál*,[19] "travel well, Théoden." The lack of exploitation of Old English is continued in the film, where the Rohirrim speak modern English to each other as well as to strangers, the primary nod to the language being lyrics in Old English on the sound track.

The use of Old English, Tolkien claims, does not necessarily imply a cultural resemblance between the Rohirrim and the pre–Conquest English.[20] The English were certainly not a nation of horse-breeders, and in some respects the description of the Rohirrim would better fit the ancient Bulgars, Hungarians, or even Mongols. But clearly the use of Old English *does* evoke early medieval England or, in general, the culture of ancient Germanic tribes. This approach is extended by using the ancient Germanic language of Gothic for the names of certain peoples related to the Rohirrim within Tolkien's fictional history. It is perhaps not so much the place (England) as the time of Old English (the seventh to eleventh century) that Tolkien wants to evoke, and the feeling that Rohan where Old English is spoken is an archaic island, a place where ancient traditions survive nearly unchanged in a world that has largely passed them by. It also associates them with the men of Gondor in a way similar to the association that the Saxons had with the Romans or Byzantines, living on a portion of formerly Roman territory and strongly influenced by the remains of Roman culture. Though the film does not portray and barely alludes to Rohan's relationship to Gondor, the styles of art and architecture portrayed are indeed reminiscent of an early medieval Germanic or Celtic culture of northwestern Europe, consistent with Tolkien's descriptions. The architecture of the film's Meduseld— the hall of King Théoden of Rohan, analogous to the "mead-hall" of the Danish king Hrothgar in *Beowulf*—is particularly well-realized in its form and decoration.

If, therefore, much in Middle-earth seems realistic, familiar though foreign, it is because Tolkien has colored his alien world with pigments drawn from a real history. If Quenya and Sindarin are more approachable than Klingon, it is because they have been made strange in familiar ways. Far from being limited to the surface of invention and such details as the author provides, readers can import into their personal images of Middle-earth all the details of our own history that may be congruent with Tolkien's descriptions. Middle-earth has depth and the appearance of authenticity because that authenticity has been borrowed from our world. If the readers do not always agree in their images or argue with the depiction provided by Peter Jackson's filmed version, it is because they have filled in the holes in Tolkien's description with different details.

By means of language as much as any other description, Tolkien has differentiated his invented peoples from each other, from the "baseline" culture of the Hobbits, and from all the nations of our own world. In the process of their quest, the Hobbits penetrate multiple layers of the alien, and in the process become alien themselves; upon their return to the Shire, they find that it has become strange to them, and they are perceived as foreigners. Even after they have been accepted back into their society, the hero, Frodo Baggins, is incapable of readjusting or even of recovering his former social identity.

The reader or viewer likewise follows the Hobbits through their perception of the alien; but he or she has to make a final step that the Hobbits do not, returning from the book or movie to the alienness of the everyday. If Tolkien and Jackson have done their work well, the everyday world will itself have become tinged with exoticism, and the reader may never regard such conventional things as his or her own language in the same way again. Certainly the response to the films—not just in terms of revenues, but in terms of increased fan interest in such things as the Elvish languages—indicates that some chord has been struck.

No movie version can possibly satisfy every reader of *The Lord of the Rings*, because all readers bring to the book out of their own knowledge that element of authenticity which they perceive in it. Yet Peter Jackson's films convey, in their own way, much the same sense of alienness that is found in the books, using Tolkien's languages and nomenclature and building upon his descriptions to create a vivid visual and musical interpretation of Tolkien's work. To many readers it may seem "inauthentic"; to others it provides another template upon which they can inscribe their own understanding of authenticity.

Notes

1. J.R.R. Tolkien, *Letters of J.R.R. Tolkien* (Boston: Houghton Mifflin, 1981), p. 239.
2. Tolkien, *Letters*, p. 211.
3. Tolkien, *Letters*, p. 210.
4. Tolkien, *Letters*, pp. 235, 288.
5. Tolkien, *Letters*, pp. 225–6.
6. Tolkien, *Letters*, p. 360.
7. J.R.R. Tolkien, *The Fellowship of the Ring* (Boston: Houghton Mifflin, 1982), pp. 197, 212.
8. Tolkien, *Letters*, p. 214.
9. "Ah, the golden leaves fall in the wind." Tolkien, *Fellowship of the Ring*, p. 394.
10. Tolkien, *Letters*, p. 213.
11. Tolkien, *Letters*, pp. 219, 426.
12. "The crystalline jewelled glory of the stars falls from heaven." Tolkien, *Fellowship of the Ring*, p. 250.
13. Tolkien, *Fellowship of the Ring*, p. 299.
14. Tolkien, *Fellowship of the Ring*, p. 320.
15. Tolkien, *Letters*, p. 229.
16. "Axes of the Dwarves! The Dwarves are upon you!" J.R.R. Tolkien, *The Two Towers* (Boston: Houghton Mifflin, 1982), p. 139.
17. "A straight road formerly went westward; now all roads are bent." J.R.R. Tolkien, *Sauron Defeated* (Boston: Houghton Mifflin, 1992), p. 247.
18. Tolkien, *Two Towers*, p. 48.
19. Tolkien, *Two Towers*, p. 127.
20. J.R.R. Tolkien, *The Return of the King* (Boston: Houghton Mifflin, 1983), p. 414.

Works Cited

Tolkien, J.R.R. *The Fellowship of the Ring*. Boston: Houghton Mifflin, 1982.
_____. *Letters of J.R.R. Tolkien*. Boston: Houghton Mifflin, 1981.
_____. *The Return of the King*. Boston: Houghton Mifflin, 1983.

_____. *Sauron Defeated*. Boston: Houghton Mifflin, 1992.
_____. *The Two Towers*. Boston: Houghton Mifflin, 1982.

Filmography

2001 *The Lord of the Rings: The Fellowship of the Ring*, d. Peter Jackson, with Elijah Wood, Ian McKellen, Viggo Mortensen, Cate Blanchett. U.S.: New Line Productions.
2002 *The Lord of the Rings: The Two Towers*, d. Peter Jackson, with Elijah Wood, Ian McKellen, Viggo Mortensen, Cate Blanchett. U.S.: New Line Productions.

Authenticating Realism in Medieval Film

WILLIAM F. WOODS

This is an essay about the authenticating features of medieval film, the ways in which we are led to accept the illusion on screen as a convincing version of the medieval world. The focus of the illusion and of this discussion is the medieval film hero. We will begin with an examination of the realism of Johan Huizinga's historical narrative and its close cousin, cinematic medievalism, which attracts us on sensible but also spiritual levels, both levels dependent upon the mundane details that create the realistic surface of the film narrative. The essay's second and third parts deal with those details and the ways in which they enhance the image, character, and thematic force of the hero.

I

"To the world when it was half a thousand years younger," Huizinga says at the beginning of his classic social history, *The Waning of the Middle Ages*, "[a]ll experience had yet to the minds of men the directness and absoluteness of the pleasure and pain of child-life.... We, at the present day, can hardly understand the keenness with which a fur coat, a good fire on the hearth, a soft bed, a glass of wine, were formerly enjoyed."[1] From sensations he passes to sentiments, concluding that emotions, too, were closer to the surface in medieval times. Everyday life had a "tone of excitement and ... passion," veering as it did "between despair and distracted joy, between cruelty and pious tenderness."[2] The authority of Huizinga's great history, not to mention its enduring popularity, rests partly on its ability to present the experience of medieval life as sensuous, immediate, and, in a basic sense, authentic. The close attention to the tiny details of mundane experience, the emphasis on human suffering, on the emotional extremes of terror, exaltation, or joy, the sense that a meaning, indeed a complex of meanings lay behind ordinary acts and perceptions, lending them a significance beyond themselves and a kind of order—these and other authenticating devices are the means by which Huizinga creates a medieval world that has the density and immediacy of lived experience and that presents an affect very similar to that of cinematic realism.

For despite their mythic overtones and romance coloring, films with medieval themes, like medieval histories, are required by their audiences to deliver a convincing picture of life. We reject out of hand costume dramas and sword-and-sorcery fantasies, just as we smile at the paradings of the Society for Creative Anachronism. Nonetheless, the authenticity we suppose we are looking for proves elusive. Would we recognize real medieval life if we saw it? And if medieval reality were revealed to us, in a sort of dream vision perhaps, what would be the charm of that artless, unaesthetic view? Some films do indeed gain our assent, but it is not the historical accuracy, necessarily, that moves our acceptance, or brilliant dialogue, or camera work. When we connect with the world of the film, when we can share some difficulty, some desire that is simplified, made a little strange, and in a way, vitalized by *what we can accept* as authentic features of medieval reality, *then* our resistance fades, and the scene breaks upon us with the force of real experience.

The most compelling medieval films have this kind of power because they invite their audience to collaborate with them in what could be called a shared cinematic medievalism. "Medievalism" may be defined as simply looking backward and, as Cervantes put it, imagining our past. When medieval films are made and when they are viewed, modern notions, emotions, and sensibilities are projected backward into the past, shaping and being shaped by what is known of the medieval world. Necessarily, what is constructed in this kind of activity is a communal fantasy, since writers, directors, viewers, and even historical consultants tacitly agree to accept—if only for the duration of the movie—the same version of medieval reality. This agreed-upon fantasy is the core truth of every medieval film. A world that lives in the imaginations of writers and directors is brought to the screen in such a way that it breaches the walls of our disbelief, and unconsciously we begin to contribute from our own experience, adapting the shared vision to create our own perception of the medieval world.

But what is it, exactly, that enables us to suspend our disbelief? In a basic sense, medieval film, like Huizinga's narrative, engages the senses and the emotions directly, heightening our sense of the ordinary. The medieval world on film is usually a romantic vision then, in a sense that

Henry V (Lawrence Olivier) in authentic period attire, with his prospective bride, in *Henry V* (1945).

Wordsworth would have recognized. Yet it is not necessarily an idealized version of primitivism—neither a pastoral idyll nor what Eco has called "shaggy medievalism."[3] Searching for immediacy in medieval experience and for authenticating features that suggest it will lead us not only through the blood and mire of medieval battles (e.g., *Henry V*, *Braveheart*), the dark, smoky interiors of peasants' huts (*The Return of Martin Guerre*), or exuberant barnyard sex (*The Advocate*), but also into experience one might call spiritual or intellectual. For there can be a piercing emotional quality to the lives of saints—Saint Joan, for instance, or Saint Francis, to mention two frequently filmed stories. Even Brother William of Baskerville (Sean Connery in *The Name of the Rose*), despite his deft intellectual style, is drawn into a crisis of identity and potential self-sacrifice.

The characteristic immediacy of medieval film attracts us on two levels, then: first, through the senses and emotions, and second, and more important, through the linked problems of loyalty, faith, and identity. Films such as *The Advocate*, *The Return of Martin Guerre*, and *The Seventh Seal* retain their peculiar sense of authentic medieval experience because they raise questions in real and insistent ways that are also our own: among them, who we are, whom we serve, and why. We confront such questions within the historical world of these films, which means we must shed much of our protective armor—our enabling but also insulating cultural sensibility—and battle imaginatively with the conflicts such stories raise as if we were peasants, princes, or saints. It is the sensible and spiritual poignancy of their vision of human experience that makes the most engaging medieval films feel authentic; and this particular form of authenticity—realistic yet reflective—is the definitive quality of cinematic medievalism. The authenticating features that we are about to examine—some of them so elementary that viewers scarcely notice them—provide us with a practical means and a vocabulary for discussing medieval films and their heroes.

II

For the most part, our sense of what is real or authentically medieval in a film depends upon perceptual realism—what we see there. Nevertheless, our first impression in a medieval film is generally formed by what we are told. There will be a voice-over or perhaps only a text crawling up the screen that frames the upcoming story by telling us when and where a conflict occurred and often what the complications were—war, plague, hunger, for example. The medieval movie tends to be framed, like certain famous works of medieval fiction. To a degree, the framing statement establishes genre, just as fairy tales have to begin with "Once upon a time" (it would be hard to know how to respond to them, how to *read* them, if they did not). Medieval movies may not necessarily be fairy tale romances like *Star Wars* ("Once long ago, in a galaxy far, far away...") yet, inescapably, they tell old stories. Implicit is the assumption that we will be testing our times, our experience, against theirs, and that is part of the fun. The opening statement of a medieval film invites our interaction with what we encounter in the story, which in turn creates a bias in favor of accepting it as a substitute for real experience. Also understood (without our thinking about it much) is that the framing assertion is a kind of truth claim. Merely by making the statement (e.g., "These are medieval times"), the narrator asserts its truth, thereby bringing to bear what Grodal, in his study of realism in audio-visual representation, has called "a central means of transmitting a feeling of reality and factuality."[4] In effect, because we are told the film is going to be authentically medieval and, at this point, we have no reason to disagree, we are prepared to accept it as so.

Very quickly the framing statement ends and the action begins, if it has not been in progress since the beginning. Often the opening shot places us in company with someone on a journey—monks, for example, riding slowly across mountain meadows toward a forbidding Benedictine abbey, as in *The Name of the Rose*. Or consider the opening of *Excalibur*, where, waiting in the Wagner-tormented dark, we see a point of brightness out in the barren lands, a torch—Merlin (!) coming to shed some light on Uther's benighted realm. The need for initial movement and more generally for on-screen action is so obvious as to escape notice, if we were not scrutinizing what feeds the roots of medieval film realism. The perceptual processes that create our basic sense of reality are linked to our "motor-based relations to the world.... Those things, those perceptions are real that can guide our (re)actions."[5] In other words, we tend to see something as real when we have already had the experience of reacting to it or something like it. In extreme cases, we find our muscles twitching as we watch, as if we ourselves had to ward off a sword stroke or enter into the dance. This basic reactivity is fundamental to our response to most movies, and when the range of action is severely restricted, as it is in Bresson's *Le Procès de Jeanne d'Arc*, where Joan and her prosecutor recite the words of the trial with frozen faces, their bodies rigid, we are acutely aware of its lack. Furthermore, given our preconceptions of the medieval world, it seems that we might associate the authentically medieval with particular kinds of physical action—men on horseback, for instance, or swordplay, plowing, prayer.

In medieval film narratives, as in medieval romances, the jousting, feasting, and journeying seize our attention, yet our ultimate concern is not the events themselves, but the inner logic that determines the sequence, severity, tonality, and finally the significance of events. The logic or relevance of the action depends upon the character or, to be precise, the agency of the medieval protagonist. That is why a discussion of cinematic medievalism must focus not merely on the experience represented by the film but on heroic experience, the way in which the action is oriented by the subjectivity—the identity, abilities, background, problems, and desires—of the film's hero.

In heroic narratives, the action occurs in precisely the ways necessary to show off the hero's courage and limitations and often to reveal the inevitability of the tragic ending. The plot mechanism is that he or she must make choices. The need for Bertrande to choose between the two men who claim to be her husband, Martin Guerre, is paradigmatic for all heroes on film. Such choices demonstrate the inner logic of the narrative but—and this is important for our sense of the authentic—they also dramatize the problematic nature of the medieval experience. Given a hostile world and their own resurgent weaknesses, human beings must make hard choices, plan carefully, deny their fears, and defer desires. Indeed, the primary way we participate in medieval film is by taking upon ourselves the hero's problems, planning, feeling his or her hesitation— trying to figure out what we would do in Lancelot's place, for example, had we his beauty and strength, his touching loyalty, and Guinevere.

Should we list just a few types of medieval hero—just the major ones, to get that medieval flavor? Surely this is the place to parade our somber knights (*The Seventh Seal*), tragic queens (*The Lion in Winter*), exalted saints (*La Passion de Jeanne d'Arc*), even an idealistic lawyer, and a philosophic monk (*The Advocate, The Name of the Rose*). They pass in review and they are splendid. After all, they are the main reason we came to the medieval movies in the first place.

What about women as heroes in medieval film? The female heroes are sometimes seen as predictable—martyred saints and tragic Guineveres, Iseults, witches, and madwomen. Marjory Kempe and Margaret Paston have yet to be seen on film. As with the male heroes, the range of roles does not seem especially broad. I myself would very much like to see a film about Margery Kempe, but the world of medieval movies is deeply dyed in the colors of romance and folktale, and it is most unlikely, although much to be hoped, that we will soon see films of the caliber of *The Return of Martin Guerre* starring heroes like Margery. Among an intriguing variety of mostly aristocratic or saintly female heroes, at least one of them is dark-hearted, if that is what one could call Morgana, the tarty villain of *Arthur's Quest*, who is a kind of anti–Wonder Woman.

More important, in any case, is the general principle that whoever the hero happens to be, he or she tends to be reflective by nature and will probably suffer in the course of the film. Let us consider actual heroic behaviors, reflective ones to begin with. At the beginning of *The Advocate*, for example, just after the framing statement and the opening credits, we are treated to a close-up of a crow. This fellow darts his head here, there, behind, with a bird's impossible quickness, while the sound track plays a brooding theme we soon come to know as "the lawyer's music." The camera then cuts to the coach where the Advocate Courtois, recently of Paris, has fallen asleep. As he peers out into the dark, drizzling night of his dream, we see the first of his long, pondering, brown-eyed gazes. These long looks recur throughout the film, carrying its major themes (the idealistic Courtois, having left the wicked city for the small, unhappy town of Abbeville, is there to see and sift everything). The crow moves us toward the idea of Courtois as an eagle-eyed representative of truth and justice, and Courtois himself shows us that there is much to ponder in fifteenth-century France.

For the viewer, these long, thoughtful glances are an invitation to enter the film, to interact, as it were, by pondering along with the advocate questions of natural law and human identity that the film raises. As we commit ourselves to weighing these questions, their context—the town of Abbeville, including the corrupt prosecutor, the lord with his frigid humor, the compromised priest—becomes real for us. Other examples of brooding looks on screen come easily to mind, the most striking of them being Renée Falconetti's silent, heartbreaking gazes in *La Passion de Jeanne d'Arc,* Tilda Swinton's very long, ambivalent gazes into the camera in *Orlando,* and even Richard Harris's gaze in his role as Arthur in *Camelot,* which reveals Arthur's agony of indecision and gives it a credibility that is mainly lacking in Malory.

Arthur is reflective but he is also in pain, torn between Guinevere, his wife, and Lancelot, who is his right hand. Courtly love by definition is almost sure to involve pain, and pain can hardly be separate from the warfare, jousts, the seven deadly sins, and famine that we have come to associate with medieval stories. But rather than being an incidental result of authentic medieval life, pain is itself a primary authenticating feature. We tend to take narrative seriously; we consider it more lifelike, more authentic, "when vital human (or animal) concerns [are] at stake," Grodal says,[6] and pain or the possibility of it raises the stakes. Grodal's analysis of this equation is illuminating:

> A consequence of the principle that a strong feeling of reality demand[s] that vital human or animal concerns be at stake is that "realism" is more often attributed to representations that portray negative emotions than those that portray positive emotions. This is perhaps based on the assumption that "pain" is more real than "pleasure," thus evoking more genuine behavior.[7]

We remember, he adds, that Freud called those (associative) mechanisms that were linked to pain the "reality principle" as opposed to the "pleasure principle."[8]

But given that pain is a universal signifier of the harsh reality of the human condition, can it also be a feature that has a particularly authenticating force in medieval film? Both trivial and more profound scenes come readily to mind. The trivial might be the sad group of extras— old men, women, children, and youths—standing in a cold rain, their rough clothing soaked, their breaths smoking in the Norwegian chill as they wait for Kirk Douglas to row up the fjord in his Viking ship (*The Vikings*). The scene seems authentic. As for the excruciating, there is richness of choice, but being burned at the stake has a ritual starkness that gives it pride of place over all the other agonies. One thinks first of the many Joan of Arcs who have died thus on film. But this motif has been used in various other contexts—the burning of the fool, the peasant girl, and the heretic monk in *The Name of the Rose,* for example, or the young girl who is burned in *The Seventh Seal.* Antonius Block, the weary, God-deserted knight, kneels over the condemned girl and with an exhausted pity, which increases our sense of the blind pointlessness of the death and its inevitability, gives her an anodyne before she is burned. Insofar as we tend to think of medieval people as being vulnerable to cold, hunger, war, pestilence, and so forth, it probably seems natural to accept life's promise of pain, the pain lending a sort of weight to that experience, a burden of the real. Virtually every medieval film provides additional examples. We have only to remember that the pain does not have to be bloody or physical to create authenticity. In the most convincing of these films, the sources of pain can be subtle indeed.

III

More commonly, however, the pain in medieval movies *is* physical and bloody, and that is because our sense of the real is fundamentally visual; we tend to believe what we see. "All other things being equal," Grodal says, "perceptual uniqueness and complexity enhance the feeling of realism, because the representation is directly simulated in our brains as if we were confronted with reality."[9] We watch the action happen on the screen and we live it for about a hundred minutes. We live it partly as Lancelot or Joan of Arc because we unconsciously react to the perceptual world as he or she (like any hero) focuses it for us.

That said, we can proceed to how we might judge the visual authenticity of a medieval film; in short, why does *The Return of Martin Guerre* look real, while *Excalibur* does not? Essentially, the more we can enjoy

The traveling players from *The Seventh Seal* (1957).

the hero's facial expressions and spoken lines, the better established and more particular his character becomes.

In *The Seventh Seal*, for instance, Antonius Block is a tall, fine-looking knight whose role is allegorical. He plays chess with Death, after all. His face is that of a man on a quest; close-up shots are unusual, and we do not miss them. But the face of William Wallace, played by Mel Gibson in *Braveheart*, is constantly before us in close-up, whether he is weeping, raging, or wearing barbaric face paint. Here it is the character we identify with, not so much the idea. We want him to be real and beautiful in close-up—hence the long hair, the face paint, the mask of battle-rage as the ragged ranks of Scots and English race toward each other with axes and claymores held high—and we also require consistency in his role. We need to see the emotional implications of that face carried out in appropriate body language (notice too how Wallace *walks* in this movie, every stride strongly separate, as if he were advancing against an enemy). His dialogue must be characteristic and all the features of the action must visually extend the reach and depth of his character.

There is much to be said for "perceptual uniqueness." We go to medieval movies for blood and iron, banners snapping in the wind, smoky banquet halls, and tragic women. Many of us will never forget the unearthly beauty of Elizabeth Taylor as Rebecca in *Ivanhoe*. Others might remember Olivia Hussey when she played the same role, or Michelle Pfeiffer in *Ladyhawke*. The point is not so much that we fall in love with Gibson's face, or Taylor's, or even that we love to identify with it, making it ours. In the banners and banquet halls, but far more through observing the faces of these medieval heroes, we experience what William Wallace feels for Scotland under the iron fist of England or we feel something of the pride and sadness of the hard life of medieval Jews. In the most compelling of our movies a face presents a layered reality, and that too contributes to the illusion of medieval realism.

When viewers argue the authenticity of a film or the lack of it, they usually mean realism based on decorum or fittingness. One hesitates to complain that a director has put a fifteenth-century bridle on a fourteenth-century horse (although that is a common sort of pretentiousness), but some flaws—a prominent anachronism, perhaps, or an accent that strongly reminds us of a modern time or place (one thinks of Kevin Costner's casual surfer-boy inflection in *Robin Hood, Prince of Thieves*)— do destroy the consistency of the illusion, eroding our emotional investment in the film. The perceptual complexity has been compromised; the sense of historical depth disappears, and we are left looking at a movie set.

What is interesting is not how seldom Hollywood makes such a mistake (experts tell us that very little of what we see is historically accurate) but how unusual it is that a lapse of authenticity tears the fabric of the viewer's sense of the authentic. As an audience, we are extraordinarily tolerant of inconsistencies, perhaps because our feeling for the authentic can be sustained by what seems typical, the kinds of clothes, gestures, and so forth that we expect of medieval reality. Our prior knowledge of the medieval, built up from watching films and from other sources, allows for a range of specificity in the unique image. There is a register of descriptive features we can accept for a Robin Hood or, for that matter, a castle in *Ivanhoe*, and we eagerly accept any version that does not clearly violate that category; many versions of a peasant's jacket would seem authentic, in other words, but not one trimmed in sumptuous fur.

Our sense of the typical in medieval life deserves special attention because it is the primary basis of cinematic medievalism—the way modern viewers conceive the Middle Ages. The medievalism of film is attractive because it is a paradox, both a comfort and an implicit threat. Presented with Camelot, we are suddenly at ease. We know pretty well what to expect from Gawain, Guinevere, and the rest. Lancelot can be Cornel Wilde (*The Sword of Lancelot*) or Franco Nero (*Camelot*), but the ground rules are the same; the loyalties and betrayals we love are replayed on the violent medieval turf, with horses thundering, men bleeding, women privileged, imperiled, scheming. What we can accept as authentically medieval, in other words, is partly what we think we know and partly what we need to think and feel about that dim medieval twilight when pain, death, and taxes were so much closer to the bone. The stereotypes found on film—medieval life was dirty, dangerous, sexy, ignorant, passionate, doomed, and so on—are important. If these medieval stereotypes strike us as regressive, too easy, perhaps as a kind of infantile projection, remember that they are a common denominator, a simple but effective device for accessing our emotions. Those who think this an unfair remark should consider the farting contest at the end of that very successful film, *A Knight's Tale.*

But if we acknowledge the murky underlying attractions of the medieval stereotypes—the excremental humor and the barnyard sex (*The Advocate* had to be edited to earn its R rating)—we must also give attention to medievalism at the other end of the scale—the overarching themes and the structures of obsessive ideas that are equally a source of authenticity in medieval movies. This is where the medieval hero, the focusing presence of the film, matters most, and this is where, if we can accept it, we feel the implicit threat. For we live the film's events and emotions through our heroic surrogate, and the blows of fortune, the lovers, the loneliness and joy are viscerally powerful for that reason. But the ideology of the film, the organizing necessities, and the unexamined assumptions of its medieval world (mingled, naturally, with modern ideologies projected onto the film by its makers and in reception by its viewers) also depend essentially on the hero. Grodal associates this aspect of cinematic realism with Plato's idealist tradition:

> The schemas are the mentally pertinent features in the experience of the ever-changing phenomenal world. Therefore I propose that there is a kind of "schematic salience" that provides a feeling of reality that is abstract and atemporal ... the power of which comes from being the mental essence of many different experiences, in contrast to the feeling of perceptual salience that is connected to the temporal, specific and unique.[10]

As Grodal explains, the perceptual and the schematic are complementary in a film. What we see creates the film's perceptual realism, while what we know (the organizing concepts that govern what we see) creates our sense of its reality.[11]

In some films, visual realism may seem to dominate, in others, the cognitive sense of reality. *First Knight* has been criticized as, if not a mindless film, then a film distinguished by "the irresolute flatness of [its] characterizations."[12] Yet the middle-aged Richard Gere still projects some of the wildness of his earlier roles, and as we watch him casually win at swordplay or ride (unhelmeted) into battle, we are entertained. *The Seventh Seal*, on the other hand, moves toward allegory. And in Bresson's *Le Procès de Jeanne D'Arc* the burden of ideas presses so heavily as to move the film toward a kind of moral didacticism. Joan sits motionless under the scrutiny of the inquisitors, returning her answers without hesitation but also without inflection or facial expression, so that finally she seems more a representative of the idea of righteous innocence than an innocent character cruelly examined.

Loyalty, faith, identity are abstract schemas and have their own sense of reality, but in medieval movies we do not experience them in the abstract. They are, after all, real to the hero, in ways that cost him or her enormous pain. But our need to see the hero torn between loyalties, faiths, identities does not arise from sadism but from a need to be torn ourselves, transfixed inescapably by the necessity of doing what we must, believing as we do, being who we are. Medieval films, like most stories, are fables of identity but they are set in a harder world than ours where the demands of loyalty and faith are absolute. This is not the unbearable lightness of being—which is a modern affliction—but its opposite, where being is the still center, and all other things fall into orbit around it, transient and relative to the ineluctable identity of the self. We need such hyperbolic terms to describe the martyrdom of Saint Joan or, for that matter, the martyrdoms of Thomas Becket and William Wallace. Like them, Richard Courtois, the advocate, in his quest for justice and William of Baskerville in his quest for the truths of earth and heaven hold to their own truth with great force despite enormous difficulties, which often—no, *always*—offer the truly frightening opportunity of recantation, betrayal, and the abandonment of self. Like no other films, medieval movies call upon us to be authentically ourselves, if only in the person of Courtois or William, if only until the final credits.

Notes

1. Johan Huizinga, *The Waning of the Middle Ages*, tr. F. Hopman (1924; New York: Doubleday, 1954), p. 9.
2. Huizinga, p. 10.
3. Umberto Eco, "Dreaming of the Middle Ages," in *Travels in Hyperreality* (1967; London: Picador, 1987), p. 69.
4. Torben Grodal, "The Experience of Realism in Audiovisual Representations," in *Realism and "Reality" in Film and Media*, ed. Anne Jerslev (Copenhagen: Museum Tusculanum Press [University of Copenhagen], 2002), p. 84.
5. Grodal, p. 83.

6. Grodal, p. 86.
7. Grodal, p. 87.
8. Grodal, p. 87.
9. Grodal, p. 70.
10. Grodal, p. 81.
11. Grodal, p. 82.
12. Robert S. Blanch and Julian N. Wasserman, "Fear of Flyting: The Absence of Internal Tension in *Sword of the Valiant* and *First Knight*," *Arthuriana* 10.4 (2000): 28.

Works Cited

Blanch, Robert J., and Julian N. Wasserman. "Fear of Flyting: The Absence of Internal Tension in *The Sword of the Valiant* and *First Knight*." *Arthuriana* 10.4 (2000): 15–32.

Eco, Umberto. "Dreaming of the Middle Ages." In *Travels in Hyperreality*. 1967. London: Picador, 1987, pp. 61–72.

Grodal, Torben. "The Experience of Realism in Audiovisual Representation." In *Realism and "Reality" in Film and Media*, ed. Anne Jerslev. Copenhagen: Museum Tusculanum Press [University of Copenhagen], 2002, pp. 67–91.

Huizinga, Johan. *The Waning of the Middle Ages*, tr. F. Hopman. 1924. New York: Doubleday, 1954.

Filmography

1928 *La Passion de Jeanne d'Arc* (*The Passion of Joan of Arc*), d. Carl Theodor Dreyer, with Renée Falconetti, Antonin Artaud. France: Société Générale des Films.

1952 *Ivanhoe*, d. Richard Thorpe, with Robert Taylor, Elizabeth Taylor. U.S.: MGM.

1957 *The Seventh Seal*, d. Ingmar Bergman, with Max Von Sydow. Sweden: Svensk Filmindustri.

1958 *The Vikings*, d. Richard Fleischer, with Kirk Douglas. U.S.: Bryna Productions, United Artists.

1962 *Le Procès de Jeanne d'Arc* (The Trial of Joan of Arc), d. Robert Bresson, with Florence Carrez. France: Agnès Delahaie Productions.

1963 *The Sword of Lancelot*, d. Cornel Wilde, with Cornel Wilde, Jean Wallace. U.K./U.S.: Emblem, Universal.

1964 *Becket*, d. Peter Glenville, with Peter O'Toole, Richard Burton. U.K./U.S.: Keep Films, Paramount.

1967 *Camelot*, d. Joshua Logan, with Richard Harris, Vanessa Redgrave. U.S.: Warner Bros., Seven Arts.

1968 *The Lion in Winter*, d. Anthony Harvey, with Katherine Hepburn, Peter O'Toole. U.K.: Haworth Productions.

1981 *Excalibur*, d. John Boorman, with Nicol Williamson. U.S.: Orion.

1982 *The Return of Martin Guerre*, d. Daniel Vigne, with Gerard Depardieu,

Nathalie Baye. France: Société Française de production cinemato-
graphique.

1985 *Ladyhawke*, d. Richard Donner, with Rutger Hauer, Michelle Pfeiffer,
Matthew Broderick. U.S.: Warner Bros., 20th Century–Fox.

1986 *The Name of the Rose*, d. Jean-Jacques Annaud, with Sean Connery. German Federal Republic/Italy/France: Neue Constantin, Cristaldifilm, Ari-
ane Productions.

1989 *Henry V*, d. Kenneth Branagh, with Kenneth Branagh, Emma Thompson.
U.K.: BBC, Renaissance Films.

1991 *Robin Hood: Prince of Thieves*, d. Kevin Reynolds, with Kevin Costner,
Morgan Freeman. U.S.: Morgan Creek.

1993 *Orlando*, d. Sally Potter, with Tilda Swinton. U.K.: Columbia, Tri Star.

1994 *The Advocate*, d. Leslie Megahey, with Colin Firth. France/U.K.: BBC
Films, CiBy 2000, British Screen, European Co-production Fund.

1995 *Braveheart*, d. Mel Gibson, with Mel Gibson. U.S.: Icon Productions, Ladd,
20th Century–Fox.

First Knight, d. Jerry Zucker, with Richard Gere, Julia Ormond, Sean Connery. U.S.: Zucker Brothers, Columbia.

1998 *Arthur's Quest*, d. Neil Mandt, with Arye Gross, Alexandra Paul, Catherine Oxenberg. U.S.: Crystal Sky Communications.

2001 *A Knight's Tale*, d. Brian Helgeland, with Heath Ledger. U.S.: Columbia,
Escape Artists/Finestkind Productions.

Kid Crusaders

Heroic Children on Film

MARTHA W. DRIVER

We read the Arthur legends through the lens of film, through Jessie L. Weston whose influential work *From Ritual to Romance* (which was first published in 1920) is still in print,[1] and through the interpretations of the Victorians. The Victorians were the first great promoters of the Arthur legends after William Caxton who first brought Sir Thomas Malory's collection of King Arthur legends into print on 31 July 1485, to which Caxton himself gave the title "Morte Darthur." In his preface, Caxton explains that Arthur was the only Englishman among the 'Nine Worthies,' the greatest heroes that have ever existed.[2] Caxton describes Malory's work as providing excellent examples of honorable behavior for his readers: "For herein may be seen noble chivalry, courtesy, humanity, friendliness, hardiness, love, friendship, cowardice, murder, hate, virtue, and sin. Do after the good and leave the evil, and it shall bring you to good fame and renommé [renown] in this life."[3]

In mid-nineteenth century Britain, the Arthur legends were revived in conjunction with a renewed interest in Gothic architecture brought about by the influential works of A. W. Pugin (1812–1852) and John Ruskin (1819–1900). The first great series of murals based on the Arthur legends was commissioned in 1841 for the interior of the Queen's Robing Room in Westminster Palace. The artist William Dyce (1806–64) was advised by Prince Albert, husband of Queen Victoria, to draw on "the widest circle of the Legend of Arthur," but Dyce himself was concerned that the main plot of the *Morte*, the affair between Lancelot and Guinevere, "turns on incidents which, if they are not undesirable for representation under any circumstances, are at least scarcely appropriate in such an apartment."[4] Later, in 1855, William Morris and Edward Burne-Jones encountered a copy of Southey's reprint of Malory's *Morte Darthur* in a Birmingham bookshop which Burne-Jones had admired but could not afford. Burne-Jones wrote, "I remember I could not buy the precious book. I used to read it in a bookseller's shop day after day, and bought cheap books to pacify the owner, but Morris got at it once and we feasted on it long." Georgiana Burne-Jones wrote in *Memorials*, her biography of her husband: "sometimes I think that the book never can have been loved as it was by those two men. With Edward it became literally a part of himself. Its strength and beauty, its mystical religion and noble chivalry of action, the world of lost history and romance in the names of people and places—it was his own birthright upon which he entered."[5] The artist and poet Dante Gabriel Rossetti, who served with Ruskin as mentor to the two young men, and as co-founder with them of the Pre-Raphaelite Brotherhood, described Malory's book, along with the Bible, as "the two greatest books in the world."[6] Judging from Burne-Jones's later reticence in illustrating any of the bawdier tales in his fabulous last collaboration with Morris, the Kelmscott Chaucer, one has the distinct impression that the pre–Raphaelites, along with the Victorians more generally, embraced aspects of Malory's stories that they thought appropriate or inspiring or spiritual, overlooking the rest.

Anyone who actually reads Malory cover to cover will be impressed with the many conflicting aspects of the legends, the poignant combination of sorrow, suffering, sin, nobility, pride as portrayed by the characters (and accurately described by Caxton in his preface) and of course by the graphically presented battle scenes. Consistency of character is not a necessary prerequisite of medieval narrative, and the same characters, whether Gawain, Guinevere, Lancelot, or Arthur himself, are disclosed as honorable, weak and sinful from story to story, or sometimes within one story, or even within one paragraph. Because of the adultery that drives the main plot and that is one central element in the destruction of Arthur's kingdom (along with the focus on battle and warfare), the Arthur legends, however, do not seem to be an ideal model for the series of paintings in the Queen's Wardrobe, as Dyce pointed out to Prince Albert, or for children.

Yet there they are. From J. T. Knowles's *The Story of King Arthur*, published in 1862, to Howard Pyle's four-book *Arthuriad*, published between 1903 and 1910, to Sidney Lanier's *The Boy's King Arthur* (1919), retellings of the Arthur legends for children simply omit the main aspects of the plot.[7] In nineteenth and early twentieth-century children's versions, Lancelot is described as worshipping the queen from afar, and his treason with the queen is never clearly identified, or else the accusations against Arthur's best knight and his queen are said to be false, caused by the envy of other less-worthy knights of the Round Table. This version of the Arthur story was recommended to child readers by Robert Stephenson Smyth Baden-Powell, who founded the Boy Scout and Girl Guide movements in 1908. Baden-Powell himself was influenced by a popular group called the Knights of King Arthur founded in 1893 by

William Byron Forbush, a Dartmouth College graduate (1888) and Congregational minister from Vermont. Members of this group, perhaps one model as well for the Society of Creative Anachronism, were led by male Merlins, met around a Round Table, took the names of Malory's knights, and transformed their picnics and games into Arthurian quests and battles.[8]

In some respects, the Arthur legends were a problem for their Victorian readers, as they remain for us. However, as the authors point out in this chapter, the Arthur legends were used, and continue to be used, as models for specific types of "chivalric" or heroic behaviors for children to emulate. While Tom Henthorne looks at the perpetuation of positive models provided by the Arthurian legends primarily for boys, Kevin J. Harty points out that Arthur legends for children could be read and acted upon by girls, too.

Notes

1. Jessie L. Weston's *From Ritual to Romance* (Garden City, N.Y., Doubleday, 1957) remains readily available through Amazon and other booksellers. Weston (1850–1928) wrote on a variety of medieval subjects, none so popular as her work on the *Grail*. Most recently, Weston's work was influential on the making of *Excalibur*, directed by John Boorman (U.S.: Orion, 1981).

2. The Nine Worthies are three pagans (Hector of Troy, Alexander the Great, and Julius Caesar), three Jews (Joshua, David, and Judas Maccabeus), and three Christians (Charlemagne, Godfrey of Bologne, and King Arthur). Caxton discusses these and Arthur's proper role among them in his preface to *The Morte Darthur* (*STC* 801).

3. D.S. Brewer, ed. *Malory: The Morte Darthur* (Evanston: Northwestern University Press, 1974), p. 45.

4. From a letter written by Dyce to Prince Arthur, 15 August 1848, cited in Muriel Whitaker, *The Legends of King Arthur* (Cambridge: D.S. Brewer, 1990), p. 179.

5. *Memorials*, vol. 1, 1833–1867 (repr. Lund Humphries, 1993) p. 117, p. 182, cited in *Edward Burne-Jones: Victorian Artist-Dreamer*, by Stephen Wildman and John Christian (NY: The Metropolitan Museum of Art and Harry N. Abrams, Inc., 1998), p. 72.

6. Wildman and Christian, p. 50.

7. Sidney Lanier, *The Boy's King Arthur* (New York: Charles Scribner's Sons, 1919); see also Lanier's earlier work, *The Boy's Froissart, Being Sir John Froissart's Chronicles of Adventure, Battle, and Custom in England* (New York: Scribner's, 1879). For more on Lanier (1842–1881), see also Julie Nelson Couch, "Howard Pyle's Story of King Arthur and His Knights and the Bourgeois Boy Reader," *Arthuriana* 13.2 (Summer, 2003): 38–53.

8. Derek Pearsall, *Arthurian Romance: A Short Introduction* (Oxford: Blackwell Publishing, 2003), p. 173, citing Mark Girouard, *The Return to Camelot: Chivalry and the English Gentleman* (New Haven, Connecticut: Yale University

Press, 1981). By 1922, the Knights of King Arthur were firmly established throughout the United States and had 130,000 members. Cited in Arthur Preuss, *A Dictionary of Secret and Other Societies* (St. Louis: B. Herder Book Company, 1924), pp. 42, 354, 514—515.

For Arjo, Don and Lissy

Shirley Temple and the Guys and Dolls of the Round Table

KEVIN J. HARTY

This essay examines four film versions of Damon Runyon's short story "Little Miss Marker," focusing especially on the Arthurian subplot in the original 1934 screen version of the story. The essay also briefly surveys the more general tradition of Arthurian films for younger audiences. Film would seem to be a natural medium for juvenile versions of the legend of King Arthur, and versions of the legend, cinematic and otherwise, aimed at younger audiences would in turn seem a ready vehicle for emphasizing the heroic ideal behind the Arthurian legend that at least partially explains that legend's enduring popularity.

Depending upon their ages, intended juvenile audiences for films might well be preliterate or, even if older, more attuned to visual image than to printed page. Yet a quick survey of cinema Arthuriana reveals at best a spotty record when it come to youth-oriented films.[1] Michael N. Salda has examined in detail Arthurian animation, suggesting that like all cartoons, animated Arthurian shorts "have always followed the money,"[2] but one could argue that quantity and quality no more go hand in hand when it comes to animated Arthurian films than they do for Arthurian cinema in general.

Two very different animated features, *The Sword in the Stone* from the novel by T. H. White, and *The Quest for Camelot*, very loosely adapted from a novel by Vera Chapman, do provide interesting moments that audiences of all ages might appreciate, but both fall victim to gender stereotypes, if not sexism. In *The Sword*, Merlin's nemesis, Mad Madame Mim, is reduced to a caricature of a witch, with all the misogynistic overtones associated with such a caricature. In *The Quest*, the central character, Kayley, after proving herself a valiant fighter and the equal of any man, is nonetheless relegated to a more traditional gender-constricted role at the end of the film. Kayley literally becomes both damsel in distress and damsel in a dress.

Mark Twain's *A Connecticut Yankee in King Arthur's Court* remains the most popular literary source for cinematic treatments of the legend of Arthur. But, from the very first film based on Twain's novel in 1920, filmmakers have refused to embrace the novel's darker side. Instead, Twain's novel, when transposed to the screen, has undergone a significant change in narrative genre. What had been, in the hands of a master novelist, a multifaceted social satire soon became, in the hands of successive film directors of markedly different stripes, the stuff of, at best, two-dimensional romantic comedy. The cultural clashes of Twain's novel, with its apocalyptic final carnage, became the tiffs of lovers eventually united and headed toward some version of the happily-ever-after.

Not content with leaving bad enough alone, more recent filmmakers have tried a new twist in their reconfiguring of Twain. They have moved beyond romantic comedy to pabulum for the young, transforming in the process Twain's Hank Morgan, "a Yankee among Yankees" according to the novel, into a teenager. Apocalypticism turned into amour now becomes adolescent angst.[3] Such angst also informs a number of more or less original Arthurian films which feature youthful protagonists, though they are clearly not always intended for younger audiences. Typical of such less-than-successful cinematic endeavors are the Canadian telefilm *Kids of the Round Table* and the direct-to-video release, *Merlin's Shop of Wonders*. In the Canadian telefilm, a modern-day juvenile cast dressed in armor encounters Merlin and Excalibur and acts out a puppy-love version of the Arthur-Guinevere-Lancelot triangle. There is much in the way of sighing and downcast looks among the three teenage cast members, but obviously no adultery. In *Merlin's Shop*, any intended juvenile audience is more likely to be unnerved rather than entertained by what they see on their video screens. Part of the film presents a version of the classic horror tale involving the monkey's paw first told by W.W. Jacobs in 1902.

More successful Arthurian films involving juvenile characters, even when they are not specifically aimed at younger audiences, approach the legend of the once and future king more indirectly. Rather than trying to superimpose the pseudomedieval on the modern, these films use the spirit of the legend to inform a modern tale in which some aspect of the Arthurian ideal eventually manifests itself. A case in point is the 1934 film version of Damon Runyon's short story "Little Miss Marker," which in its print version has no connection with the Arthurian legend.

Damon Runyon's "Little Miss Marker" was first published in 1934.[4] Written in a style characterized as "Runyonese,"[5] this story of Broadway involves, as the original subtitle promises, "the softer side of a number of very hard citizens."[6] Chief among these "hard citizens" is "a guy by the name of Sorrowful. This guy is called Sorrowful because this is the way he always is about no matter what, and especially about the way things are with him when anybody tries to put the bite on him."[7] Contrary to his usual practice, Sorrowful advances two dollars to cover a bet to a "young guy [who] is a steady customer for several days, and has an honest pan."[8] As surety for repayment of his bet, "the young guy" leaves his young daughter as a marker. When "the young guy" fails to return, Sorrowful is left with the little girl, who soon enough acquires the nickname "Marky."

As one might predict, Marky does have an unexpected effect on Sorrowful, who has previously been meanness (in both senses of the word) personified. Sorrowful takes Marky in hand, feeds her, rents an expensive apartment overlooking Central Park for her to live in, and hires or otherwise presses into service a number of his cronies to act as her chauffeur, guardian, nurse, and governess. Marky in turn becomes almost immediately attached to Sorrowful, to the surprise of his friends, who are not all as enamored of the tike as Sorrowful is: "Many citizens are commencing to consider Marky something of a nuisance and are playing the duck for her and Sorrowful."[9]

Marky likes to dance to big-band music; indeed, the only words she ever utters in the story are "Marky dance," which are repeated on a number of occasions. But, as Runyon's first-person narrator makes clear, what she lacks in skill as a dancer, she makes up, in part, with enthusiasm:

> Then she begins hopping and skipping around among the tables, holding her little short skirt up in her hands.... Personally, I like Marky's dancing very much, although of course she is no Pavlowa, and finally she trips over her own feet, and falls on her snoot.[10]

Marky and Sorrowful soon prove inseparable, to the growing concern, consternation, and annoyance of Sorrowful's fellow "hard citizens." Increasingly, Sorrowful's cronies look with alarm on his refusal to turn Marky over to the police or "to put an ad in the Lost and Found columns of the morning bladders, the same as people do when they lose or find Angoras cats, and Pekes and other animals which they do not wish to keep."[11]

Marky's fondness for Sorrowful eventually leads to her undoing. The management of the Hot Box, Sorrowful's and Marky's favorite hang out, also does not share Sorrowful's enthusiasm for his ward's terpsichorean feats: "Henri, the manager of the Hot Box, once tells me he will just as soon Marky does not do her dancing there"[12] after an incident involving the less-than-respectful reaction some Park Avenue types have to her falling "on her snoot."[13]

Marky does inadvertently end up saving Sorrowful's life. Sorrowful is locked in a dispute over a bet placed by Milk Ear Willie, a prizefighter, who comes to the Hot Box to shoot Sorrowful. As Milk Ear draws a bead on Sorrowful, Marky suddenly rushes into the club wearing only her nightgown and jumps into Sorrowful's arms. Milk Ear refuses to shoot for fear of hitting Marky. It turns out Marky has run several blocks barefoot through the snow to the club because she missed Sorrowful. The next day finds her hospitalized, suffering from pneumonia. As Marky's condition worsens, the hospital is overwhelmed by gifts and visits from the "hard citizens" and "many other prominent characters, especially as these characters keep trying to date up the nurse."[14]

The newspapers soon learn of the commotion at the hospital, and Marky and her visitors become front-page stories, as the little girl's condition worsens. Marky's only hope seems to be Doc Beerfeldt, the now retired great pneumonia specialist whom it is impossible to see "unless you are somebody like John D. Rockefeller or maybe President Hoover"[15]—or Milk Ear Willie, who simply kidnaps Beerfeldt at gunpoint and brings him to Marky's bedside. Unfortunately, things have progressed too far, and Marky succumbs, her last words being her near mantralike "Marky dance."

But at the moment of her death, her father suddenly appears at the hospital with his mother and sister in tow. The melodrama that follows is best indicated by quoting directly from Runyon's story:

> "I leave my little girl with you one day while I go on an errand, and while I am on this errand everything goes blank, and I wind up back in my home in Indianapolis with my mother and sister here.... We will be rich," the young guy says. "We just learn that my darling child will be sole heiress to her maternal grandpa's fortune, and the old guy is only a hop ahead of the undertaker right now."[16]

The family's lack of sorrow at Marky's death and their enthusiasm for their imminent newfound wealth disgust Sorrowful and his cronies. Indeed, Sorrowful changes on the spot: "a very strange thing seems to happen to his kisser, for all of a sudden it becomes the sad, mean-looking kisser that it is in the days before he ever sees Marky, and furthermore it is never again anything else."[17] And the guy who "is doing the best job of sobbing of all is nobody but Milk Ear Willie."[18]

Runyon's story is hardly the stuff of great literature. It is at best romanticized melodrama designed to have mass appeal to the readership of a popular weekly. The Depression and its continuing effects may be looming large, and America may be terrorized by all-too-real gangsters, but a "little doll" with "big blue eyes and fat pink cheeks, and a lot of yellow curls hanging down her back"[19] is able to bring out the best in gamblers, killers, and high-priced society doctors. The gap here between fantasy and reality is all the greater when one considers that at the time organized crime had a stranglehold on America and that the vicious tactics of a new breed of criminals (those who now comprise "organized crime") were grabbing the headlines daily. Al Capone finally went to jail only in late 1931, and John Dillinger was shot down outside Chicago's Biograph Theatre on July 22, 1934.[20] In comparison to the likes of Capone and Dillinger, even Milk Ear Willie seems a caricature. As J.C. Furnas notes, Runyon, in portraying his underworld characters, follows a fairly simple principle, "the reasonable well-worn device of making a hard-boiled enemy of society behave like St. Francis of Assisi, demonstrating for all and sundry that the softest hearts beat beneath the latest fashions in bullet-proof vests."[7]

Such sanitizing of crime doubtless explains in part Hollywood's embrace of Marky's story, which has been brought to the screen four times—as *Little Miss Marker* in 1934, as *Sorrowful Jones* in 1948, as *40 Pounds of Trouble* in 1962, and again as *Little Miss Marker* in 1980.[8] In each case, filmmakers make significant changes to the plot of Runyon's story. In none of the four movies, for instance, does Marky die, although in each case her father dies under a variety of circumstances. Also in all four films, Marky and Sorrowful end up living together happily ever after as Sorrowful settles down and marries a love interest whom each film introduces to provide the orphaned Marky with a proper home. In the original story and the four film versions, Marky's mother is already dead before the story opens. But more interestingly, the original film version of Runyon's story adds to its source an Arthurian subplot found only in the 1934 film.

The original Little Miss Marker was five-year-old Shirley Temple in her first starring role. Temple was a natural choice for the role: her physical features were an almost perfect match for those of Runyon's Marky, who like Temple was a real life "little doll" with "big blue eyes and fat pink cheeks, and a lot of yellow curls hanging down her back."[22] But Temple's mother had to lobby hard to get her daughter the part; Paramount had bought the rights to Runyon's story with the idea of changing the diminutive central character to a boy and offering the role to Jackie Cooper.[23]

As it turned out, the film guaranteed Temple's future career—she had previously played only bit parts in film shorts—and rescued Paramount from the brink of financial doom.[24] Temple soon proved a formidable presence both on and off the screen. Interestingly, Shirley Temple and Adolph Menjou, the film's Sorrowful Jones, had strikingly different recollections about their working together. Temple wrote that "Adolphe Menjou was wonderful to work with and he used to play jacks with me on the dressing-room floor. The studio would never allow any photographs made of our games because it might destroy his reputation as 'Hollywood's best-dressed man.'"[25] Menjou, on the other hand, told an interviewer:

> I've played with a lot of actresses, and I've learned how to defend myself. You know, troupers who step on your lines and steal your scenes. But this child frightens me. She knows all the tricks. She backs me out of the camera, blankets me, crabs my laughs—she's making a stooge of me. Why, if she were forty years old and on the stage all her life, she wouldn't have had the time to learn all she knows about acting. Don't ask me how she does it. You've heard of chess champions at eight and violin virtuosos at ten? Well, she's an Ethel Barrymore at six.[26]

With *Little Miss Marker*, Temple's career as an American icon was clearly launched.[27] The film is hers from the moment she first appears on screen. And Menjou's comments reflect, almost bitterly, the old acting saw suggesting that actors are foolish to share the stage or the screen with children or dogs because they will always be upstaged.

The 1934 film opens in the office of Big Steve Holloway, small-time mobster and nightclub owner, who is attempting to muscle in on the racing business by fixing a race so that he can win big and pay off his own gambling debts. To do so, he leans on New York's bookies, including a reluctant Sorrowful Jones, to join him in the scheme. Big Steve threatens to ruin the bookies if they do not go along with his plans. Big Steve owns a horse named Dream Prince whose jockey will hold him back in an initial race. In the second race, a veterinarian will give the horse a speedball that will allow him to win but cause him to drop dead after the race. Big Steve then lets it be known that he is betting big on Dream Prince in the first race, and suckers line up at their favorite bookies to place bets on the horse to win.

Among one of those suckers is an unnamed man who, short of cash to bet on Dream Prince, leaves his young daughter, Martha Jane, as surety for the bet that he places with Sorrowful. The man never returns—we learn later that he commits suicide after Dream Prince loses the race—and Sorrowful is stuck with Martha Jane, whom an associate dubs "Marky," as a shortened form of her given name. As the incredibly precocious Marky walks around the betting parlor, she begins to address people she meets with chivalric names and titles. Dizzy, the black janitor, becomes the Black Knight. Sorrowful's assistant, Regret, becomes Sir Lancelot. Bennie the Gouge, another of Sorrowful's associates, becomes Sir Perceval. Even Big Steve becomes the Strong Knight, and Sorrowful, Sir Sorry. Bangles Carson, Steve's girlfriend, becomes Lady Guinevere. When questioned by Bangles as to why she bestows these names on the people whom she meets, Marky tells her that her mother used to read her bedtime stories every night about King Arthur. But Marky's gesture here is clearly more significant. There is a transformative power to this renaming process. Changing underworld nicknames to chivalric identities imposes romance signifiers on criminals with positive effects. Never really all that threatening to begin with, Sorrowful and company are now positioned to embrace the heroic.

Unclaimed by her father, Marky joins Sorrowful and his cronies at Big Steve's nightclub where Bangles is the featured singer. Without singing a note—or dancing a step—Marky is soon the center of attention in the nightclub. She helps Sorrowful win a bet and ends up staying at his rather seedy apartment for the night. Soon, however, she is having a noticeable effect on Sorrowful, and he and his cronies are having an effect on her. Marky adopts the patter of the "mugs," and Sorrowful begins to show that he may have a bit of a heart after all. An investigation of Dream Prince's first race leads to Big Steve's being banned from racing, so Sorrowful hits upon the idea of registering the horse in Marky's name. Marky continues her chivalric fairy tale by dubbing the horse "the Charger." Big Steve, meanwhile, leaves town for Chicago so that he can bet against Dream Prince in his second (and last) race from a safe distance, entrusting Bangles to Sorrowful's care.

Because he needs Marky until after the second race, Sorrowful refuses to turn her over to the police or to the child welfare authorities, setting her up in a rather posh apartment instead and somewhat begrudgingly buying her some new clothes. At night, he reads her stories about King Arthur, just as her mother did, at first improvising from news reports in the *Racing Form* by substituting Arthurian names for the names of the horses.

Marky continues to melt street-hardened hearts. Cast here for the first time as the quintessential screen moppet she would subsequently always be known as, Temple sings, cries, and charms everyone she meets, causing them to go "just plain sappy over her." She also continues to develop some rough edges, thanks to her further association with Sorrowful and his "mugs." Among the presents Bangles buys her, with an eye toward teaching her how to behave better, is a copy of Sidney Lanier's *The Boy's King Arthur*, from which Sorrowful now reads her more traditional Arthurian tales.[28]

Sorrowful Jones (Adolphe Menjou) reads Martha Jane (Shirley Temple) a bedtime story from Sidney Lanier's *The Boy's King Arthur* in *Little Miss Marker* (1934).

Further concerned about the bad influence that hanging out with the "mugs" is having on Marky, Bangles convinces Sorrowful to throw an Arthurian costume party for her in Big Steve's club. Bangles hopes this Arthurian pageant will have a civilizing effect on Marky—and on Sorrowful and his cronies. At a horse-shoe-shaped "round table," Runyon's "hard citizens" sit dressed in chivalric finery as Marky, clearly the princess of King Arthur's knights, parades around the club riding on Dream Prince. An ecstatic Princess Marky dubs Sorrowful "Sir Galahad, the greatest knight of all." As my colleague, Dr. John Christopher Kleis, pointed out to me, Sorrowful should more properly be dubbed Sir Tristan, whose name comes in legend from the sad circumstances of his birth. His mother died in childbirth. But Tristan is a problematic hero because of his doomed love affair with the fiancée, Isolde, of his uncle King Mark. In contrast, the always pure Galahad is always above

Bangles Carson (Dorothy Dell) as Lady Guinevere, Sorrowful Jones (Adolphe Menjou) as Sir Galahad, and Martha Jane (Shirley Temple) as the Princess in the party scene in *Little Miss Marker* (1934).

reproach. And this change of names clearly signals a total change in Sorrowful's character. He goes from becoming a "hero" in the underworld to a true hero thanks to the influence of a young girl who introduces him to the legend of King Arthur.

Having grown suspicious of Sorrowful and Bangles, Big Steve suddenly arrives from Chicago intent on teaching them both a lesson. But Big Steve's mere presence scares Dream Prince, who bolts, throwing Marky to the ground and knocking her unconscious. She is rushed to the hospital, and her condition is diagnosed as critical. In a scene that parallels one in Runyon's original short story, Sorrowful kidnaps the leading child surgeon, Dr. Ingalls, from his wedding and forces him to come to the hospital to treat Marky. Ingalls wants to operate immediately, but Marky first needs a blood transfusion. No one at the hospital, however, is a suitable donor, and all despair for Marky's life until Big Steve shows up still intent upon teaching Sorrowful a lesson. Regret disarms Big Steve, who reluctantly agrees to have his blood typed.

Meanwhile Sorrowful—in a scene that definitely casts Menjou against type—is in the waiting room offering a sappy prayer for Marky's recovery. When it turns out that Big Steve's blood type is a perfect match for Marky's, he agrees to provide Marky with the blood that she needs for her operation. Once it is clear that she will survive, Dr. Ingalls assures Big Steve that he has good, strong blood. Marky briefly awakens to dub Big Steve the Strong Knight once again, and a clearly changed Big Steve almost dances out of the operating room, announcing to all that he has given life for a change because he has "good blood" in him. It is perhaps not too much of a stretch to see Steve's good blood as a parallel to the "royal blood" of the Arthurian heroes, yet another sign of the power of the Arthurian legend to transform a member of the underworld into a hero.

The centrality of the Arthurian story and of its role in helping to mold proper behavior to the 1934 film version of Runyon's short story is even more apparent when the original film is compared to its three remakes. Each of these films marginalizes the original central character, Marky, although certain details about her remain the same. She is always, for instance, left behind by a father who does not return, and her mother is in each case already dead. But the Marky character becomes the means to an end in each of the three film remakes. These remakes are romantic comedies, and the Marky character functions simply as a means to join two reluctant adult characters together romantically.

The 1948 *Sorrowful Jones*, for instance, is primarily a vehicle to display the comedic talents of Bob Hope and Lucille Ball. Nonetheless, Bruce Cabot's Big Steve Holloway is truly a sinister character. He has Martha Jane's father, Orville Smith, killed after he intercepts a telephone call in Big Steve's office and learns that the upcoming big race is fixed. Later, when he discovers that Martha Jane is Smith's daughter, Big Steve tries to get rid of her as well. She is injured when she falls from a fire escape. Rushed to a hospital in a coma, she awakens not because she receives a blood transfusion but because Sorrowful brings the horse in the film, Dreamy Joe, to visit her. The horse nuzzles the little girl and she suddenly wakes up, as an unrepentant Big Steve is arrested and led off in handcuffs for the murder of Orville Smith.

In the 1962 *40 Pounds of Trouble*, Sorrowful is transformed into Tony Curtis's suave, womanizing Steve McCluskey, who manages a Lake Tahoe hotel-casino complex for Bernie "the Butcher" Friedman. The little girl's father leaves her behind at the casino, although not as a marker, and dies in an automobile accident before he can return to pay a gambling debt and collect his daughter. The Chicago-based Bernie (read potential gangster by geography) sounds threatening enough, but he turns out to be really a meat cutter, not a thug. This film's Steve is the hero, who spars with Chris Lockwood, Bernie's niece; the two are brought together at Disneyland by Penny, the film's Martha Jane.

The 1980 *Little Miss Marker* also stars Tony Curtis who plays the rather benign thug, Blackie Ryan, suitor of the impoverished society widow Amanda Worthington, played by Julie Andrews. Blackie wants to use her estate as a venue for a fancy illegal gambling salon that caters to the rich. Amanda's only other possession is a horse called Sir Galahad, to whom Blackie wants to give a speedball so the horse can win a race to underwrite Blackie's gambling enterprises. Sorrowful, played by Walter Matthau, takes the Kid as a marker from her father who commits suicide when his horse loses. Blackie's plans fail, but he extracts no greater revenge on Sorrowful than throwing him in the river. Sorrowful and Amanda marry to prevent the Kid from having to go to an orphanage, and all three honeymoon together at Coney Island. Missing in all three films is any Arthurian thread. Amanda's horse in the 1980 film is named Sir Galahad for no apparent thematic reason.

Missing too in all three films are characters in need of reforming or capable of being reformed. The 1948 Big Steve is carted away to prison for murder. The 1962 "villain," Bernie "the Butcher" Friedman, turns out to be nothing more than a blowhard meat cutter. In the 1980 film, Tony Curtis's Blackie Ryan does at one point shoot a dog to impress people that he means business, but he is essentially more a caricature of a gangster than even Runyon's original characters were. His biggest flaw is his affectation that he is somehow better than the "mug" he really is.

The Shirley Temple film is, however, part of an established Arthurian tradition, using Lanier as a subtext. By 1934, the story of King Arthur already had an accepted role in the proper education of young boys. Arthurian youth groups were popular in America in the late nineteenth and early twentieth centuries.[29] These youth groups were in turn partially the inspiration for the Boy Scouts, whose founder, Lord Baden-Powell, encouraged his boys to read stories of King Arthur to find role models for their lives.[30] And the Boy Scouts were in part responsible for a 1917 film, *Knights of the Square Table; or, The Grail,* which parallels the adventures of two groups of boys, a group of Scouts and a group of ne'er-do-wells, whose leader's prize possession is another boy's King Arthur book, Howard Pyle's *The Story of King Arthur and His Knights* (first published in 1903), which was given to him by his mother on her deathbed.[31]

In the 1934 film version of his story, Runyon's gangsters are reduced to wrongheaded bad boys with hearts of gold. They simply need to learn to behave better, and their principal corrective text is Lanier's version of the Arthuriad to which a five-year-old moppet introduces them.[32] Lobby cards and advertisements for the film proclaimed "She Made Softies out of Hard Guys and Dolls," and she made "Broadway Mugs Believe in Fairies." Coincidentally, the same little girl learns how better to mind her manners. But the real-life little girl who played Martha Jane on screen herself recognized that stories of King Arthur were really designed for boys, not for girls. In an early autobiography distributed by Paramount, an eight-year-old Shirley Temple wrote: "There's another story which I like almost as much as *Heidi*. It's one of the first stories that Daddy ever read to me. He read it while I was making *Little Miss Marker*. It's *King Arthur*. That's not a girl's story at all, but I like it still."[33] Temple's comment is especially interesting given the original intention in Hollywood of recasting Runyon's story to make the central character a boy (played by Jackie Cooper) rather than a girl. The 1934 film *Little Miss Marker* has generally not been discussed as an example of cinema Arthuriana.[34] It turns out, however, to be a rather good example of a film that uses the story of Arthur to advance its plot while also underscoring the continuing appeal that the story of the once and future king has had for audiences of all ages.[35] One of the reasons that the story of Arthur makes such a good read and still has a central place in Western culture is its grounding in an heroic ideal. In the 1934 film, America's sweetheart, Shirley Temple, uses the Arthurian text as retold by Lanier to transform a group of "mugs"—and herself—into genuine heroes at a time when Depression-era America could use a touch of the heroic.

Notes

1. For the most recent catalogue of cinema Arthuriana, see Kevin J. Harty, "Cinema Arthuriana: An Overview" and "Cinema Arthuriana: A Comprehensive Filmography and Bibliography," in Kevin J. Harty, ed., *Cinema Arthuriana, Twenty Essays* (Jefferson, NC: McFarland, 2002), pp. 7–33, 252–301.

2. "'What's Up, Duke?' A Brief History of Arthurian Animation," in Kevin J. Harty, ed., *King Arthur on Film, New Essays on Arthurian Cinema* (Jefferson, NC: McFarland, 1999), p. 203.

3. For how well Twain has fared at the hands of filmmakers, see Kevin J. Harty, "Cinematic Legends Lost and Found: The Film Versions of Mark Twain's *A Connecticut Yankee in King Arthur's Court* and George Romero's *Knightriders*," in Kevin J. Harty, ed., *Cinema Arthuriana, Twenty Essays* (Jefferson, NC: McFarland, 2002), pp. 96–109; and Elizabeth S. Sklar, "Twain for Teens: Young Yankees in Camelot," in Kevin J. Harty, ed. *King Arthur on Film: New Essays on Arthurian Cinema* (Jefferson, NC: McFarland, 1999), pp. 97–108.

4. Damon Runyon, "Little Miss Marker," *Collier's* 89 (26 March 1932): 7–9, 40, 43, 44.

5. For a discussion of Runyon's use of cant, jargon and argot, see Jean Wagner, *Runyonese: The Mind and Craft of Damon Runyon* (Paris: Stechert-Hafner, 1965), pp. 84–108; and John Lardner, "The Secret Past of a Popular Author," *New Yorker* 25 (27 August 1949): 58–63.

6. Runyon, p. 7.

7. Runyon, p. 7.

8. Runyon, p. 8.

9. Runyon, p. 9.

10. Runyon, p. 8.

11. Runyon, p. 8–9.

12. Runyon, pp. 9, 40.

13. Runyon, p. 40.

14. Runyon, p. 40.

15. Runyon, p. 43.

16. Runyon, p. 44.

17. Runyon, p. 44.

18. Runyon, p. 44.

19. Runyon, p. 7.

20. For an indication of the volume of coverage afforded both Capone, even after he went to jail, and Dillinger, see *The New York Times Index [for 1932]* (1933; rpt. New York: Bowker, 1964), p. 438; *The New York Times Index [for 1933]* (1934; rpt. New York: Bowker, 1964), p. 498; and *The New York Times Index [for 1934]* (1935; rpt. New York: Bowker, 1964), pp. 440 and 710–13.

21. The original source for Furnas's comment is unclear. I quote it from Wagner (p. 48). When Wagner interviewed Furnas (pp. 146–47), Furnas himself was unsure where and when he made the comment. Wagner subsequently argues that the gangland respectability imposed in "Little Miss Marker" is an exception to the rule in Runyon's stories (pp. 48–80). Wagner's conclusion is echoed by Guy Szuberla in his comments about the film versions of "Little Miss Marker," which are the subject of the balance of my essay. See Guy Szuberla, "Damon Runyon at the Movies," *Literature/Film Quarterly* 21 (January 1993): 71–79.

22. The original film version was directed by Alexander Hall for Paramount. It starred Adolphe Menjou as Sorrowful, Dorothy Dell as his love interest Bangles Carson, Charles Bickford as gangster Big Steve Holloway, and Shirley Temple as Martha Jane, the film's title character. The 1948 version was directed by Sidney Lanfield for Paramount and starred Bob Hope as Sorrowful, Lucille Ball as his love interest Gladys O'Neill, Bruce Cabot as gangster Big Steve Holloway, and Mary Jane Saunders as Martha Jane Smith, the abandoned gambling marker. The 1962 version was directed by Norman Jewison for Curtis Enterprises and Universal-International and starred Tony Curtis as Steve McCluskey, a stand-in for Sorrowful who manages a casino and is dodging alimony payments to his former wife. The casino is run by Bernie "the Butcher" Friedman (Phil Silvers), whose niece Chris Lockwood (Suzanne Pleschette) becomes Steve's love interest. The two eventually marry to prevent the orphaned Penny Piper (Claire Wilcox as the film's Little Miss Marker) from going to an orphanage. The 1980 version was directed by Walter Bernstein for Universal and starred Walter Matthau as Sorrowful, Julie Andrews as his love interest Amanda Worthington, Tony Curtis as mobster Blackie Ryan, and Sara Stimson as the Kid.

23. Runyon, p. 7.

24. See Patricia King Hanson, ed., *The American Film Institute Catalog of Motion Pictures Produced in the United States. Feature Films, 1931–1940* (Berkeley, CA: University of California Press, 1993), p. 1211.

25. On the film's role in establishing Temple's career—she would soon become Hollywood's highest paid film star—see Patsy Guy Hammontree, *Shirley Temple Black, A Bio-Bibliography* (Westport, CT: Greenwood, 1998), pp. 39–60. On the

film's effect on Paramount's previously precarious finances, see Robert Windeler, *The Films of Shirley Temple* (Secaucus, NJ: Citadel, 1978), p. 131.

26. Shirley Temple and the Editors of *Look*, *My Young Life* (Garden City, NY: Garden City Publishing, 1945), p. 50.

27. Quoted in Jeanine Basinger, *Shirley Temple* (New York: Pyramid Publications, 1979), p. 34.

28. Temple's role as American icon has been the subject of some continuing debate and reassessment. The brief against her—or at least against her public persona—is complicated. Critics have objected to the fact that her public persona was used to exploit her, to commodify her, to anesthetize the country during the Depression, and even to reinforce racial stereotypes. For representative discussions of the various aspects of the brief against Temple's public persona, see Charles Eckert, "Shirley Temple and the House of Rockefeller," *Jump Cut* 2 (July-August 1974): 1, 17–20; Lori Merish, "Cuteness and Commodity Aesthetics: Tom Thumb and Shirley Temple," in Rosemarie Garland Thomson, ed., *Freaking: Cultural Spectacles of the Body Extraordinary* (New York: New York University Press, 1996), pp. 185–203; and Karen Orr Vered, "White and Black in Black and White: Management of Race and Sexuality in the Coupling of Child-Star Shirley Temple and Bill Robinson," *The Velvet Light Trap* 39 (Spring 1977): 52–65.

29. Lanier's popular book was first published in 1880 with illustrations by Alfred Kappes. It was then reissued in 1917 with new illustrations by N. C. Wyeth. In the 1934 film, Sorrowful reads to Marky from the reissued edition.

30. For an extensive discussion of the role of the story of King Arthur in programs designed to educate boys properly, see Alan Lupack, "Visions of Courageous Achievement: Arthurian Youth Groups in America," *Studies in Medievalism* 6 (1994): 50–68; and Alan Lupack and Barbara Tepa Lupack, *King Arthur in America* (Cambridge, U.K.: D. S. Brewer, 1999), pp. 60–68.

31. The 1908 edition of Baden-Powell's *Scouting for Boys* specifically recommended that scouts read Uriel W. Cutler's *Stories of King Arthur*, an expurgated version of Malory first published in the United States in 1904. See Robert H. MacDonald, *Sons of Empire: The Frontier and the Boy Scout Movement, 1890–1918* (Toronto: University of Toronto Press, 1993), p. 249. I am grateful to Dan Nastali, who answered an April 2002 query I posted on Arthurnet about *Stories of King Arthur and His Knights*, for additional information about Cutler.

32. For a discussion of the film, see Kevin J. Harty, "*The Knights of the Square Table*: The Boy Scouts and Thomas Edison Make an Arthurian Film," *Arthuriana* 4 (Winter 1994): 313–23.

33. Apparently, Temple's performance in the film also charmed a real life thug. In his biography of Runyon, Jimmy Breslin reports that Benito Mussolini was a big fan of Temple after he saw the film. See Jimmy Breslin, *Damon Runyon* (New York: Ticknor & Fields, 1991), p. 326.

34. Shirley Temple, *Now I Am Eight* (Akron, OH: Saalfield Publishing Co., 1937), n.p.

35. Alan Lupack and Barbara Tepa Lupack very briefly discuss Runyon's short story and the four films based upon it in *King Arthur in America*, pp. 323–24.

36. Other films that use the Arthuriad to advance their plots while also underscoring the continuing appeal that the story of the once and future king has include the more recent *Knightriders*, *The Four Diamonds*, *The Mighty*, and *The Sixth Sense*—the last three are youth-centered. See Kevin J. Harty, "Looking for Arthur in All the Wrong Places: A Note on M. Night Shyamalan's *The Sixth*

Sense," *Arthuriana* 10 (Winter 2000): 57–62; and "'Arthur? Arthur? Arthur?'—Where Exactly Is the Cinematic Arthur to Be Found?" in Alan Lupack, ed. *New Directions in Arthurian Studies* (Woodbridge, Suffolk: Boydell & Brewer, 2002), pp. 135–48.

Works Cited

Basinger, Jeanine. *Shirley Temple*. New York: Pyramid Publications, 1979.
Breslin, Jimmy. *Damon Runyon*. New York: Ticknor & Fields, 1991.
Eckert, Charles. "Shirley Temple and the House of Rockefeller." *Jump Cut* 2 (July-August 1974): 1, 17–20.
Hammontree, Patsy Guy. *Shirley Temple Black, A Bio-Bibliography*. Westport, CT: Greenwood, 1998.
Hanson, Patricia King, ed. *The American Film Institute Catalog of Motion Pictures Produced in the United States. Feature Films, 1931–1940*. Berkeley, CA: University of California Press, 1993.
Harty, Kevin J., ed. *Cinema Arthuriana, Twenty Essays*. Jefferson, NC: McFarland, 2002.
_____. *King Arthur on Film, New Essays on Arthurian Cinema*. Jefferson, NC: McFarland, 1999.
_____. "*The Knights of the Square Table*: The Boy Scouts and Thomas Edison Make an Arthurian Film." *Arthuriana* 4 (Winter 1994): 313–23.
_____. "Looking for Arthur in All the Wrong Places: A Note on M. Night Shyamalan's *The Sixth Sense*." *Arthuriana* 10 (Winter 2000): 57–62. Lardner, John. "The Secret Past of a Popular Author." *New Yorker* 25 (27 August 1949): 58–63.
Lupack, Alan. "Visions of Courageous Achievement: Arthurian Youth Groups in America." *Studies in Medievalism* 6 (1994): 50–68
_____, ed. *New Directions in Arthurian Studies*. Woodbridge, Suffolk: Boydell & Brewer, 2002.
_____ and Barbara Tepa Lupack. *King Arthur in America*. Cambridge, U.K.: D.S. Brewer, 1999.
MacDonald, Robert H. *Sons of Empire: The Frontier and the Boy Scout Movement, 1890–1918*. Toronto: University of Toronto Press, 1993.
Runyon, Damon. "Little Miss Marker." *Collier's* 89 (26 March 1932): 7–9, 40, 43, 44.
Szuberla, Guy. "Damon Runyon at the Movies." *Literature/Film Quarterly* 21 (January 1993): 71–79.
Temple, Shirley. *Now I Am Eight*. Akron, OH: Saalfield Publishing Co., 1937.
_____ and the Editors of *Look*. *My Young Life*. Garden City, NY: Garden City Publishing, 1945.
Thomson, Rosemarie Garland, ed. *Freaking: Cultural Spectacles of the Body Extraordinary*. New York: New York University Press, 1996.
Vered, Karen Orr. "White and Black in Black and White: Management of Race and Sexuality in the Coupling of Child-Star Shirley Temple and Bill Robinson." *The Velvet Light Trap* 39 (Spring 1977): 52–65.
Wagner, Jean. *Runyonese: The Mind and Craft of Damon Runyon*. Paris: Stechert-Hafner, 1965.
Windeler, Robert. *The Films of Shirley Temple*. Secaucus, NJ: Citadel, 1978.

Filmography

1934 *Little Miss Marker*, d. Alexander Hall, with Adolphe Menjou, Dorothy Dell, Charles Bickford, Shirley Temple. U.S.: Paramount Pictures.

1949 *Sorrowful Jones*, d. Sidney Lanfield, with Bob Hope, Lucille Ball. U.S.: Paramount Pictures.

1963 *40 Pounds of Trouble*, d. Norman Jewison, with Tony Curtis, Suzanne Pleschette. U.S.: Curtis Enterprises and Universal-International Pictures.

1980 *Little Miss Marker*, d. Walter Bernstein, with Walter Matthau, Julie Andrews, Tony Curtis, Sara Stimson. U.S.: Universal Pictures.

Boys to Men: Medievalism and Masculinity in *Star Wars* and *E.T.: The Extra-Terrestrial*

TOM HENTHORNE

In the 1950s historians apparently decided that the Dark Ages were not so dark after all.[1] Such revisionism is not unusual, of course. Historians frequently rewrite history, concluding, for example, that Alexander the Great was not so great, that the American Revolution was no revolution, and that Nero could not possibly have fiddled while Rome burned since fiddles had not been invented yet. What made the reinvention of the Middle Ages unusual was its rapid popularization. As Joerg O. Fichte notes, since World War II there has been "a great revival of interest in the Middle Ages," a revival that has transformed not only medieval studies, but popular culture.[2] This has been particularly true in the United States, a nation that, ironically, has no medieval past to celebrate. By the 1970s medieval-themed restaurants such as Round Table pizza parlors and White Castle hamburger stands were commonplace, and Americans began playing games such as Dungeons & Dragons and Swords and Sorcerers. In the United States at least, neomedievalism had become a part of mainstream culture.[3]

To an extent, the neomedievalism in mid-to-late twentieth-century America can be understood as a reaction to the social transformations that followed World War II, particularly those related to gender. At a time when traditional values were increasingly coming under attack, this new medievalism tended to affirm the existing social order by idealizing the Middle Ages as a period of peace and order, when both convention and authority were respected. It also promoted supposedly chivalric values—faith, loyalty, courage, and, for women at least, chastity—by reducing

complex medieval narratives such as those of Chrétien de Troyes and
Robert de Boron to simpler tales about knights in shining armor and
damsels in distress. Not every neomedieval work was set in the Middle
Ages, of course. By the seventies and eighties, one could read about alternative medieval worlds in fantasy novels such as *The Chronicles of Amber*,
"joust" with others atop flying ostriches at the local video arcade, and
see Indiana Jones quest after the Holy Grail at the theater.[4]

Science fiction films increasingly adopted neomedieval themes as
well, especially those that featured coming-of-age stories such as the original *Star Wars* film (1977) and *E.T.: The Extra-Terrestrial* (1982).[5] Like
the reformulated Camelot stories, these films were directed primarily at
boys, though they were popular with girls and adults as well. They suggested that faith, loyalty, and courage were the basis for true masculinity and that women were simply victims to be rescued or prizes to be
won.

This essay analyzes the neomedievalism of the late seventies and
early eighties in its original cultural context in order to identify its role
in the construction of masculinity. In particular, I hope to show how
coming-of-age films such as *Star Wars* and *E.T.* redeploy themes and
motifs of medievalism that themselves were developed in the late nineteenth century in order to promote conservative models of masculinity.[6]
Ultimately, I argue that it is no coincidence that the popularity of such
films peaked during Ronald Reagan's first term as president: neomedievalism and neoconservatism were both reactions to the supposed
excesses of the late sixties and early seventies, particularly those associated with the feminist and other liberation movements. Although filmmakers such as George Lucas and Steven Spielberg were hardly Reagan-
ites, their films are products of a reactionary period when even the
so-called liberals expressed nostalgia for imaginary, simpler times when
men were knights and warriors, and women were damsels and princesses.

Before addressing neomedieval film's ideological function, I want to
discuss medievalism in general and American medievalism in particular.
The history of medievalism dates all the way back to the early Renaissance when thinkers first began to differentiate their own "modern"
period from "darker," older times.[7] Although the Middle Ages was
generally thought of as a period of ignorance and stagnation, medieval
models were used intermittently throughout the Renaissance and the
Enlightenment to posit alternatives to the existing social order. It was not
until the nineteenth century, however, that medievalism was assimilated
into the dominant culture. As Alice Chandler observes in *A Dream of
Order*, this medievalism was essentially a reactionary movement, a response to both the French and the Industrial revolutions. According to
her:

the medievalism of the mid-nineteenth century demanded a renewed commitment from the "natural leaders" of society. The upper classes and the Church were asked to bestir themselves once again and to restore that great chain of feudalism in which each of the estates of the realm owed reciprocal allegiance to the others. Only under such guidance, they believed, could the disintegration of society be checked and the rule of order revived.[8]

As Chandler's work suggests, nineteenth-century European medievalism was essentially a social movement, one that idealized feudalism as a means of addressing the social problems associated with industrialization and the rise of the bourgeoisie.

Nineteenth-century medievalism manifested itself differently in America, of course, because the United States had no feudal order to return to and because its own national myths valued social mobility and opportunism rather than class privilege and *noblesse oblige*. Although some American medievalists, including Charles Eliot Norton and Henry Adams, idealized communal elements of feudal society, they did so in hopes of reforming American democracy rather than replacing it.[9] In the popular culture, the difference between European and American medievalism was even more pronounced; whereas Europeans tended to emphasize social relations, Americans emphasized individual conduct. James Russell Lowell's popular "The Vision of Sir Launfal" (1848), for example, is a didactic poem about a vain knight who, after years of questing for the Holy Grail, returns to England, having learned the true meaning of Christian charity. Although as Leon Howard notes, Lowell did not particularly care for the poem, it was widely disseminated both as a pamphlet and in children's textbooks, where it was used to provide moral instruction.[10]

Sidney Lanier's *A Boy's Froissart* (1879) and *A Boy's Arthur* (1880) were even more pointedly directed towards boys, as Marya DeVoto demonstrates in "The Hero as Editor: Sidney Lanier's Medievalism and the Science of Manhood." According to her, Lanier "viewed the encounter with medieval literature, history, and language as a crux in the formation of manhood,"[11] a belief reflected in his "Introduction" to *A Boy's Froissart*, where he writes: "Now, Froissart sets the boy's mind upon manhood.... In reading him the young soul sifts out for itself the splendor, the hardihood, the daring, the valor, the boundless conflict, and unhindered actions, which makes up the boy's early ideal of the man."[12] Lanier goes on to identify particular medieval behaviors that boys must develop if they are to become true men:

> To speak the very truth; to perform a promise to the utmost; to reverence all women; to maintain right and honesty; to help

the weak; to treat high and low with courtesy; to be constant
to one love; to be fair to a bitter foe; to despise luxury; to preserve simplicity, modesty, and gentleness in heart and bearing: this was in the oath of the young knight who took the
stroke upon him in the fourteenth century, and this is still the
way to win love and glory in the nineteenth.[13]

As the above passage suggests, Lanier idealizes the medieval knight as a
model of masculinity; in his view, every boy should aspire to be a "modern knight," emulating characters such as Froissart's Edward III and Malory's Lancelot.[14]

As one might expect, there are a number of important similarities
between American medievalism of the late nineteenth century and that
of the late twentieth century, particularly with regards to the construction of masculinity. There is also at least one important difference:
whereas nineteenth-century medievalists such as Lanier regarded the
Middle Ages as essentially "dark," emphasizing the ability of certain indi-
viduals to transcend the corruption and decadence of their times, many
twentieth-century American medievalists considered the period itself to
be superior to the modern age. In *A Boy's Arthur*, for example, Lanier
finds Launcelot to be not only heroic but singular:

I will but ask you to observe specially the majestic manhood
of Sir Launcelot during those dolorous last days when King
Arthur, under the frenzied advice of Sir Gawaine, brings two
great armies in succession to besiege Joyous Gard. Day after
day Gawaine, and sometimes Arthur, call out the vilest taunts
and dares and accusations over the walls; but ever Sir Launcelot, though urged even by his own indignant followers within,
replies with a grave and lordly reasonableness which shames
his enemies beyond measure; twice he fights a great single-
handed battle with Sir Gawaine and, although Gawaine is
miraculously helped, wounds him sorely, yet spares his life; he
charges his knights to be still loyal to King Arthur, and to do
the king no hurt, upon pain of death; and one day in a general engagement when King Arthur is unhorsed Sir Launcelot
himself flies to the rescue, places the king on horseback again,
and sees him safe, with perfect tenderness and loyalty.[15]

For Lanier, Launcelot is an ideal model of masculinity for boys because
he rises above the darkness around him. Post–World War II popular
medievalism tends to be very different in this regard; films such as
Camelot (1967) and *Excalibur* (1981) represent the Middle Ages as a time
when greatness was more common than it is now. Although individual
knights in these films have flaws, sometimes serious ones, together they
form a community of heroes capable of overcoming their evil adversaries. Late-twentieth-century American medievalism hence has a far

Han Solo (Harrison Ford) strikes a pose in *Star Wars* (1977).

stronger social element than the medievalism of the previous century since it calls for not only the emulation of particular heroes but a return to times when heroes abounded, when honor, integrity, and selflessness were valued, and when good prevailed over evil.

Late-twentieth-century nostalgia for the medieval is particularly evident in science fiction films such as *Star Wars* and *E.T.* Although neither film is set in the Middle Ages, both employ neomedieval themes in order to suggest that things were better in the past. *Star Wars*, a neomedieval

Obi-Wan Kenobi (Alec Guinness) in *Star Wars* (1977).

romance with a futuristic setting, reached a wider audience than any previous medieval film, entering into the popular consciousness very deeply. Within a year of its release in 1977, *Star Wars* became the most lucrative film ever, earning hundreds of millions of dollars in ticket sales and billions more in merchandizing.[16] Its sequels, *The Empire Strikes Back* (1980) and *The Return of the Jedi* (1983), were nearly as successful, and the series' popularity continues into the twenty-first century, when, as Glen Kenny notes, "most reasonably comfortable, reasonably media-savvy Americans don't go through a single day without hearing some passing *Star Wars* reference, in conversation or over the television or radio, or without seeing some ad or headline or Internet graphic that refers to it, or without coming upon a piece of *Star Wars*–related merchandise—book, comic, coffee mug, what have you."[17]

The popularity of George Lucas's *Star Wars* can be explained in part by its skillful exploitation of a number of medieval and neomedieval texts, including stories, narrative poems, science fiction thrillers, adventure films, and Westerns. As Jay Cocks suggests, *Star Wars* is "a combination of *Flash Gordon*, *The Wizard of Oz*, the Errol Flynn swashbucklers of the '30s and '40s and almost every Western ever screened—not to mention *The Hardy Boys*, *Sir Gawain and the Green Knight* and *The Faerie-Queene*."[18] It also borrows freely from popular tales about King Arthur. In essence, the film is a coming-of-age story about an orphaned boy, Luke Skywalker, who endeavors to become a Jedi Knight like his father before him. Just as King Arthur discovers his identity only after pulling a sword from a stone, Skywalker learns of his own past only after Obi-Wan Kenobi presents him with his father's lightsaber.[19] Skywalker soon finds, however, that becoming a man involves more than just possessing a sword[20]; he must learn to wield it properly, something he can learn only from other men.

Since his own father is unavailable, Skywalker turns to surrogates, namely Kenobi and Han Solo. Kenobi, who, as Sylvia McCosker notes, resembles "a medieval hermit-knight, doing penance in the wilderness for some great error," becomes Skywalker's spiritual advisor, teaching him the faith, reverence, and selflessness that a Jedi needs.[21] Solo, who is an adventurer rather than a hermit, teaches Skywalker audacity, courage, and personal loyalty. Guided by such mentors, Skywalker matures into a great warrior and leader, rescuing Princess Leia, helping to deliver the plans of the Death Star to the Rebel Alliance, and eventually leading the assault upon it. In the end, the community of heroes prevails; with the help of Kenobi, Solo and others, including Chewbacca, R2-D2, and C-3PO, Skywalker destroys the Death Star, and the dark knight, Darth Vader, is defeated, at least for the time being.

Star Wars is more than just a coming-of-age story modeled on medieval and neomedieval romances, of course; it is also a product of the late 1970s, a time when Americans were increasingly conscious of their diminishing military power, rising crime, and decreasing standard of living. Many Americans—including James Dobson, Jerry Falwell, and Ronald Reagan—associated the problems America faced with the erosion of traditional beliefs and values.[22] When considered within such a context, the reactionary function of *Star Wars* becomes apparent: Lucas seems to be calling for a return to traditional values just as conservative leaders of the late 1970s did. Lucas, however, addresses children rather than parishioners and voters. Like Lowell's "Sir Launfal" and Lanier's *A Boy's Arthur* and *A Boy's Froissart*, *Star Wars* provides appealing models of proper behavior to children, especially boys. Indeed, Lucas is explicit about his story's didacticism, just as Lanier was: "I wanted to make a kids' film that would strengthen contemporary mythology and introduce a kind of basic morality. Nobody's saying the very basic things; they're dealing in the abstract. Everybody's forgetting to tell kids, 'Hey, this is right and this is wrong.'"[23] As Dale Pollack notes, Lucas wanted to "present positive values" to children at a time when "traditional religion was out of fashion and the family structure was disintegrating."[24] In *Star Wars*, Lucas does this by creating an adventure story in which the "good guys" fight for a return to the traditional social order. Lucas's rebels are not revolutionaries but conservatives who hope to restore the old Republic where proper authority and the rule of law are respected.[25]

The fact that, except for the ever-in-distress Princess Leia, Lucas's "good guys" are almost entirely male is also significant. In *Star Wars* it

Princess Leia (Carrie Fisher) consoles Luke Skywalker (Mark Hamill) in *Star Wars* **(1977).**

is up to men to save the galaxy. Although Leia is initially represented as being an important rebel leader, it soon becomes apparent that she is more of "a drag" and "a nuisance" than an asset to the Rebellion, to borrow Lucas's own terms.[26] Indeed, her leadership results in capture or death for others and situations from which she herself needs to be rescued. At the very beginning of the film, for example, she not only fails in her mission to deliver the plans of the Death Star to the Rebel Alliance but is captured by Darth Vader and imprisoned aboard the Death Star. After being freed from her cell by Skywalker, Solo, and Chewbacca, she leads her rescuers into a giant trash compacter from which she must again be saved. When she and her rescuers finally manage to escape the Death Star, she has Solo take her directly to Rebel Headquarters, even though she knows that a transmitter has been placed aboard the ship, thereby endangering the entire Rebellion.

It is only when she relinquishes her leadership role that the Rebel Alliance has any success. Rather than issue commands, near the end of the film she gives Skywalker a chaste kiss before he flies away into battle and then silently watches the climactic assault upon the Death Star from a bunker. Still wearing what Peter Biskind calls a "Guinevere hairdo" and a "Pre-Raphaelite white gown," she has become a conventional damsel in distress: passive, dignified, yet never losing her regal bearing.[27]

The change in Leia has a powerful effect on those around her. Indeed, one could argue that it is her transformation from a comrade-in-arms into a conventional princess that enables Skywalker to become a powerful warrior; like Lanier's Launcelot, he sublimates his desire for an unattainable woman into feats of arms, something that Lucas underscores by having Skywalker emit what appears to be a postejaculatory groan after he fires a torpedo through a small exhaust port and into the depths of the Death Star. In the victory celebration that follows Skywalker's triumphant return to the Rebel Base, Leia fully embraces her ceremonial role as princess; now wearing jewelry and a revealing formal gown, Leia presents Skywalker and Solo with medals before the assembled rebel forces, all of whom appear to be male. Although the rebels have not yet succeeded in restoring the old social order throughout the galaxy, they have succeeded in restoring the old order among themselves. The Rebel Alliance, at least, is a place where men are warriors and leaders, and women are mere ornaments when they are visible at all.

If it is the Rebel Alliance's righteous battle to restore the old Republic that aligns *Star Wars* with a broad conservative movement that led to Ronald Reagan's election in 1980, it is Leia's transformation that marks the film as a reactionary response to the women's movement. In the beginning of the film, Leia is represented as being a "tomboy" of sorts, someone who has transgressed traditional gender roles by behaving like a man.[28] In order to reinforce this idea, Lucas desexualizes Leia, costuming the actor who plays her, Carrie Fisher, in a loosely fitting gown that covers her entire body and binding her breasts to her body with gaffer's tape.[29] In effect, Lucas makes Leia a "female man," to borrow Jonathan Swift's term: she shoots lasers, issues orders, challenges Solo for the role of alpha male, and refuses to be intimidated by Darth Vader. As I suggested earlier, such "unnatural" behavior only leads to disaster for Leia and those allied with her.

Once Leia accepts her place in the traditional order, however, giving up her tomboy ways to become a ceremonial princess, Lucas resexualizes her, removing not only the gaffer's tape but Fisher's bra, so that her femininity is evident when she runs to congratulate Skywalker after he returns from his assault upon the Death Star. No longer a female man or even a liberated woman, Leia now resembles a noble lady in a neomedieval romance: she is an object to be protected and admired. Rather than lead a community of heroes, she has become their inspiration—and a potential prize.

Like *Star Wars*, Steven Spielberg's *E.T.: The Extra-Terrestrial* uses the neomedieval romance to address problems associated with the social

Elliott (Henry Thomas) on a quest with the concealed E.T. from *E.T.: The Extra-Terrestrial* (1982).

transformations that occurred in the 1960s and 1970s. Released midway through Ronald Reagan's first term, the film seems to affirm the conservative call for a return to older, simpler times and traditional values. Unlike *Star Wars*, however, which values certain adults as mentors and allies, *E.T.* represents adults as being a part of a debased, corrupt world that ultimately must be rejected. Directed primarily at boys, *E.T.* suggests that by adopting the chivalric ideals that are represented in the film by Dungeons & Dragons, a popular role-playing game in which players create characters and go adventuring in neomedieval fantasy worlds, adolescent boys can achieve manhood without the assistance of adult males.[30] To Spielberg, who himself grew up in a fatherless home, delivering such a message was important[31]; he wanted to make a film that not only depicted "a young child's reaction to his parent's divorce" but demonstrated how a boy can become the ideal man by choosing virtue over vice.[32]

In terms of structure, *E.T.* resembles other neomedieval romances. The protagonist, Elliott, a ten-year-old child who, along with an older brother and a younger sister, is being raised by a divorced mother, must put chivalric ideals into practice in order to fulfill a quest—the rescue of an extra-terrestrial from the government. In particular, he must demonstrate courage, faith, initiative, selflessness, and even chastity. More important, perhaps, like King Arthur he must create a community of heroes—a twentieth-century version of the Knights of the Round Table—in order to overcome all adversaries and save the extra-terrestrial.

Spielberg signals the film's neomedievalism by introducing the main characters in the context of a raucous Dungeons & Dragons game that is being played in Elliott's kitchen by his brother and three of his brother's friends. Ideally, in D&D players work together so that their characters can overcome obstacles, acquire fame, fortune, and power, and complete quests. Michael and his friends, however, are anything but cooperative: they complain, squabble among themselves, and even throw things at each other. Their immature, unchivalrous behavior extends beyond the game, too; one of the boys, for instance, makes a lewd gesture at Elliott's mother when she bends to load the dishwasher. Ironically, only Elliott, who has been excluded from the game because of his age, is prepared to undertake a real-life quest and put the chivalric values D&D teaches into practice. Sent out by the older boys to pay for the pizza they have ordered, he encounters what he thinks is a goblin in the backyard.[33] Although initially frightened, he eventually establishes contact with the extra-terrestrial, leading it to his home. Rather than seek assistance from adults, Elliott hides the extra-terrestrial from them, taking the initiative and offering it his protection.

As the relationship between the extra-terrestrial and Elliott develops, it becomes increasingly complex. At first E.T. is simply a companion to a lonely child. Elliott shows him his toys and then feigns illness so he can stay home from school and play with his new friend. By the next day, however, the extra-terrestrial becomes a father figure of sorts, wearing Elliott's father's robe and drinking beer[34]; he even acts in a parental manner, mentoring Elliott in masculinity by telepathically inducing Elliott to free the frogs his class is about to dissect and then kiss the girl who Spielberg describes as "the prettiest in class."[35] In effect, the extra-terrestrial reinforces the lessons of D&D, teaching Elliott how to put chivalric ideals into practice and become a hero and a man. Finally, towards the end of the film, the extra-terrestrial himself is refigured as a damsel in distress, an event which is foreshadowed in the film when Elliott's sister puts a blonde wig and jewelry on E.T. and dresses it in women's clothes.[36] In terms of structure, it is this last relationship between Elliott and the extra-terrestrial that is most important, since it leads not only to the film's dramatic climax but also to Elliott's passage into manhood.

Once the extra-terrestrial is captured by the government, Elliott is

again forced to put the chivalric ideals he learned from D&D into practice. This time the stakes are much higher, however: it is E.T. who faces
death and dissection rather than frogs. In order to prevent this, Elliott
must again demonstrate strength, courage, and selflessness. More importantly, perhaps, he must also become a leader and evoke the same virtues
in others, organizing the very people who excluded him from the earlier
D&D game into a real-life community of heroes. Like King Arthur, Elliott
leads his modern-day knights against his adversaries. Mounted on bicy-
cles rather than horses, Elliott and the other boys rescue the extra-terrestrial, evading his armed captors, and carry him to the landing site,
where they are met by the alien spacecraft. The film ends with an affirma-
tion of the importance of masculine identity: Elliott stands before an
assembly of his own people and claims his place in society as a man.
Representing not only his quest companions but also society at large, he
bids the extra-terrestrial farewell and watches as the alien ship departs,
leaving behind only a rainbow-colored vapor trail.[37]

By almost any measure, *E.T.* represented the high-water mark for
neomedieval science fiction films, earning more than $700 million in the-
aters and receiving almost universal critical acclaim.[38] Although *Return
of the Jedi*, which was released in the following year, did very well at the
box office, the genre was already declining in popularity, and by the
mid–1980s dystopian films such as *The Terminator* (1984) and *Aliens*
(1986) were the top-grossing science fiction films. To an extent at least,
the change in public taste may be explained by changes in the culture.
With Ronald Reagan's reelection in 1984, the Reagan Revolution was
complete, and as a result there was less of a market for films that called
for a return to older, better times, since those times had already been
restored, at least in theory. Although neomedieval science fiction films
continued to be made throughout the 1980s, such films tended to affirm
the existing order rather than subvert it.

In the *Star Trek* films, for example, the crew of the *Enterprise* struggles to maintain the status quo, rather than alter it, by protecting the Fed-
eration from internal and external enemies.[39] In their representation of
masculinity, however, the *Star Trek* films resemble other neomedieval science fiction films. Like *Star Wars* and *E.T.*, they feature an almost exclusively male community of heroes whose individual deficiencies are offset
by their general adherence to a neochivalric code of conduct, one that
demands not only individual honor and courage but selflessness and a
commitment to preserving the social order. In *Star Trek II: The Wrath of
Khan* (1982), for instance, the threat from the past that Khan represents
is ultimately defeated through the combined efforts of the *Enterprise*
officers, who, after a series of errors and miscalculations, put into practice the repeatedly voiced idea: "The needs of the many outweigh the

needs of the few—or the one."[40] By framing the film's message in such terms, the film emphasizes the importance of community, just as the works of James Russell Lowell and Sidney Lanier did at the turn of the last century. In order for boys to become men, they suggest, boys must learn not only individual heroism but to subordinate their own interests to those of society.

Notes

1. Although Charles Haskins argued in *The Renaissance of the Twelfth Century* (Cleveland: World Publishing, 1957), p. vii, that the Middle Ages were "less dark and less static" than previously thought as early as 1927, a keyword search of academic works on Expanded Academic database suggests that the term "Dark Ages" fell into disuse only after World War II. See, for example, the introduction to Peter Brown's *The Rise of Western Christendom*, rev. ed. (Oxford: Blackwell, 2003), pp. 1–34. See also Marcia Colish, *Medieval Foundations of the Western Intellectual Tradition* (New Haven: Yale University Press, 1997); Robert Bartlett, *The Making of Europe: Conquest, Colonization, and Cultural Change, 950–1350* (Princeton, NJ: Princeton University Press, 1993); and Norman Cantor's *Inventing the Middle Ages* (New York: Morrow, 1991).

2. Fichte, "The End of Utopia—The Treatment of Arthur and his Court in Contemporary German Drama," in *Mediaevalitas: Reading the Middle Ages*, ed. Piero Boitani and Anna Torti (Rochester, NY: D.S. Brewer, 1996), p. 153.

3. In this paper I will use the term "medieval" to refer to physical and cultural products of the Middle Ages and the term "neomedieval" to things derivative thereof.

4. *Nine Princes of Amber*, the first book of Roger Zelazny's *The Chronicles of Amber* series, was published in 1970. In "Joust," a popular arcade game of 1982, players could duel with lances atop giant flying birds. *Indiana Jones and the Last Crusade* was released in 1989.

5. Other neomedieval science fiction films include *The Last Starfighter* (1984), *Starman* (1984), and *Highlander* (1986).

6. Following John Simons, I will use the term "medievalism" to denote "the process by which the Middle Ages is transformed into a useful discourse out of which can be produced ideas and practices which comment upon or contest other contemporary beliefs"; John Simons, ed. *From Medieval to Medievalism* (New York: Macmillan, 1992), p. 6.

7. See, for example, the "Introduction" to *The Portable Medieval Reader* by James Bruce Ross and Mary Martin McLaughlin (New York: Penguin, 1977), p. 5.

8. Chandler, *A Dream of Order: The Medieval Ideal in Nineteenth-Century English Literature* (Lincoln: University of Nebraska Press, 1970), pp. 4–5.

9. See Peter Williams "The Varieties of American Medievalism," *Studies in Medievalism* 11 (1982): 10; see also James P. Young, *Henry Adams: The Historian as Political Theorist* (Lawrence: University Press of Kansas, 2001).

10. Howard, *Victorian Knight-Errant: A Story of the Early Literary Career of James Russell Lowell* (Berkeley: University of California Press, 1952), p. 272.

11. *Studies in Medievalism* 9 (1997): 148–49.

12. Lanier, "A Boy's Froissart," in *Centennial Edition of the Works of Sidney*

Lanier, ed. Charles M. Anderson (Baltimore, MD: Johns Hopkins University Press, 1945), p. 346.

13. Lanier, "A Boy's Froissart," in *Centennial Edition*, p. 349.

14. Lanier, "A Boy's Arthur," in *Centennial Edition*, p. 369.

15. Lanier, "A Boy's Arthur," in *Centennial Edition*, p. 368.

16. Peter Biskind, *Easy Riders, Raging Bull: How the Sex-Drugs-and-Rock 'n' Roll Generation Saved Hollywood* (New York: Simon & Schuster, 1998), p. 135.

17. Kenny, "Introduction: Jedi Mind Tricks," in *A Galaxy Not so Far Away*, ed. Glenn Kenny (New York: Henry Holt and Company, 2002), p. xiii.

18. Quoted in John Baxter's *Mythmaker: The Life and Work of George Lucas* (New York, Avon, 1999), p. 243. For a detailed discussion of the relationship between science fiction and the medieval, see Kathryn Hume's "Medieval Romance and Science Fiction: The Anatomy of a Resemblance," *Journal of Popular Culture*, 16.1 (Summer 1982): 15–26.

19. For more on twentieth-century representations of King Arthur, see Raymond H. Thompson, "Conceptions of King Arthur in the Twentieth Century," in *King Arthur: A Casebook* (New York: Routledge, 2002).

20. For more on the lightsaber as a phallic symbol, see Biskind, p. 127.

21. Sylvia McCosker, "The Lady, the Knights and 'the Force' or How Medieval Is *Star Wars*," Culture@Home, available at http://www.anglicanmediasydney .asn.au/cul/StarWars.htm.

22. James Dobson founded Focus on the Family in 1977 and Jerry Falwell founded the Moral Majority in 1979, along with Paul Weyrich and Richard Viguerie. Ronald Reagan began focusing on "family values" as early as 1977. In a speech at the Fourth Annual CPAC Convention on February 6, 1977, in which he outlines the principles of the "New Republican Party," for example, he said: "Families must continue to be the foundation of our nation.... Families—not government programs—are the best way to make sure our children are properly nurtured, our elderly are cared for, our cultural and spiritual heritages are perpetuated, our laws are observed and our vales are preserved." "The New Republican Party," available at http://www.townhall.com/REAGAN/speeches/newrepublicanparty.htm.

23. Quoted in Dale Pollock's *Skywalking: The Life and Films of George Lucas* (New York: Da Capo Press, 1999), p. 144.

24. Dale Pollock, *Skywalking*, p. 143.

25. Biskind, p. 137.

26. Pollock, p. 165.

27. Biskind, p. 113.

28. Pollock, p. 165.

29. The gaffer's tape prompted Fisher to remark later, "No breasts bounce in space, there's no jiggling in the Empire." Pollock, p. 165.

30. In the original script, Dungeons & Dragons is mentioned by name. The production company was unable to acquire rights to the name, however, and so when *E.T.* was filmed, direct references to the game were omitted. See Linda Sunshine, ed., *E.T.: The Extra-Terrestrial from Concept to Classic* (New York: New Market Press, 2002), p. 53.

31. Spielberg, who describes himself as having grown up "in a house with three screaming younger sisters and a mother who played concert piano with seven other women" was very conscious of the lack of male influences when growing up; Michael Sragow, "A Conversation with Steven Spielberg," in *Steven Spielberg: Interviews*, ed. Lester Friedman and Brent Notbaughm (Jackson: University of Mississippi Press, 2000), p. 108.

32. Quoted in Sragow, p. 108.

33. The fact that he initially thinks that the extra-terrestrial is a "goblin" indicates the extent to which D&D has become a part of his conceptual system: goblins are a very common monster in the game. Spielberg reinforces this point by having Elliott make direct references to D&D throughout the film. For example, when one of his brother's friends calls him "a cintus suprimus," Elliott insults him back by repeatedly shouting "Zero charisma" at him, a term taken from the game's numerical system for measuring the attractiveness of a character.

34. For more on the extra-terrestrial as a father figure, see Marina Heung, "Why E.T. Must Go Home: The New Family in American Cinema," *Journal of Popular Film and Television* 11.2 (1983): 83–4.

35. Sragow, p. 110.

36. Even though it was crucial to the film's structure, refiguring E.T. as a damsel in distress was potentially problematic, of course, given American attitudes towards homosexuality in the early 1980s: any hint of homoerotic attraction between Elliott and the extra-terrestrial might have prevented the film from being a popular success. Spielberg seems to address this in two ways: by marking Elliott as a heterosexual in the kissing scene with the "pretty girl" and by having him use the term "penis-breath" when insulting his brother earlier in the film. Spielberg's own comments on the term make its homophobic connotations clear: "It's not the most popular word in the Pac Man generation's vernacular, but it's a word that's used every once in a while, and it conjures up quite gross and hilarious images" (Sragow, p. 112).

37. The original ending to the film makes explicit what is here only implied: Elliott has become a man. According to screenwriter Melissa Mathison: "There was a final scene we shot where Elliott and the boys are playing Dungeons and Dragons again, echoing the beginning. However, now Elliott is the ringmaster rather than the annoying little brother. He's grown. He has confidence. He's the master of his own destiny." The scene was cut because Henry Thomas, the actor who played Elliott, "was so emotional" in the farewell scene "that it was hard to go anywhere else" (Sunshine, p. 148).

38. Sunshine, p. 168.

39. The first Star Trek film, *Star Trek: The Motion Picture*, was released in 1979. The following Star Trek films were released in the 1980s: *Star Trek II: The Wrath of Khan* (1982), *Star Trek III: The Search For Spock* (1984), *Star Trek IV: The Voyage Home* (1986), and *Star Trek V: The Final Frontier* (1989). *Star Trek II: The Wrath of Khan*, which was released early in Reagan's presidency, earned $79,912,963 in the United States. *Star Trek IV: The Voyage Home*, which was released towards the end of Reagan's presidency, earned significantly more— $109,713,132; see http://www.the-numbers.com/movies.

40. These words are first spoken when, towards the beginning of the film, Spock transfers command of the *Enterprise* to Kirk. They are repeated towards the end of the film as Spock is dying after sacrificing himself for the sake of the ship. In both cases, Spock says, "The needs of the many outweigh the needs of the few" and Kirk adds, "or the one."

Works Cited

Bartlett, Robert. *The Making of Europe: Conquest, Colonization, and Cultural Change, 950–1350*. Princeton, NJ: Princeton University Press, 1993.

Baxter, John. *Mythmaker: The Life and Work of George Lucas.* New York: Avon, 1999.
Biskind, Peter. *Easy Riders, Raging Bull: How the Sex-Drugs-and-Rock 'n' Roll Generation Saved Hollywood.* New York: Simon & Schuster, 1998.
Brown, Peter. *The Rise of Western Christendom.* London: Blackwood, 1996.
Cantor, Norman. *Inventing the Middle Ages.* New York: Morrow, 1991.
Chandler, Alice. *A Dream of Order: The Medieval Ideal in Nineteenth-Century Literature.* Lincoln: University of Nebraska Press, 1970.
Colish, Marcia. *Medieval Foundations of the Western Intellectual Tradition.* New Haven, CT: Yale University Press, 1997.
DeVoto, Marya. "The Hero as Editor: Sidney Lanier's Medievalism and the Science of Manhood." *Studies in Medievalism 9* (1997): 148–70.
Fichte, Joerg O. "The End of Utopia—The Treatment of Arthur and his Court in Contemporary German Drama." In: *Mediaevalitas: Reading the Middle Ages,* ed. Piero Boitani and Anna Torti. Rochester, NY: D.S. Brewer, 1996, pp. 153–69.
Haskins, Charles. *The Renaissance of the Twelfth Century.* Cleveland, OH: World Publishing, 1957.
Heung, Marina. "Why E.T. Must Go Home: The New American Cinema." *Journal of Popular Film and Television* 11.2 (1983): 79–85.
Howard, Leon. *Victorian Knight-Errant: A Story of the Early Literary Career of James Russell Lowell.* Berkeley: University of California Press, 1952.
Hume, Kathryn. "Medieval Romance and Science Fiction: The Anatomy of a Resemblance." *Journal of Popular Culture* 16.1 (Summer 1982): 15–26.
Kenny, Glenn. "Introduction: Jedi Mind Tricks." In: *A Galaxy Not so Far Away,* ed. Glenn Kenny. New York: Henry Holt and Company, 2002.
Lanier, Sidney. "A Boy's Arthur." In: *Centennial Edition of Works of Sidney Lanier,* ed. Charles M. Anderson. Baltimore, MD: John Hopkins University Press, 1945, pp. 355–69.
Lanier, Sidney. "Introduction to *A Boy's Froissart.*" In: *Centennial Edition of Works of Sidney Lanier,* ed. Charles M. Anderson. Baltimore, MD: Johns Hopkins University Press, 1945, pp. 346–54.
McCosker, Sylvia. "The Lady, the Knights and 'the Force' or How Medieval Is *Star Wars.*" Cuture@Home. Available at http://www.anglicanmediasydney.asn.au/cul/StarWars.htm.
Pollock, Dale. *Skywalking: The Life and Films of George Lucas.* New York: Da Capo Press, 1999.
Reagan, Ronald. "The New Republican Party." Available at http://www.townhall.com/REAGAN/speeches/newrepublicanparty.htm.
Ross, James Bruce, and Mary Martin McLaughlin. "Introduction." In: *The Portable Medieval Reader.* New York: Penguin, 1977, pp. 1–29.
Simons, John. "Introduction." In: *From Medieval to Medievalism,* ed. John Simons. New York: Macmillan, 1992.
Sragow, Michael. "A Conversation with Steven Spielberg." In: *Steven Spielberg: Interviews,* ed. Lester Friedman and Brent Notbaughm. Jackson: University of Mississippi Press, 2000.
Sunshine, Linda. *E.T.: The Extra Terrestrial" from Concept to Classic.* New York: New Market Press, 2002.
Thompson, Raymond, H. "Conceptions of King Arthur in the Twentieth Century." In: *King Arthur: A Casebook.* New York: Routledge, 2002.
Williams, Peter. "The Varieties of American Medievalism." *Studies in Medievalism 2* (1982): 7–20.

Young, James P. *Henry Adams: The Historian as Political Theorist.* Lawrence: University Press of Kansas, 2001.

Filmography

1967 *Camelot,* d. Joshua Logan, with Richard Harris, Vanessa Redgrave. U.S.: Warner Bros., Seven Arts.

1977 *Star Wars,* d. George Lucas, with Mark Hamill, Harrison Ford, Carrie Fisher. U.S.: 20th Century–Fox.

1980 *The Empire Strikes Back,* d. Irvin Kershner, with Mark Hamill, Harrison Ford, Carrie Fisher. U.S.: 20th Century–Fox.

1981 *Excalibur,* d. John Boorman, with Nicol Williamson. U.S.: Orion.

1982 *E.T.: The Extra-Terrestrial,* d. Steven Spielberg, with Dee Wallace Stone, Henry Thomas, Peter Coyote, Robert MacNaughton, Drew Barrymore. U.S.: Universal.

1983 *The Return of the Jedi,* d. Richard Marquand, with Mark Hamill, Harrison Ford, Carrie Fisher. U.S.: 20th Century–Fox.

Star Trek II: The Wrath of Khan, d. Nicholas Meyer, with William Shatner, Leonard Nimoy, DeForest Kelley, Ricardo Montalban. U.S.: Paramount.

Last Starfighter, d. Nick Castle, with Lance Guest, Dan O'Herlihy, Catherine Mary Stewart. U.S.: Universal.

The Terminator, d. James Cameron, with Arnold Schwarzenegger, Michael Biehn, Linda Hamilton. U.S.: Orion.

1985 *Starman,* d. John Carpenter, with Jeff Bridges, Karen Allen. U.S.: Columbia.

1986 *Aliens,* d. James Cameron, with Sigourney Weaver. U.S.: 20th Century–Fox.

Highlander, d. Russell Mulcahy, with Christopher Lambert, Roxanne Hart. U.S.: 20th Century–Fox.

Iron Maidens

Medieval Female Heroes on Film

MARTHA W. DRIVER

The woman warrior continues to fascinate us. Praising the Old Testament warrior heroine Deborah in his treatise *On Widows*, St. Ambrose (ca. 339–397) says that Deborah "undertook to perform the duties of a man.... A widow, she governed the people; a widow, she led armies; a widow, she chose generals; a widow, she made military decisions and had charge of triumphs.... It is not sex, but valor that gives strength."[1] Writing almost fifteen hundred years later, John Stuart Mill, in his famous treatise *The Subjection of Women* (1869), observed that "In the feudal ages ... war and politics were not thought unnatural to women, because not unusual; it seemed natural that women of the privileged classes should be of manly character, inferior in nothing but bodily strength to their husbands and fathers."[2] Women engaged in, or financially supported, major political and religious battles throughout the Middle Ages, shaping the course of history. The wars that raged in Europe, as well as the various unsuccessful Crusades in the Holy Land, were not only fought by a few aristocrats but affected people on all levels of society. Though war and the battlefield are idealized in medieval literature and art, the daily reality must have been altogether different. The physical and intellectual challenges posed to women living in a warrior society, who must themselves become warriors, is one subject of the essays in this chapter.

Medieval women lived in uncertain times, when raids on property, homes, and castles were common, and they were often called upon to lead, direct, and organize their defense. In the eleventh century, Donna Jimena, the widow of Le Cid, held the city of Valencia for more than a year, fending off the Muslims. Ermengarde, a twelfth-century vicountess, led her troops against the count of Toulouse who had attempted to seize her lands. During the Scottish wars in the fourteenth century, the Countess of Buchan defended Berwick Castle against Edward I. To humiliate her after her defeat, Edward hung her in a cage, suspended from the ramparts.

Classical warrior women like Penthesilea and the Amazons gave inspiration and guidance to actual women warriors in the Middle Ages. Matilda, Countess of Tuscany (1046–1115), fought on the side of Pope Gregory VII against the German emperor Henry IV, providing troops and lending the Pope her fortress at Canossa for his historic confrontation with Henry. The Emperor stood barefoot in the snow outside Matilda's fortress, from 25 to 27 January, before being admitted and receiving absolution from the pope. A wealthy, pious aristocrat who was literate in German, French, Italian, and Latin, Matilda herself often joined her troops, making her first foray on the battlefield as a young girl. Her epitaph reads in part: "This warrior-woman disposed her troops as the Amazonian Penthesilea is accustomed to do. Thanks to her—through so many contests of horrid war—man was never able to conquer the rights of God."[3]

Eleanor of Aquitaine (1122?–1204), another strong-willed aristocrat, put on the garb of Penthesilea when she accompanied her first husband, Louis VII of France, on the Second Crusade. By consciously imitating the Amazon warrior queen, Eleanor simultaneously encouraged the troops and stylishly surmounted the rule forbidding concubines on the Crusade.[4] Subsequently, however, all women were forbidden to take part in the Third Crusade by general agreement of all Christian monarchs, including Eleanor's first husband, Louis VII!

In a world in which war and warfare were glorified, were indeed central to human experience, men were often away fighting for their lords or for the Church. The women were left behind to cope with everything else, taking on tasks traditionally thought masculine, a situation we have also seen in the twentieth century. With some stellar exceptions, physical warfare was generally the prerogative of men, though there are many examples of tough-minded women coming to the defense of their homes. In 1449, for example, while her husband, John, was away, Margaret Paston was left to defend Gresham Manor from a rival claimant, Lord Moleyns, "who sent to said mansion riotous people to the number of a thousand." Moleyn's men quickly subdued Margaret's small retinue, carrying Margaret bodily from the house, after which they robbed, looted, and "broke up all the rooms and chests."[5] Whether they endured plundering raids, as was Margaret's experience, or outright battle, war was a fact of life for women as well as men. Under adverse conditions, and in the absence of fathers, husbands, and sons, women continued to maintain and protect their homes and lands, working to preserve the family's stability and economic well-being.

Medieval history and literature are replete with powerful women characters who are decisive and independent, and in that respect, modern film reflects portrayals of women that are as old as those described by Chrétien de Troyes and Marie de France in the twelfth century. In modern renditions, however, the warrior women are perhaps seen as more anomalous, misfits who are great leaders of men, like St. Joan, for example. The essays that follow (by Anke Bernau, "Girls on Film: Medieval Virginity in the Cinema," Diana Slampyak, "*Crouching Tiger, Hidden Dragon*'s Wudan Warrior Princess," and Susan Butvin Sainato, "Not Your Typical Knight: The Emerging On-Screen Defender"), explore sometimes contradictory notions about female heroes on film.

Notes

1. Alcuin Blamires, Karen Pratt, and C. W. Marx, eds., *Woman Defamed and Woman Defended: An Anthology of Medieval Texts* (Oxford: Clarendon Press, 1992), p. 60. The description of a woman as "man-like" was considered the highest praise in late classical works like *The Golden Ass* by Apuleius and is frequently found in narrative accounts of the female saints. Petrarch uses the term as approbation in his Latinized story of patient Griselda. The word Petrarch uses is "virago," a man-like woman (*vir* is Latin for man), originally a compliment of the highest order, which has now become debased to mean a scold or domineering female.

2. John Stuart Mill, "from *The Subjection of Women*," in *Victorian Literature: Prose*, ed. G. B. Tennyson and Donald J. Gray (New York: Macmillan Publishing Co., Inc., 1976), p. 570.

3. Antonia Frasier, *The Warrior Queens* (New York: Vintage Books, 1990), p. 148.

4. Amy Kelly, *Eleanor of Aquitaine and the Four Kings* (Cambridge, MA: Harvard University Press, 1971), pp. 38–39, 47–48, 234, 257.

5. Emily Amt, ed., *Women's Lives in Medieval Europe: A Sourcebook* (New York: Routledge, 1993), pp. 173–174.

Girls on Film:
Medieval Virginity
in the Cinema

ANKE BERNAU

This compulsion towards liquidity, flow, and an accelerated
circulation of what is psychic, sexual, or pertaining to the body
is the exact replica of the force which rules the market value:
capital must circulate; gravity and any fixed point must disappear; the chain of investments and reinvestments must never
stop; value must radiate endlessly and in every direction.[1]

In Luc Besson's 1999 production, *The Messenger: The Story of Joan
of Arc*, an advisor to the Dauphin responds with the following statement
to the Dauphin's uncertainty as to whether Joan should be trusted or
not: "She claims to be a virgin. Well, that's something we can examine
and be absolutely certain about." What follows is one of the few chastity-
testing scenes in films dealing with medieval subject matter; arguably,
one of the few virginity-testing scenes in cinema *per se*.[2] The confident
assertion of the Dauphin's advisor that Joan's virginity is something that
can be tested and proven beyond doubt—something that can be rendered *visible*—brings together the main concerns of this article: How is
the medieval virgin heroine represented in contemporary cinema, and,
more fundamentally, how is virginity understood today? Can medieval
virginity be represented in a meaningful way, considering the cultural and
historical disparities between a medieval, Christian worldview and a
twenty-first-century, secular one?[3] How can a twenty-first-century cinematic audience read or recognize a virgin on screen, and are virginity
and heroism in any way connected? While I will be referring to a range

of films, my main focus will be on Joan of Arc, the medieval, virginal heroine most frequently and consistently represented in contemporary cinema.

Throughout the medieval period in Western Europe, the virginal identity was central and idealized. Understood as the most "natural" of identities in that it was believed to resemble most closely a prelapsarian condition, virginity—particularly female virginity—was highly valued, in both the religious and the secular spheres. For the former, it provided proof of God's mercy and grace, raising the lowly, carnal woman to a privileged position of *sponsa Christi*; for the latter, it functioned as the guarantor of patrilineal descent. The virgin figured frequently in religious writings as well as romance, her ongoing purity viewed as heroic in itself, or as a direct cause of others' heroism: the undaunted and defiant protagonist in saints' lives; the inspiration for knightly deeds of prowess and chivalry.[4]

Clarissa W. Atkinson divides the approaches of early Christian writers to virginity into roughly two categories: on the one hand there are those (such as St. Jerome) who see virginity "as a physiological state," the virgin being someone "who has never had sexual intercourse"; on the other, there are those (like St. Augustine) by whom "virginity is defined as a moral or spiritual state—as purity, or humility."[5] In other words, virginity fluctuates on the boundaries of a model that founds itself on two regulating categories that are seen (and constructed) as separate: the physical body and social performance. According to this schema, a virgin might be physically "intact" but not possess the correct "inner" disposition, whereas another person might not be a virgin technically but qualify as one spiritually. As this model indicates, the "proofs" of virginity are not necessarily physically ascertainable.

One of the central questions when discussing the medieval virgin heroine in contemporary cinema is the possibility of such an undertaking. Does the virgin whose virginity is a vocation rather than a transient state appeal to the audience of mainstream Hollywood cinema? Margaret Miles argues that "a religion of romantic love has replaced religion as the force that creates and attracts commitment," and that "[s]alvation through romance has replaced Christian salvation and occupies its place in the film's cultural psyche."[6] Laura Mulvey, in a groundbreaking article, states that "[w]oman displayed as sexual object is the *leitmotif* of erotic spectacle."[7] While there are problems with Miles's assumptions, heroines in mainstream cinema are undoubtedly presented as pneumatic and sexually desirable. How can the supposedly nonsexual virginal heroine be made to signify in such a system?

It is certainly the cause for uneasy moments within different films on Joan. The title of Cecil B. DeMille's film on Joan, for instance, gestures very clearly towards this: *Joan the Woman* (1917). This, along with the film's opening words ("The patriot who fought with men, was loved by men and killed by men, yet retained the heart of a woman!"), leaves no uncertainty about its project to locate and "fix" Joan, placing her story in a framework of thwarted love and barely overcome desire. In fact, from the definite *lack* of overt references to virginity, one could be forgiven for thinking that it is actually not that important in a twentieth- and twenty-first-century context and that virginity today is on the whole nothing but an adjunct to the heroine's identity—a clear shift from a medieval viewpoint, which placed it very much in the center. Yet Besson's recent film, which does focus explicitly on Joan's virginity, has been criticized for not doing so *enough*. Director Ronald F. Maxwell (*Gettysburg*), who is planning his own film on Joan, comments scathingly that Besson has "barely alluded" to Joan's virginity and concludes that Joan "was authentic," presumably seeing her virginity as evidence of this.[8] The title of his proposed film further underlines this point: *Joan of Arc: The Virgin Warrior*.

It is possible to see Besson's chastity-testing scene as an attempt to "deal" with the issue of virginity, which, once ascertained, can then be ignored. In the film, Joan's virginity is tested in front of the court, with numerous members of the clergy present. An emphatically old woman, dressed wholly in white and with vigorous, no-nonsense movements, washes her hands briskly and marches towards the terrified Joan, looking vulnerable and childlike in a white shift. Other women dressed in white (though with less filmy veils than Joan) fold up the front of her shift, and it appears for a brief second that we will catch a glimpse of her pubic hair. A clergyman (and scribe) begins to chant. The old woman places a hand on each of Joan's naked inner thighs—her face is shown framed by them—and she looks up, presumably at Joan's genitalia. The camera gives us a close-up shot of Joan's face as the woman does *something*—presumably inserts her fingers into Joan's vagina. Joan flinches. The woman turns away and pronounces her intact: "There is no sign of corruption."

This scene can work only on the assumption of a *presence* of something physical that "proves" virginity, an assumption that everyone watching must share in order for it to make sense. The tension that is deliberately created in this scene (we all know Joan to be a virgin but we nonetheless breathlessly await the verdict) can work only in a context that agrees that testing virginity is *possible*. This assumption, as well as Maxwell's insistence that virginity should be given more emphasis in the film, are views echoed in current North American discussions of virginity more generally.

Virginity is once again becoming a focal point for Western culture, raising the question whether it ever really was not. An article in the British *Observer* from October 27, 2002, claims that in "America, chastity is the fastest growing youth movement," with groups such as True Love Waits boasting more than 500,000 members.[9] In the United States there are numerous similar groups with such names as "Clean Teens," based in California, or the "Free Teens," who are "funded by the state of New Jersey."[10] Miss America 2003, Erika Harold, "announced that she will spend the following year promoting abstinence to teenagers."[11] In the United States virginity is a hot political issue, with George W. Bush's government planning to "spend millions of dollars promoting the 'no sex is safe sex' campaign."[12] These campaigns are aimed at persuading teenagers to remain virgins until they marry, and in February 2002, Bush "laid out a budget for [the] next year that would raise federal spending on 'abstinence only' education by $33 million to $135 million." Bush repeated his election promise to spend an equal amount on abstinence programs as on "medical services that provide contraception to teenagers."[13] An article in the *Washington Times* this year reported that abstinence "gain[ed] record funding," at a total of $120 million.[14] The $15 billion five-year AIDS combating plan, passed by the U.S. House of Representatives at the end of April 2003, specified that one third—$5 billion—be used for abstinence programs, not allowing "countries to distribute that money as they see fit."[15]

And there are signs that this renewed interest in abstinence and premarital virginity may be crossing the Atlantic. In Britain, Catholic groups such as Youth 2000 have organized so-called "chastity workshops" that see thousands of eager young attendants,[16] and a story entitled "'Virginity' Scheme under Fire" on the BBC news Web site on October 10, 2000, talks about a "controversial new government campaign aimed at tackling high teenage pregnancy rates" that is, according to the report, aimed at persuading specifically "teenage girls to consider the consequences of having sex."[17]

Yet despite these trends and official recommendations of virginity and abstinence, the ontology of virginity, while implicitly assumed, still goes largely ignored, implying that there is a tacit acceptance that what virginity is and means are commonly known and understood, as suggested by Besson's film. This is not just the case in reports focusing on Western chastity movements. Numerous articles in the international press in the past few years have related the newly popular practice of testing virginity in some African countries, most notably the KwaZulu-Natal Province in South Africa. Journalist Rena Singer, writing for the *Christian Science Monitor*, states that while exact figures are difficult to obtain, "[g]overnment officials and Zulu leaders ... estimate that tens of thousands [of women and girls] are being examined each month."[18] The explosive spread of AIDS/HIV is cited as the reason for these tests, which exist alongside the popular belief in South Africa, Zambia, Mozambique, and Malawi (to name some countries) that intercourse with a virgin—preferably a child—can heal a man of AIDS.[19]

While some journalists and commentators acknowledge the difficulties of testing virginity accurately, none of the articles I read questioned what exactly it is that is being looked for and apparently found that "proves" incontrovertibly the young woman's virginity.[20] The implied belief that there *is* a physical marker of virginity seems to point to the hymen as the primary candidate for furnishing the desired proof. As Jocelyn Wogan-Browne has pointed out, both the absence and the presence of the hymen—a contentious membrane at the best of times—are continuously reified.[21] Wogan-Browne refers to the "Somali justification for female excision and infibulation ... that it is necessary because of 'the inability of women to find other ways of establishing virginity'" as an example of the former, while there are a growing number of clinics in the West offering hymenoplasty—the surgical reconstruction of the hymen—often in the name of women's liberation, as an example of the latter. [22] One Web site offering such a procedure, from the Liberty Women's Health Care of Queens, New York (motto: "The freedom to choose ... the freedom to care"), offers a wide range of related services: "We also perform expert hymen repair surgery ..., restoration of the hymenal ring, or vaginal rejuvenation for patients in need of these services."[23]

Intactness, tightness, wholeness—these are the familiar if ambiguous signifiers of virginity that hymenoplasty promises to deliver and that, presumably, chastity tests promise to ascertain. And the need is clearly great, for, according to this site, the hymen is apparently so fragile that it can be "disrupted" not just through penetrative sex but through rather vaguely defined "strenuous physical activity" or even "tampon use."[24]

Despite these positivist assumptions, one of the most fundamental and persistent concerns about female virginity—present also in Besson's film—remains the question of how the virgin can be recognized. After all, no one within the film or watching it actually *sees* Joan's proven virginity. As Monica Green has pointed out, while "womanhood" has historically been viewed according to a "sexuality/reproduction link," the visible markers of which are, for example, menstruation, pregnancy, lactation, and childbirth, the virgin cannot be read or determined in this way.[25] Is the female virgin a woman? This question is taken up in Otto Preminger's *Saint Joan* (1957), where there are two moments that highlight the problems of categorizing the virgin within a binary gender construction.

When she arrives to join the French troops, one of the commanders, "the Bastard," says to Joan, "You can't be a woman and a soldier, maid." She replies, "I am a soldier. I do not want to be thought of as a woman. I will not dress as a woman. I do not care for the things women care for—they dream of lovers and money. I dream of leading a charge and of placing the big guns." Yet those around her continuously try to force her back into the "woman" category, telling her to go home and find a husband when the battles are won. In another, later exchange with "the Bastard," Joan says wistfully, "I wish you were one of the village babies ... I could nurse you for a while." Pulling her close, he replies, "Oh, you are a bit of a woman after all," at which point she draws away in anger, exclaiming, "No! I am a soldier and nothing else. Soldiers always nurse children." She explicitly identifies herself along the lines of a profession (soldier) rather than along gender lines. Virginity here appears to enable her self-identification as soldier ("You can't be a *woman* and a soldier"), but its position is elided in the process.

An online news Web site announced last year that "only half [of Church of England clergy] are convinced of the truth of the Virgin birth," demonstrating the doubt surrounding one of the most central narratives of Western culture, even from within the religious establishment.[26] It also signals an uncertainty about the nature of virginity and its "knowability," pointing towards the central problem of the representation of virginity. Medieval writers countered this by creating lists of recognizable characteristics that promised to reveal a "true" virgin, for example clear urine, breasts shaped a certain way, blushing, and posture.

Kathleen Kelly has argued that "just as Ambrose and Jerome constructed a semiotics of virginal behavior for the early Church, so did the PR machine of 50s Hollywood create their version of the virginal," citing Sandra Dee and Doris Day as examples.[27] A survey of contemporary views on virginity in the United States shows that American teenagers are confident that there are ways of determining whether one of their peers is a virgin or not. Accordingly, a virgin is a girl (always a girl) who "will be able to peel the label from a bottle of beer in one piece, to peel the foil from a chewing-gum wrapper in one piece, and [intriguingly], the cartilage at the end of her nose will feel as if it's in two pieces."[28] Without wishing to conflate these "tests" in any simplistic manner, it is striking that both medieval and modern ways of identifying a virgin rely heavily on physical attributes or visible actions that then serve as externalized and recognizable proofs and performances marking the spotless virgin.

These beliefs, alongside the many jokes that center on ascertaining the verifiable presence of a woman's virginity, paradoxically signal the *absence* that lies at the very heart of the virginal identity as its enabling condition. When used as an adjective, the term "virgin" conveys a sense of the unknown; virgin territory, virgin snow, and virgin rock all indicate that the nouns described as "virginal" are somehow pure, untouched. Once the land is cultivated, the rock quarried, the snow trodden on, "virginity" is lost. In this logic, virginity *must* be absent, residing in places unexplored and lost the very moment they are approached. Hence the (female) virgin is understood to be a woman who is "unknown." In Luce Irigaray's description of the "cultural stereotype of the female virgin" she states that, for men, "'virgin' means one as yet unmarked by them, for them. Not yet a woman in their terms ... Not yet penetrated or possessed by them ... A virgin is but the future for their exchanges, their commerce, and their transports."[29] The woman who refuses to be such a future resource becomes relegated to the category of "eternal virgin," a term that no longer possesses the positive connotations of a chosen vocation that it could in medieval culture. Similarly, the power of virginity to cause both intense desire and anxiety has much to do with questions of position: What is a virgin? Does "she" fit into a binary gender structure at all? And how does virginity affect our understanding of that structure?

Virginity in the cinema today tends to be found mainly in the horror genre, as Wes Craven's *Scream* (1996) acknowledges knowingly. In typical scenarios the virgin—inevitably a young woman—is safe from the lurking danger and death until the moment when she has sex and thus loses the purity that has so far protected her. A recent film that focuses explicitly on this theme, though in reverse, as the killer actively preys on virgins, is *Cherry Falls* (dir. Geoffrey Wright, 2000), for which the tagline reads, "If you haven't had it ... you've had it." Here the tantalizing question of how one can actually tell who is a virgin and who is not is addressed as the suspense of the film centers on the uncertainty as to who the next victim will be—it could be anyone. As virginity is never in itself *visible*, it must be made so, and this usually happens either through a particular performance that encodes "virginal" behavior, or through a displacement of the central signifier of virginity—the hymen—onto other, external objects that then stand in metaphorically for the virgin state. In films on Joan of Arc, this tends to be her suit of armor, which is almost always accompanied (especially in the earlier films) by a white garment of some kind.

In fact, white clothing appears to be the preferred signifier of purity and chastity in cinematic representations of virginity.[30] Alternately, virginity is established through a mirroring process, in which the subject in question is explicitly and repeatedly likened to a known virginal figure, primarily the Virgin Mary. A very explicit of example of this is to be found in Cecil B. DeMille's *Joan the Woman*, when Bishop Cauchon is shown in his chambers, plotting Joan's downfall. A gust of wind sweeps in from the open window, causing an oil lamp to spill onto a statue of the Virgin Mary, which immediately catches fire. It is evident as he watches the statue burn with satisfaction that this has given him a very clear idea of how to dispense with Joan.

In the films I surveyed, the main visible symbols of virginity were remarkably consistent: youth, white clothing, slight physique, and, frequently though not exclusively, blonde hair. In Ingmar Bergman's *Virgin Spring* (1959), Karin, the virginal (Christian) protagonist, is blonde and rides a white pony, sitting demurely

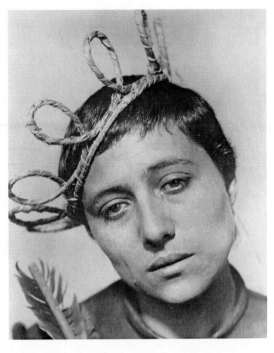

Renee Falconetti in close-up as the imprisoned Joan tormented by her captors in *La Passion de Jeanne d'Arc* (1928).

sidesaddle, whereas Ingeri, her pregnant and sullen counterpart, has unkempt, dark hair, dabbles in pagan rituals, and rides astride her pony, bare legs showing. In his article, "Jeanne au Cinéma," Kevin J. Harty refers to several occasions when directors were troubled by the question of which actress should be chosen to play Joan. He cites Carl Theodore Dreyer, director of *La Passion de Jeanne d'Arc* (1927–1928) as stating that he wanted "huge closeups of Jeanne, whose *pure features* would reveal that she alone found strength in her faith in God."[31] While films may draw on similar symbols of virginity, as Kelly has pointed out, "[p]roperly contextualised, *any* sign is capable of signifying virginity and its presence or absence."[32]

Is virginity—now rendered "visible"—to be understood as a purely physical state, as opposed to the medieval understanding of it outlined above? It seems not. A teen advice Web site makes the following assertion in response to the question: "what does it mean to lose your virginity?":

> In the strictest term; [*sic*] you are a virgin until you've had sexual intercourse with a member of the opposite sex. But this definition leaves a lot of people out of the loop. While the social

policy makers look to redefine marriage to include same sex partnerships, maybe it is time we also revisited what it means to be a virgin.[33]

Virginity is here understood as a *social* category, defined by "policy makers" or even the teens themselves, who are encouraged to write in with their views. It points out that "the standard definition of virginity lets you *get away with* having a lot of different kinds of sex [while] still being able to call yourself a virgin" (my emphasis), and that the term is therefore in "desperate need of a rewrite." It goes on to ask its readers to consider the following points when thinking of a "new definition":

• Is someone who is raped or molested no longer a virgin?
• Is actual intercourse the only act that counts when determining one's virginity?
• If you willingly engage in other intimate sexual acts but do not have intercourse, is it fair to still consider yourself a virgin?
• How would you define losing your virginity if you were/are homosexual or bisexual?

The list is lengthy and therefore rather daunting, continuing to ask the (teenage) reader to consider whether "being a virgin is based on your feelings"; whether one loses one's virginity only when engaging in a sex act that carries emotional significance, and finally, whether virginity is a subjective or objective state of being, depending either on how the person sees him/herself or how the individual is viewed by others. While these questions apparently attempt to redress the relentlessly heterosexist nature of the virginity debate as well as to offer a more nuanced definition of the term, the site does not explain why it is so necessary to work with this term at all.[34]

Some of this overlaps in interesting and perhaps unexpected ways with current discussions on virginity by medical experts. Two "co-directors of the Female Sexual Medical Centre at the UCLA Department of Urology,"[35] doctors Jennifer and Laura Berman, hosted a talk show on virginity in May 2002, which was then aired on the Discovery Health Channel later in the same month.[36] On it they discussed the "pros" and "cons" of virginity. Dr. Jennifer Berman states the "obvious" medical benefits ("avoiding pregnancy, avoiding sexually transmitted diseases, HIV....").[37] The physiological quickly slides into the psychological when the two doctors claim that: "[women who choose virginity] can feel confident that the partners that they're with are not with them just for sex and that gives them a certain kind of comfort." They praise the creativity that comes from avoiding intercourse: "You can try lots of different, what I call VENIS, Very Erotic, Non-Insertive Sex activities."

Here the difference between a sexually active woman and a virgin—supposedly being delineated—actually becomes increasingly difficult to ascertain.

Reading through these sites, one gets the impression that virginity is something that can be maintained, ascertained—even regained—unproblematically. Later on in the Bermans' program, Lisa Marie, a 35-year-old "secondary virgin," is interviewed. According to the Canadian priest Father Rolheiser, anyone can become a secondary virgin through the process of "revirginization," which designates a "two-to-three-year period of celibacy for those who have been separated, divorced, or widowed, or who have been sexually promiscuous," at the end of which period the individual is successfully "revirginized."[38] Lisa Marie explains that she has managed to revirginize by avoiding specific social situations: "I don't hang out in the bars I used to hang out in. I don't do drugs and alcohol.... And the company I keep is different." She no longer watches "dirty films" or "talk[s] dirty" or even "listen[s] to music." She does not masturbate, does not even think about it. She says that she has "shut off" that part of herself, and that whereas her soul used to be "empty" and "lonely," secondary virginity has made her feel "righteous."[39] In a register reminiscent of an advertising jingle, she claims enthusiastically that she is now "full of joy ... always energetic ... with that glide in my stride, that skip in my step."

The Bermans conclude the show by stating that "virginity can mean many things for many people," again echoing the teen advice Web site and the Christian sites. The implications of this indeterminacy can be understood in terms of Jean Baudrillard's argument that sexuality is "an element in the economy of the subject."[40] In her feminist reading of Baudrillard's work, Victoria Grace explains this in the following way:

> [A]s the body becomes that which is signified, or represented, sexuality becomes individualised as a function of the subject: sexuality becomes a function of self-expression or the expression of subjectivity.... Sexuality becomes a kind of individualised production.[41]

Where does that leave the vexed question of virginity's definition and its proofs, which is continuously being presented as answerable?

It is noticeable that fundamentalist Christian sites employ similarly ambiguous terms as the others discussed here, despite being the main proponents of virginity and supporters of abstinence programs in the West. While they tend to be scathing about hymenoplasty, their emphasis on "values" does not provide a more conclusive or comprehensive understanding of virginity.[42] Virginity and chastity, the argument goes, prevent the social disorder resulting from disease and criminality. In one online article, "Virginity in Vogue," its author Leilani Corpus states that the sociologist George Gilder has shown in his book *Men and Marriage* that "men who respond to short term sexual desires are apt to have significantly higher rates of suicide, drug and alcohol addiction, mental disease, arrest and accidental death."[43] These misdemeanors can all be avoided if one remains a virgin "until marriage to gratify that desire in its *proper* context" (my emphasis).[44]

This site, like the proponents of chastity tests in Africa and of abstinence programs in the United States and Britain, claims that chastity tests prevent teenage pregnancy, AIDS, and STDs, but furthermore that virginity also prevents the development of emotional problems, such as "guilt, frustration [and] jealousy." Virginity has therefore "proven to be a sound answer throughout the ages ... a very viable solution," concluding with the grim reminder that should we choose to ignore this evidence, we will "reap what we sow." But how to maintain that desirable state and how to know whether one still "has" it or whether one has already "lost" it remains nebulous.[45]

The question raised throughout this essay is what virginity signifies and how it is understood, defined, represented, and read in a contemporary context.[46] As the various debates on virginity have shown, a hymen, imperforate or otherwise, is not enough to mark the virgin. Sarah Salih has pointed out, with reference to a medieval context, that "an intact body is inferred from outward signs: the bodily stylisation of dress and demeanour; [for instance] the modest gait and the downcast eyes."[47] In a modern context, virginity is also believed to be a conscious, willed, individual *choice* that is then enacted.[48] The virginal performance is, however, *always* dependent on being watched and *read*, and these acts shape virginity even while virginity also transmits to the viewer types of social knowledge.

Where does all of this leave Besson's chastity-testing scene? It struggles with some of the ambiguities I have outlined here. For instance, the "revealing"—the display—of Joan's virginity is not actually *seen* by any of the viewers, either within the film or outside the film. The test occurs behind a cloaking white sheet that shields Joan from the audience's gaze. Additionally, while the camera lingers in a close-up shot of what appear to be surgical instruments nestling threateningly on a white silk pillow, conveying the impression that these will be used in the verification of Joan's intactness, they are ultimately not shown being used at all. They become empty, lurid signifiers whose purpose it is to remind viewers both of Joan's virginity and presumably of the barbarism of the medieval, denying the investment that Western culture still has in this identity.

Virginity in the cinema is conjured up in a complex interaction between the screen and the viewers, not all of whom will see, read, or understand it in the same way.[49] Its meanings are also constructed and contested in the range of other contemporary media, increasingly cinema's powerful intertexts.[50] And it is the very *performativity* of virginity that ensures the ceaseless circulation of its proliferating significations.[51] In Besson's film, for example, Joan is alternately sulky, petulant, and childish, throwing temper tantrums and vacillating clumsily between bloodthirstiness and mawkish sentimentalism. As a virgin saint, she has to be shown to be *different*, yet as a product of mainstream, secular cinema, she must still be "feminine" and still desirable, not too *unheimlich*.[52] One almost has the feeling when viewing Joan of Arc films that the directors, along with the Burgundians and the English, heave a sigh of relief when the problematic virgin can be resigned to becoming and silent martyrdom at the end.

As historically and culturally specific, divergent, and multiple as the meanings of virginity undoubtedly are, definitions of virginity are based on the separate categories of both the "natural" body and its "cultural" performances. These categories, while being constructed as separate, are continually conflated in the discussions of virginity. This reveals the lability of such categories, bringing into question the epistemological and ontological grounds of gender identity itself. Virginity, as it is currently being discussed in a North American context, is posited as a definite identificatory position, the striving for and promotion of which reveal a yearning—a desire—for a "real" manifested (for instance) in an absolute, verifiable physiological state.

At the same time virginity is presented as a commodity that can be acquired either financially (through surgery) or as a do-it-yourself enactment, following the instructions provided in manuals, videos, talks, workshops, TV programs, and Web sites. Virginity-as-commodity (like Nike sneakers, consumers are told to "just do it") promises its consumer success, freedom, popularity, and fulfillment. In this it functions like other consumer objects, taking part in "a system of signs that differentiates the population."[53] Virgins are happier, more intelligent, more confident than those who do not possess "it." Virginity is overtly linked to questions of social organization and economy in the ubiquitous parallel drawn between virginity and the maintenance of social as well as individual welfare and order. In this sense the virgin is also heroic; remaining chaste is a central element of the individual's success story—the main signifier of belonging to a moral elite.

While those promoting and selling virginity firmly maintain that the value of the product is known by God (who guarantees the image that provides meaning), the slippages and negotiability recall Baudrillard's concept of simulation: "To simulate is not simply to feign [to have what one has not] ... someone who simulates an illness [for example] produces in himself [*sic*] some of the symptoms."[54] As Grace argues, citing Baudrillard, "[i]f ... paralysis is simulated, i.e. actually produced—then the relation of truth and falsity, real and appearance, implodes."[55] The same can be said for virginity today, and this has radical implications for the question of representation itself. In the logic of this argument, it follows that "within an order of simulation, 'the whole edifice of representation (is) itself a simulacrum,'" as "the simulated and the true are one and the same thing."[56] The recent proliferation of debates and renewed emphasis on virginity are evidence of "the frantic production of the 'real' in the hyperreal mode, as simulation, as the 'natural-real' loses its potency as a discursive construct."[57] Presented as a guarantor of social as well as personal order and coherence, virginity can be read as a symptom of profound nostalgia, which generates "a proliferation of myths of origin and signs of reality; of ... objectivity and authenticity."[58]

Simultaneously, the "lack of distinction" enacted in simulation, which collapses oppositions such as "true" and "false," "performance" and "authenticity," is also "the worst form of subversion."[59] Certainly virginity in the cinema—particularly *medieval* virginity, which gestures towards a time that is presented in many ways as other but also as prelapsarian, when gender identities still signified meaningfully—points toward the conclusion that in the end, in a contemporary context, the film virgin is arguably the *only* "true" virgin, functioning as an example of hyperreality, where the "(simulated) real" comes to be "more real than (the old, natural, material) real."[60] The fluid interaction of various media— cinema, Web sites that provide audience responses, suggestions for variations on plot lines, reviews, associated merchandise—mean that a film (a mainstream film in particular) is less than ever a product that can be evaluated in isolation.[61]

The resurgence of virginity movements and debates on virginity demand an engagement with them in order to begin to understand the ways in which virginity signifies today. The manifold definitions of virginity, mutable and often vague, suggest that the trope demands collective and concerted acts of disavowal in order to exist: "We know it is not *really* there ... and yet...."[62] Like desire, to which it has an intrinsic connection and similarity, virginity—medieval and modern—is "a contradictory, fluid arena in which identities are written and rewritten."[63] It exemplifies Baudrillard's argument that sex "does not have a calculable status" and is certainly not something one should ever claim to be "absolutely certain about."[64] As Wogan-Browne notes, "[l]ike many other stories the modern scholarly narrative of virginity begins with women but rapidly develops implications for everyone."[65]

Acknowledgments

I would like to thank Martha Driver and Sid Ray for inviting me to contribute to this collection, as well as for their helpful comments. Many thanks also to all those who listened patiently to various drafts of this paper, particularly John Anderson, Gail Ashton, David Matthews, Elizabeth Oakley-Brown, and Sarah Salih.

Notes

1. Jean Baudrillard, *Forget Foucault: An Interview with Sylvere Lotringer* (New York: Semiotext(e), 1988), p. 25.

2. See Kathleen Coyne Kelly's discussion of the chastity-testing scene in the film *A Summer Place* (1959; Delmer Daves) in *Performing Virginity and Testing Chastity in the Middle Ages* (London and New York: Routledge, 2000), pp. 131–33.

3. The shift from virginity idealized as lifelong vocation to its idealization as transient state is located in the early modern period by Theodora Jankowski. She argues that as opposed to a medieval Catholic virgin, "any early modern Protestant virgin who chose unduly to prolong her virginity—or especially to adopt it as a permanent condition—had no place in the sex/gender system. She was a queer virgin and occupied an officially unnamed position that was both dissident and highly resistant." She also relates this change to the needs posed by a "newly emerging capitalist/bourgeois family and only applied to the transitory state of premarital virginity"; Jankowski, *Pure Resistance: Queer Virginity in Early Modern English Drama* (Philadelphia: University of Pennsylvania Press, 2000), p. 113. While I feel that the differences Jankowski outlines are not straightforward, the perception of virginity as an impermanent, solely premarital state, as well as its imbrication with capitalist discourse, is one that is recognizable and prominent in the debates on virginity today.

4. As Kelly has shown, this is still the case. Her assertion that "virginity pursued is capable of generating endless plot lines and complications—whether the setting is the ancient Aegean, the Roman court, the medieval countryside, or modern Los Angeles" holds true for virginity more generally; see Kelly, *Performing Virginity*, p. 139. I am much indebted to Kelly's incisive and stimulating discussion of "contemporary virginities."

5. Clarissa W. Atkinson, "'Precious Balsam in a Fragile Glass': The Ideology of Virginity in the Later Middle Ages," *Journal of Family History* 8.2 (1983): 131–43, 133. For a survey of the meaning of virginity in the Middle Ages, as well as its tradition, see John Bugge, *Virginitas: An Essay in the History of a Medieval Ideal*, International Archives of the History of Ideas, Series Minor, 17 (The Hague: Martinus Nijhoff, 1975).

6. Margaret R. Miles, *Seeing and Believing: Religion and Values in the Movies* (Boston: Beacon Press, 1996), p. 150.

7. Laura Mulvey, "Visual Pleasure and Narrative Cinema," in *Feminism and Film*, ed. E. Ann Kaplan (Oxford University Press, 2000), pp. 34–47, p. 40. While it lies outside the scope of this article to do so, it is worth noting how virginity in the cinema may be used to problematize Mulvey's argument concerning scopophilia; see also notes 49 and 62.

8. See www.ronmaxwell.com/virginwarrior.html.

9. Rebecca Fowler, "Just Say No," *Observer Special Magazine: Sex Uncovered* (London), October 27, 2002: 56–61, 58. See www.lovematters.com/truelove-waits.htm. For further links to sites dealing with the issue of abstinence, from a range of perspectives, see www.excite.co.uk/directory/Kids_and_Teens/Teen_Life/Teen_Sexuality/Abstinence.

10. Ed Vulliamy, "Bush Promotes Virgin Values to Curb Teen Sex," *Observer* (London), April 28, 2002.

11. See www.ChristianityToday.com.

12. Vulliamy, "Bush Promotes Virgin Values."

13. Vulliamy, "Bush Promotes Virgin Values." For the potentially devastating impact of these programmes on AIDS/HIV awareness, see Joanne Mariner, "Smells like Teen Censorship," at www.IndexonCensorship.com.

14. Cheryl Wetzstein, "Abstinence Education Gains Record Funding," *Washington Times*, March 24, 2003. Her article, "Teen Pregnancies, Abortions Lowest in Years," *Washington Times*, May 11, 2003, claims that the Guttmacher Institute (AGI) report, released on May 1, 2003, shows a decline in teen pregnancy and abortions over the past year, a success claimed by some researchers to be due in large part to abstinence programs.

15. "Third of $24bn AIDS Plan Tied to Abstinence," *Sydney Morning Herald*, May 3, 2003, at www.smh.com.au/articles/2003/05/02/1051382095811.html. See also Rupert Cornwell, "$15bn Aids Bill Pushes for Sexual Abstinence," May 2, 2003 at http://news.independent.co.uk/world/americas/story.jsp?story=402304; and Gaby Hinscliff, "Aids Fear as Bush Blocks Sex Lessons," *Observer* (London), May 5, 2002.

16. Fowler, "Just Say No."

17. See http://www.bbc.co.uk/1/hi/health/964146.stm. This campaign is part of the government's £60 million Teenage Pregnancy Scheme. A spokesperson for the British Pregnancy Advisory Service (BPAS) commented rather drily, "I really worry that government advertising to promote virginity is about as good an investment as the investment in the Millennium Dome" ("'Virginity' Scheme under Fire," BBC News, October 10, 2000, at http://www.bbc.co.uk/1/hi/health/964146.stm. Another article points to a "mixed reaction" to the scheme; "Like a Virgin," (BBC News, October 10, 2002, at http://news.bbc.co.uk/1/low/uk/965697.stm).

18. Rena Singer, "Chastity Tests: Unusual Tool for Public Health," *Christian Science Monitor* at www.csmonitor.com/durable/2000/06/02/fp1s4-csm.shtml. Although they do exist, chastity tests for boys are rare. See also Jo Stein, "Virginity Tests in AIDS War," September 2, 2000, at www.news24.com/City_Press/City_Press_News/0,1885,186-187_906042,00.html; "Zulu Maidens Put Safety First," July 11, 2000, at http://old.smh.com.au/news/specials/intl/aids/aids12.html; "Women's Virginity Test in Uganda and Turkey," at www.archives.healthdev.net/gender-aids/msg00054.html. An article, entitled "Virgin on the Ridiculous," claims that "[a]uthorities in Turkey have rescinded a controversial law that forced school girls suspected of having sex to undergo virginity tests." It goes on to say that '[f]orced gynaecological examination were common practice until five students attempted suicide by taking rat poison rather than be subjected to the test"; see "Virgin on the Ridiculous," *World View* 19, March 1, 2002, at www.worldvision.org.uk/worldviewarchive/worldview19.html.

19. See the report on this by the international development charity, Voluntary Services Overseas (VSO), at http://www.vso.org.uk/raisa/mainstreaming.pdf, par-

ticularly pp. 16 and 22 of the file. This has also been reported on www.Truthor-Fiction.com/rumors/aids-virgins.htm.

20. Those who "fail" the test are not discussed in these reports. While questions of civil liberties and the reinforcement of gender inequalities that such tests raise are addressed to some extent, the central question of ontology is veiled in silence, both by those who promote the tests and by those who report on them.

21. Wogan-Browne notes that in her examination of recent medical writings on virginity, she "found the hymen as evanescent and problematic as at any other stage of its history." She demonstrates how the hymen is "still a now-you-see-it, now-you-don't phenomenon"; see "Virginity Now and Then: A Response to *Medieval Virginities*," in *Medieval Virginities*, ed. Anke Bernau, Ruth Evans, and Sarah Salih (Cardiff: University of Wales Press, 2003), pp. 234–50, 242.

22. Jocelyn Wogan-Browne, "Virginity Now and Then," p. 247, citing Lillian Passmore Sanderson, *Against the Mutilation of Women: The Struggle to End Unnecessary Suffering* (London: Ithaca Press, 1981), p. 53.

23. See www.libertywomenshealth.com. See also Kelly's discussion of vulvaplasty and other surgical procedures; *Performing Virginity*, pp. 135–36.

24. The latter feeds into the popular myths about tampons destroying virginity that companies such as Tampax have had to consider in their advertising campaigns for some countries. The associations found in writings on virginity with the notion of "fake," "counterfeit," or "feigned" virginity are also mirrored here: the surgery is "virtually undetectable," the virgin-like patient can "pass."

25. Monica H. Green, "Female Sexuality in the Medieval West," *Trends in History* 4 (1990): 127–58, 131.

26. Jonathan Petre, "One Third of Clergy Do Not Believe in the Resurrection," July 31, 2002, at www.telegraph.co.uk.

27. Kelly, *Performing Virginity*, p. 131.

28. Alleen Pace Nilsen, "Virginity: A Metaphor We Live By," *Humor: International Journal of Humor Research* 3.1 (1990): 3–15, 9.

29. Luce Irigaray, "When Our Lips Speak Together," *Signs* 6.1 (1980): 69–79, 74.

30. On the ambiguities of the color white in relation to purity and virginity, see Sarah Salih, *Versions of Virginity in Late Medieval England* (Cambridge, U.K.: D. S. Brewer, 2001).

31. Kevin J. Harty, "Jeanne au Cinéma," in *Fresh Verdicts on Joan of Arc*, ed. Bonnie Wheeler and Charles T. Wood (New York and London: Garland Publishing, 1996), pp. 237–64, p. 244.

32. My emphasis; Kelly, *Performing Virginity*, p. 130.

33. Mike Hardcastle, "Losing It," at www.teenadvice.about.com/library/weekly/aa072300a.htm.

34. The heterosexist assumptions that frequently inform discussions of (female) virginity have led Kathleen Coyne Kelly to suggest that the possibility of homosexuality is denied through the privileging of virginity; *Performing Virginity*, p. 122. A recent cinematic example of this is the controversial French director Catherine Breillat's *À ma Soeur!* (2001), in which the fifteen-year-old Elena is convinced by her holiday romance, the older Italian law student Fernando, that if he penetrates her anally she will remain a virgin, as that "doesn't count."

35. Rachel Cooke, "Sexual Chemistry," *Observer Special Magazine: Sex Uncovered* (London), October 27, 2002: 24–31, 29. Cooke adds that they are also said to be two of the "best-known researchers into female sexual dysfunction" (p. 29).

36. For a transcript of the show, see "Virginity," at www.newshe.com/virginity1.shtml.

37. The list continues: "syphilis, gonorrhea, chlamydia which ...can lead to ...Pelvic Inflammatory Disease, which ... can lead to infertility." She adds quickly that one should not forget "Human Papaloma [*sic*] Virus ... another sexually transmitted disease that can lead to cervical cancer." The doctors Berman go on to warn that these diseases can be contracted in other ways: "Right, [with] oral sex you are at risk from herpes as well ...You can also contract AIDS from oral sex."

38. Nilsen, "Virginity," p. 6. The Christian Women Today Web site also offers information on "Renewed Virginity." Listing "seven steps to help you regain and maintain your virginity," the third suggests: "Discover why you had sex so you can correct the problem"; see Dr. Greg and Michael Smalley, "A Renewed Virginity," at www.christianwomentoday.com/womenmen/virginity.html.

39. This echoes the findings of sociologist Peter Bearman of Columbia University on teens who take a virginity pledge: "By pledging, they have an important sense of identity, and belong to an elite moral community"; see Vulliamy, "Bush Promotes Virgin Values."

40. Baudrillard, *Symbolic Exchange and Death* (1976), tr. Iain Hamilton Grant, intro. Mike Gane (London: Sage, 1993), p. 115.

41. Victoria Grace, *Baudrillard's Challenge: A Feminist Reading* (London and New York: Routledge, 2000), p. 44.

42. See, for instance, Leilani Corpus, "Virginity in Vogue," at www.forerunner.com/forerunner/X0865_Virginity_in_Vogue.html. The piece itself was written in the late 1980s.

43. Corpus, "Virginity in Vogue"; the quotation is from Corpus, not Gilder. For more on Gilder, his work and his political leanings, see www.discovery.org/fellows/gilder/index.html.

44. Corpus, "Virginity in Vogue."

45. See Greg and Smalley, "A Renewed Virginity."

46. As Nilsen states in her survey, "[o]ne of the surprises that I had was that there's a lack of agreement on what a virgin is"; "Virginity," p. 5.

47. Salih, *Versions of Virginity*, p. 21.

48. See also Kelly, who argues that "the desire to revirginize and/or to discount past sexual activity as a 'loss' of virginity arises out of a prevailing popular belief that one can reinvent or construct oneself at will." She locates the "foundations of this belief" in "good old American individualism"; *Performing Virginity*, pp. 120–21.

49. I am arguing here that female virginity in the cinema is not just determined by a "male gaze," pointing, with Judith Mayne to "the complex nature of identification and recognition in film viewing"; see Judith Mayne, "The Female Audience and the Feminist Critic," in *Women and Film*, ed. Janet Todd (New York: Holmes and Meier, 1988), pp. 22–40, p. 37. This problematizes Mulvey's discussion of scopophilia, as it seems to deny both active scopophilia as well as, for the majority of viewers, the narcissistic aspect of scopophilia.

50. A prescient example of how television, Web sites and films interrelate is *The Blair Witch Project* (1999); see www.blairwitch.com. While this was a highly self-conscious and deliberate setup, it served to uncover the crisscrossing that inevitably and increasingly occurs between various media and also increasingly between "fictive" film and reality television. Other recent films that deliberately play in various ways with the complex and problematic relationship between

"reality" and "fiction" are, for instance, *The Truman Show* (dir. Peter Weir, 1998), *Donnie Darko* (dir. Richard Kelly, 2001) and *S1m0ne* (dir. Andrew Nicole, 2003).

51. As the various discussions of virginity show, it is an identity that relies on continuous performance, a performance that renders virginity "visible" and in this confers a status on the body that the body itself cannot adequately provide. It is clear that the performance itself cannot ultimately provide the desired guarantee.

52. The choice of supermodel Milla Jovovich to play Joan surely also says something about the importance placed on attractive appearance above and beyond the need for a competent actor.

53. Mark Poster, ed., "Introduction," in *Jean Baudrillard: Selected Writings* (Cambridge, U.K.: Polity Press, 1988), pp. 1–9, p. 3.

54. Baudrillard, "Simulacra and Simulations," in Poster, ed., *Jean Baudrillard*, pp. 166–84, pp.167–68.

55. Grace, *Baudrillard's Challenge*, p. 84.

56. Grace, *Baudrillard's Challenge*, p. 85; quoting from Baudrillard, *Simulations*, tr. Paul Foos, Paul Patton, and Philip Beitchman (New York: Semiotext(e), 1983), p. 11.

57. Grace, *Baudrillard's Challenge*, p. 62.

58. Baudrillard, "Simulacra and Simulations," p. 171.

59. *Baudrillard*, p. 168.

60. Grace cites the example of the "synthesized emerald, which simulates a model of the perfect emerald; the structural perfection of the emerald does not precede its representation but rather the *most* real emerald is preceded by its own model"; *Baudrillard's Challenge*, p. 25.

61. Groups such as "True Love Waits" offer a range of products to their followers, from t-shirts, to books and bumper stickers. The "What Would Jesus Do?" site offers bracelets, bible covers, books, postcards and the "WWJD game"; see www.wwjd.com. My thanks to Anna Feigenbaum for this reference.

62. This can also be read as complicating Mulvey's reading of disavowal and film. When she states that "the meaning of woman is sexual difference," it raises the question: How does this apply to the female virgin? Virginity demonstrates Lorraine Gamman's and Merja Makinen's point that "in postmodern terms ... gender is the perfect simulacrum—the exact copy of something that never existed in the first place"; Gamman and Makinen, *Female Fetishism: A New Look* (London: Lawrence and Wishart, 1994), p. 217.

63. Tamsin Spargo and Fred Botting, "Re-Iterating Desire," *Textual Practice* 7.1 (1993): 379–83, 383.

64. Grace, *Baudrillard's Challenge*, p. 38.

65. Wogan-Browne, "Virginity Now and Then," pp. 234–35.

Works Cited

Atkinson, Clarissa W. "'Precious Balsam in a Fragile Glass': The Ideology of Virginity in the Later Middle Ages," *Journal of Family History* 8.2 (1983): 131–43.

Baudrillard, Jean. *Forget Foucault: An Interview with Sylvere Lotringer*. New York: Semiotext(e), 1988.

Baudrillard, Jean. "Simulacra and Simulations." In: *Jean Baudrillard: Selected Writings*, ed. Mark Poster. Cambridge, U.K.: Polity Press, 1988, pp. 166–84.

Baudrillard, Jean. *Symbolic Exchange and Death* (1976), tr. Iain Hamilton Grant, intro. Mike Gane. London: Sage, 1993.

Bugge, John. *Virginitas: An Essay in the History of a Medieval Ideal.* International Archives of the History of Ideas, Series Minor, 17. The Hague: Martinus Nijhoff, 1975.

Gamman, Lorraine, and Merja Makinen. *Female Fetishism: A New Look.* London: Lawrence and Wishart, 1994.

Grace, Victoria. *Baudrillard's Challenge: A Feminist Reading.* London: Routledge, 2000.

Green, Monica H. "Female Sexuality in the Medieval West." *Trends in History* 4 (1990): 127–58.

Harty, Kevin J. "Jeanne au Cinéma." In *Fresh Verdicts on Joan of Arc,* ed. Bonnie Wheeler and Charles T. Wood. New York and London: Garland Publishing, 1996, pp. 237–64.

Irigaray, Luce. "When Our Lips Speak Together." *Signs* 6.1 (1980): 69–79.

Jankowski, Theodora. *Pure Resistance: Queer Virginity in Early Modern English Drama.* Philadelphia: University of Pennsylvania Press, 2000.

Kelly, Kathleen Coyne. *Performing Virginity and Testing Chastity in the Middle Ages.* New York: Routledge, 2000.

Mayne, Judith. "The Female Audience and the Feminist Critic." In: *Women and Film,* ed. by Janet Todd. New York: Holmes and Meier, 1988, pp. 22–40.

Miles, Margaret R. *Seeing and Believing: Religion and Values in the Movies.* Boston: Beacon Press, 1996.

Mulvey, Laura. "Visual Pleasure and Narrative Cinema." In: *Feminism and Film,* ed. by E. Ann Kaplan. Oxford: Oxford University Press, 2000, pp. 34–47.

Nilsen, Alleen Pace. "Virginity: A Metaphor We Live By." *Humor: International Journal of Humor Research* 3.1 (1990): 3–15.

Poster, Mark, ed., *Jean Baudrillard: Selected Writings.* Cambridge, U.K.: Polity Press, 1988.

Salih, Sarah. *Versions of Virginity in Late Medieval England.* Cambridge, U.K.: D. S. Brewer, 2001.

Spargo, Tamsin, and Fred Botting. "Re-Iterating Desire." *Textual Practice* 7.1 (1993): 379–83.

Wogan-Browne, Jocelyn. "Virginity Now and Then: A Response to *Medieval Virginities.*" In: *Medieval Virginities,* ed. by Anke Bernau, Ruth Evans, and Sarah Salih. Cardiff: University of Wales Press, 2003, pp. 234–50.

Web Sites and Newspaper Articles

Cooke, Rachel. "Sexual Chemistry." *Observer Special Magazine: Sex Uncovered* (London). October 27, 2002: 24–31.

Cornwell, Rupert. "$15bn Aids Bill Pushes for Sexual Abstinence." May 2, 2003. Available at www.news.independent.co.uk/world/americas/story.jsp?story=402304.

Corpus, Leilani. "Virginity in Vogue." Available at www.forerunner.com/forerunner/X0865_Virginity_in_Vogue.html.

Fowler, Rebecca. "Just Say No." *Observer Special Magazine: Sex Uncovered* (London). October 27, 2002: 56–61.

Hardcastle, Mike. "Losing It." Available at www.teenadvice.about.com/library/weekly/aa072300a.htm.

Hinscliff, Gaby. "Aids Fear as Bush Blocks Sex Lessons." *Observer* (London), May 5, 2002.

"Like a Virgin." BBC News. October 10 2002. Available at www.news.bbc.co.uk/ 1/low/uk/965697.stm.

Mariner, Joanne. "Smells like Teen Censorship." Available at www.IndexonCensor ship.com (copyright 2002).

Petre, Jonathan. "One Third of Clergy Do Not Believe in the Resurrection." July 31, 2002. Available at www.telegraph.co.uk.

Singer, Rena. "Chastity Tests: Unusual Tool for Public Health." *Christian Science Monitor*. Available at www.csmonitor.com/durable/2000/06/02/fp1s4-csm. shtml.

Smalley, Michael, and Dr. Greg. "A Renewed Virginity." Available at www.christianwomentoday.com/womenmen/virginity.html.

Stein, Jo. "Virginity Test in Aids War." September 2, 2000. Available at www. news24.com/City_Press/City_Press_News/0,1885,186-187_906042,00.html.

"Third of $24bn AIDS Plan Tied to Abstinence." *Sydney Morning Herald*. Available at www.smh.com.au/articles/2003/05/02/1051382095811.html.

"Virgin on the Ridiculous." *World View* 19, March 1, 2001. Available at www.world vision.org.uk/worldviewarchive/worldview19.html.

"Virginity." Available at www.newshe.com/virginity1.shtml.

"'Virginity' Scheme under Fire." BBC News. October 10, 2000. Available at www .bbc.co.uk/1/hi/health/964146.stm.

Vullimay, Ed. "Bush Promotes Virgin Values to Curb Teen Sex." *Observer* (London). April 28, 2002.

Wetzstein, Cheryl. "Abstinence Education Gains Record Funding." *Washington Times*. March 24, 2003.

Wetzstein, Cheryl. "Teen Pregnancies, Abortions Lowest in Years." *Washington Times*. May 11, 2003.

"Women's Virginity Test in Uganda and Turkey." Available at www.archives.healthdev.net/gender-aids/msg00054.html.

www.blairwitch.com.

www.ChristianityToday.com.

www.discovery.org/fellows/gilder/index.html.

www.excite.co.uk/directory/Kids_and_Teens/Teen_Life/Teen_Sexuality/Abstinence.

www.libertywomenshealth.com.

www.lovematters.com/truelovewaits.htm.

www.ronmaxwell.com/virginwarrior.html.

www.TruthorFiction.com/rumors/aids-virgins.htm.

www.vso.org.uk/raisa/mainstreaming.pdf.

www.wwjd.com.

"Zulu Maidens Put Safety First." July 11, 2000. Available at www.old.smh.com.au/ news/specials/intl/aids/aids12.html.

Filmography

1917 *Joan the Woman*, d. Cecil B. DeMille, with Geraldine Farrar, Raymond Hattan, Wallace Reid. U.S.: Paramount.

1928 *La Passion de Jeanne d'Arc*, d. Carl Theodore Dreyer, with Renée Falconetti, Antonin Artaud. France: Société Générale des Films.

1957 *Saint Joan*, d. Otto Preminger, with Jean Seberg, Richard Widmark. U.S./U.K.: Wheel Productions, United Artists.

1960 *The Virgin Spring*, d. Ingmar Bergman, with Max Von Sydow, Brigitta Valberg. Sweden: Svensk Filmindustri.

1996 *Scream*, d. Wes Craven, with Neve Campbell, Drew Barrymore, David Arquette. U.S.: Miramax.

1998 *The Truman Show*, d. Peter Weir, with Jim Carrey, Ed Harris, Laura Linney. U.S.: Paramount Pictures.

1999 *The Blair Witch Project*, d. Daniel Myrick and Eduardo Sanchez, with Heather Donahue, Joshua Leonard. U.S.: Artisan Entertainment.

The Messenger: The Story of Joan of Arc, d. Luc Besson, with Milla Jovovich, John Malkovich. France/U.S.: Gaumont.

2000 *Cherry Falls*, d. Geoffrey Wright, with Brittany Murphy, Gabriel Mann. U.S.: USA Films.

2001 *Á Ma Soeur! (Fat Girl)*, d. Catherine Breillat, with Anais Reboux, Roxane Mesquida. France/Italy: Cowboy Booking International.

Donnie Darko, d. Richard Kelly, with Jake Gyllenhaal, Jena Malone. U.S.: IFC Films.

2002 *SImOne*, d. Andrew Nicole, with Al Pacino, Winona Ryder. U.S.: New Line Cinema.

Chivalric Virtues in Female Form: *Crouching Tiger, Hidden Dragon*'s Wudan Warrior Princess as Medieval Hero

DIANA E. SLAMPYAK

This essay focuses on Ang Lee's *Crouching Tiger, Hidden Dragon* (*CTHD*, 2000) and explores how Lee alters his source material so that the nineteen-year-old Jen Yi, daughter of a governor, becomes the film's hero. Lee, I argue, relies upon medieval tropes to fashion a Chinese version of a European "exile and return" romance, wherein Jen must undergo incredible trials of *aventure* and learn chivalric values such as trust and devotion before she can achieve her desired place in society. In doing so, moreover, Lee subverts the traditional outcomes of the main film genres with which he works, the Hong Kong action-film genre of *wuxia pian* and the Hollywood contemporary romance, positing that trying to live by either genre's confines becomes impossible. Ultimately, *CTHD* shows Lee's frustration with the genres in which he works, offering an ironic take on the conventions he deconstructs and rebuilds through his focus on Jen.

To begin to explore these ideas, I start with the final scene, for it best exemplifies the problems Lee has in constructing his film as he does. Here, the main plot's young lovers, Jen (Zhang Ziyi) and Lo (Chang Chen), consummate their love on Wudan Mountain for one last time, reunited after many physical and emotional struggles. To reach this climax, they have also endured societal struggles caused by their different class backgrounds. Jen is supposed to marry a social equal to help her father maintain his position in the aristocracy and gain more power and prestige. However, during Jen's cross-country relocation through the Gobi Desert, Lo, a warrior-thief, albeit a very chivalric one, attacks her and her entourage, and the two fall in love.[1] Since social stratification in the fictional Qing dynasty of the nineteenth century forbids such a relationship, this consummation suggests that the two have overcome their obstacles, and thus the picture fades out as the lovers climax. We almost expect the credits to start rolling. But then the picture fades in again, showing Lo wake to find Jen gone, her comb his only relic of the night before—and the whole of his romance with her. Fearfully he leaves the hut and searches for her, finally finding her in contemplation before the inviting waterfall. As the two converse for the final time, a sequence of shot/reverse shot combinations ensues. Meanwhile, Lee incorporates other shots into the scene; most importantly, when a shot focuses on Lo, Jen is always in frame, in the right lower corner.[2] However, when the focus turns to Jen, Lo is out of frame completely; she is the film's hero, after all, so focus must remain on her.[3]

CTHD contains three plots including the main one between Jen and Lo, on whom, claims Lee, the title is based.[4] Two subplots center on Li Mu Bai (Chow Yun-Fat):[5] an equally forbidden romance between him and Yu Shu Lien (Michelle Yeoh),[6] and his desire and attempts to leave the Wudan/Giang Hu life because it no longer brings him peace. Leaving the life is only possible after he avenges his master's death by killing Jade Fox (Cheung Pei Pei).[7] Lee unites these three narrative strands through Jen; as her importance to the weave of plots ascends, so too the relationships between her and the other characters become pivotal. Most of the important interactions leading up to the final scene arise during the many fight scenes, almost all of which involve Jen and one or more of her costars.[8] To make Jen the hero, Lee altered his original source, the fourth part of a five-part 1945 *wuxia* novel by Wang Du-lu called *Crouching Tiger, Hidden Dragon*, making Lo a secondary player while virtually inventing the characters Shu Lien and Jade Fox, who become foils for Jen. Shu Lien urges her to take her rightful place in society while Jade Fox influences her to develop into the depraved vengeance-seeker Jade Fox herself has become. Meanwhile, in the second part of the novel,[9] Mu Bai is the hero yet earns a supporting role here. Lee ends the film as he does because of problems with Jen being a hero; her romance with Lo leads to the denouement.

"Do you remember the legend of the young man?" asks Jen.

"A faithful heart makes wishes come true," Lo replies, reminding us of their escapade in the desert we've encountered as a flashback earlier in the film.[10]

"Make a wish," she tells him, to which he asserts, "to be back in the desert together again." With that, Jen flies over the wall, floating down into the waterfall. The camera, first at worm's-, then bird's-eye views, shows her slow-motion descent into the water.[11]

We might think this a happy ending for the couple, for Jen's leap supposedly represents her freedom from the societal forces preventing her from living the life she craves with Lo. We might also assume that Jen's act parallels that of the little boy who wishes for his parents' health and takes a similar plunge to be free from the horrors he faces, recounted in the flashback.[12] Indeed, Lee states that Jen's jump is not self-sacrifice but "liberation from human entanglements that dash her dreams" of leaving aristocratic life and becoming a Wudan warrior, living in the Giang Hu subculture about which she romanticizes and perceives as "free" from societal obligations she resents and resists.[13] Hence, equating the jump with psychological freedom, many accept this "happy" ending as just that. Most scholars seem to do so.[14] Even when placed in the Hong Kong action cinema (HKAC) genre to which it belongs, we might see this ending as heroic. However, if we look at it through the lens of a less apparently influential literary genre—the medieval European romance— we might discern pessimism, irony, even disdain, for this "forced" ending that posits the impossibility of a woman living free from constraints in any relationship.

To tell this story, Lee does something that few, if any, filmmakers have successfully done, creating a daring hybrid of Western and Eastern film genres. In fact, he blends Hollywood film genres, such as the Western, the musical, and the contemporary romance,[15] with an HKAC genre likely little known by American or European audiences, the *wuxia pian*. This form uses knightly codes of ethics and old stories from Chinese history to show how chivalric virtue is upheld and wrongs are righted, without harm to the warriors' code of morals or the fulfillment they desire.[16] It also incorporates supernatural elements, gender role reversals (i.e., a woman can be a hero, a man her heroine), and the motif of disguise to allow the plot to move forward.[17] Indeed, in both the *wuxia* film and the medieval romance, separation from one's beloved runs contrary to a conventional ending; in both, the hero always restores order. He wins the heroine in the end.

To date, although many recognize *CTHD*'s hybridity, only one critic, William Leung, offers any reading behind it, although he sees the *wuxia* competing with nineteenth-century romance (especially Jane Austen's *Sense and Sensibility*, which Lee himself filmed in 1995), and he praises the ending as well.[18] Of the end, Leung cites the co-author of the screenplay, James Schamus, who claims: "The Taoism that the film embodies says that sometimes you have to tragically acknowledge the strength of your human ties—and you have to transcend them." Leung then claims that the "success" of *CTHD* comes from "the bold willingness ... to experiment with the juxtaposition of Eastern and Western knowledge and traditions: here bringing to the fore feminist politics in a *wuxia* story, there investing a Jane Austen plot with a Taoist twist."[19] Yet I see Jen's "transcendence" of her human ties, as well as Mu Bai's death by poison (delivered by Jade Fox and leaving Shu Lien craving the human tie she wants but cannot have) as unsuccessful, even pessimistic, for no one in the film gets what she or he wants. Death by poison or suicide surely cannot satisfy an audience expecting a woman to win in romance or a near-superhuman fighter to win her battles, the traditional outcome for the hero in both *wuxia* and romances, particularly medieval ones.

Indeed, the *wuxia* tradition of Chinese literature and film and medieval European romances, particularly those produced in England, share common features. Romances such as *King Horn, Havelok the Dane, Bevis of Hampton*, and even Marie de France's *Lai le Fresne* and its four-teenth-century translation, all focus on the "exile and return" theme,[20] in which heroes, displaced from their aristocratic place in society, must fight to regain their positions, thrones, betrothed/beloved, trusted friends, and so on, through trials of *aventure*, or the journeys/ stages a hero must endure to secure his or her fate. Each *aventure* exemplifies a different trait or characteristic which helps the hero reach internal spiritual harmony. Journeys and adventures similar to *aventures* are a common theme in *wuxia*, wherein the "roaming hero [is] not only strong and skillful; he or she also [has] an obligation to right wrongs, especially when the situation seem[s] dire. The hero [fights] for *yi* (the Chinese concept of right-eousness)—not for rights in the abstract, or for society as a whole, but for fairness in a particular situation."[21]

Additionally, both genres set their stories in lands exotic or historic that have been mystified in story after story. For example, the Arthurian legends take place "somewhere mystical" in either medieval France or England, on Breton or Celtic land, depending upon who tells the romance, while *wuxia* such as *Swordsman II* and its sequel, *The East is Red*, take place in "Ming China," a dimension parallel to the real China.[22] *CTHD*, too, exists in a netherworld of half-invention, the "Qing Dynasty" of the 1800s. In fact, "[t]he film is a kind of dream of China, a China that probably never existed, except in my childhood fantasies of Taiwan," Lee claims.[23]

Similarly, both forms of storytelling became prominent in early medieval times; although the Chinese tradition began over five thousand years ago, it gained legendary and popular status around 800 AD, when the T'ang Dynasty ruled, while medieval romances began circulating in the 1000s.[24] And both were either "literary efforts composed by men of learning" or "oral tales and ballads in colloquial prose or simple verse."[25] Also, when orally performed, both rely upon music to add power to the story, and here again *CTHD* follows suit, for the music—sometimes mournful, sometimes energetic, a blend of styles appropriately matched to each scene—becomes, according to Lee, an important character informing the action throughout the film.[26] One crucial difference is that a *xia* is a knight-errant from *any* class and *any* gender, and hence *wuxia* narratives focus on Chinese concepts of knightly chivalry much akin to their English medieval romance counterparts: courage beyond compare, honor to the point of vengeance, and supreme fighting skills.[27] Most romances, however, deal with these virtues but retain aristocratic *male* heroes,[28] even after the mid–1300s when social structures changed after years of war and the Black Death epidemic.[29]

Nevertheless, both genres add elements of magic; the *wuxia*, for instance, grants skilled knight-errants the ability to attain the "weight-less leap" that comes only from intense mastery of *wuxian* Confucian or Taoist principles. Lee explains this concept of "flying" that many view-ers find hard to swallow, calling it "vulge" kung fu, enabled by an "enlight-ened body" that "weighs less" than those of fighters with unenlightened souls. Romances in the eleventh through fifteenth centuries also incor-porate magical elements—sometimes increased fighting prowess, but also items such as weapons, rings, or other talismans which represent the hero and his lover and grant them supernatural powers while simultaneously serving as symbols of the characters. In *CTHD*, we see two symbols typ-ical of medieval English romance: the Green Destiny sword and the comb Jen gives to Lo. These artifacts typify both genres, linking the *wuxia* and romance elements at work in the film.

The comb obviously serves a distinct purpose; its plainness makes it aesthetically uninteresting, but its importance cannot be overlooked, for it links the hero, Jen, with her beloved. For example, in the desert flashback, she chases after him when he steals it, wanting it back "because it's [hers]," causing her to suffer exhaustion and illness.[30] He takes care of her; they fight more as she shows off her martial arts skills, and even-tually they fall in love and have sex—in a romantic, highly charged scene.[31] Though reluctant to leave their desert hideaway, Jen realizes she must do just that, since her parents are searching for her; to show her love for Lo, she gives the comb to him, and it serves as a reminder to us (and Lo) of their seemingly impossible reunion. When he returns it, trig-gering memories of their happenstance romance, the flashback scene arises; when he subsequently claims he will prove himself worthy to marry her, we hope he can magically do so, for that's what medieval romance and *wuxia* audiences expect. Ironically, this never happens, for when Jen leaps from the cliff, the comb becomes an empty icon signifying only the implausibility of blending the two genres so that they offer viewers a traditional, expected, "happy" ending—Lo may still possess the comb but he can no longer share it with her.

The Green Destiny, however, weighs more heavily in the drama, for it is the only weapon everyone reveres, and the only one imbued with a history equal to that of Sir Gawain's pentangle in *Sir Gawain and the Green Knight*, which is explained in minute detail in the romance. The pentangle stands for many things: the five joys of the Virgin Mary, whose image adorns the inside of the shield, the five wounds Christ received during his crucifixion, and Gawain's five noble virtues, among others, which all link up to become an "endless knot" of "five fives" that can never fail him.[32] The pentangle is a central symbol, almost functioning as a character all its own. Equally revered and powerful, the Green Destiny makes its importance known when Yu Shu Lien places the sheathed sword in Jen's hands and explains its surprising weight ("The handle is heavy. And the sword is no ordinary metal") and its awesome history, saying, "Beautiful but dangerous. Once you see it tainted with blood, its beauty is hard to admire. It's four hundred years old." As she rips it out of the scabbard to show Jen, the sword emits a wobbly, almost cartoonish sound, impressing Jen even more. We can see that Jen covets it. Similarly, as Sir Te, the man entrusted with the sword, unsheathes the Green Destiny to show it to Governor Yu, Jen's father, it illuminates the darkness with a blue tint. Te provides the weapon's dimensions, then explains that it has "seven rubies missing from the hilt. You can tell the design dates back to before the Chin era. Engraved with a technique lost by the time of the Han Dynasty." Like Gawain's pentangle, the Green Destiny becomes a crucial character in the film.

Not only does the weapon emit sound and provide illumination,[33] more important, it also represents the struggle Jen must undertake to reach her full potential as a Wudan warrior and become who she wants to be—a woman free of societal obligations that thwart her desire to be with Lo. Although the sword at first belongs to Mu Bai, when Jen commands it, she shows a "supernatural" ability handling it. For example, in her warrior persona, she can fight off many adversaries as the mythical "Invisible Goddess armed with the Invincible Green Destiny" at the bar/restaurant she visits, saying, "Be you Li Mu Bai or Southern Crane, lower your head. I am the desert dragon; I leave no trace."[34] Here she has learned the moves of a Wudan warrior but does not understand the rules that come with them, even those that Mu Bai has already tried to instill in her during their first fighting encounter, after Jade Fox kills Tsai, an officer. In this earlier scene, after Mu Bai starts to fight Jade Fox to save May and Bo, two characters who are still in danger, Jen steps out from the shadows in her all-black "thief" attire to help Jade Fox, her master. Though it is a tough fight, she takes on Mu Bai and almost defeats him until, by sleight of hand, he regains control of the Green Destiny, leaving her stunned but undeterred. "No growth without assistance. No action without reaction. No desire without restraint. Now give yourself up and find yourself again. There is a lesson for you," he tells Jen.

At this point, Mu Bai sees Jen's potential to become a master warrior like himself and offers to train her at the retreat in Wudan Mountain, fearing that if he does not, she'll become a "poisoned dragon." He realizes she must renounce the societal ties that bind her to the aristocrat life she abhors and "find herself," the true warrior she seems destined to become. Jen shows she would be a worthy disciple because she allows May and Bo to escape unharmed, proving she is a humanitarian at heart. Knowing that he is right yet being headstrong, she declines, despite realizing that she cannot yet compete with Mu Bai. She eventually does get the Green Destiny back, and ensuing fights between them, particularly the "bamboo" fight sequence, reinforce for Mu Bai that Jen must train with him, despite the Wudan rule that women cannot train at the mountain hideaway.[35] Because Jen naïvely thinks that the Green Destiny may be a fast ticket to the success she desires, Mu Bai continually uses it to show her that she needs to keep learning the laws of the warrior.[36] Coveting the very sword that brings Mu Bai pain and keeps him trapped in a neverending cycle of violence at least as old as the sword itself (another theme in medieval literature, i.e., the cyclicality of history and events) shows that Jen is too undisciplined to possess such a weighty weapon.

Indeed, Jen has many lessons to learn before she can meet her "green," or naïve, destiny, and doing so requires her to split herself into various personas, for she must use another medieval romance trope—disguise, a trick Jade Fox has taught her by hiding in Jen's aristocratic world as Jen's governess—to maneuver her way around the people and situations she encounters. As she wends her way through her *aventures* in disguise, she becomes a medieval hero in a self-imposed and socially defiant exile. Her quest resembles that of Marie de France's le Fresne because both rely on the power of "sisterhood" to survive their *aventures*. *Lai le Fresne* tells the story of a child abandoned at birth because her mother has twins; before her mother gets pregnant, an aristocratic neighbor has twins, and le Fresne's mother claims she must have been unfaithful, for how else could she have had two children at once? Hence, to save face and avoid being accused an adulterer when she herself gives birth to twins, she sends one of them, le Fresne, to an abbey, providing only a luxurious blanket and expensive bejeweled ring as tokens of the aristocratic birth of which the child has been cruelly stripped. Through various *aventures* le Fresne becomes the concubine of a prince. Her tokens help her to prove she is an aristocrat and can marry her beloved, who coincidentally is set to marry le Fresne's sister, le Codre. A happy ending ensues, thanks to her aristocratic manners and the tokens le Fresne carries with her.

As in *Lai le Fresne*, our first view of Jen is as a Chinese "princess"— a long shot of Jen with her back to the camera shows off a beautiful formal silk gown. She appears radiantly proud of her nobility and lords it over Shu Lien, Te's servant De Lu, and us. At this point, we start to realize that Jen is the hero, for the camera tells us so by always privileging Jen through selective focus and her placement in the lower-left-hand corner of the screen, traditionally held as the place of power in cinematic framing. Shu Lien makes her first attempt at dissuading Jen from taking the dangerous path about which she fantasizes, asking her if the Giang Hu books in which *wuxia* stories are written ever mention sleeping in flea-infested beds without bathing for days and reminding her that the warrior lifestyle requires adherence to many rules, including friendship, trust, and integrity—things about which the selfish Jen has yet to care. Shu Lien also seems jealous of Jen's impending marriage. "It's the most important step in a woman's life, isn't it?" she asks. With that, we see in her expressive face the intense passion and conviction she puts behind her statement, and we realize that Shu Lien, though not an aristocrat, yearns for the fulfillment of a more "traditional" female role. In contrast, Jade Fox tells Jen in the next scene that Shu Lien is "one of *those*" her mother "wouldn't want [Jen] consorting with." Jade Fox's disdain for Shu Lien is obvious.

Together Shu Lien and Jade Fox represent the separate paths Jen might take in her journey of self-fulfillment, one, the voice of tradition and stability, the other, the promise of danger and excitement. In the next scene, we see Jen choose the latter; the film's first fight sequence ensues after Bo, Te's head of security, discovers the theft of the Green Destiny, and Shu Lien chases after the black-clothed, masked burglar. Here Jen gives us a glimpse of the thief inside her as well as her desire to become a Wudan warrior.[37] Though Shu Lien suspects Jen, others in the compound believe the thief is the renowned and feared Jade Fox. Thus Jen has learned the power disguise wields—she can be who she needs to be, and when. Repeatedly she proves that she can convincingly move from one role to another with little suspicion.

For a while, only Shu Lien sees through Jen's disguises. She thinks she recognizes Jen's body in her black thief attire, but to be sure, she visits Jen the next day as the young woman is practicing calligraphy. Jen writes Shu Lien's name "just for fun," the camera cutting away to a close up of her hand's sleek and polished moves.[38] Shu Lien comments, "I didn't realize my name looks like 'sword,'" and the camera dollies forward for a more intimate shot of the two, revealing Jen's slight freeze.[39]

Deftly noticing this faux pas, Shu Lien says, "You write so gracefully. Calligraphy is so similar to fencing," and again Jen tips her hand, realizing that Shu Lien knows she is the thief.

Later, although Shu Lien knows that Jen is both the thief and an adept swordswoman, she tries to upset the aristocratic girl again, toying with the Fox's "pup." In this scene, Madam Yu, Jen's mother, passes out tea, and the three of them talk about Fox and the thief. Madam Yu is astonished to learn that Jade Fox is not only a murderer but also a female, which strains Jen's cool façade slightly. When Jen learns that Jade Fox has killed a policeman the night before, she becomes even more unsettled. Her mother suggests that perhaps Jade Fox and the thief are the same person, but Shu Lien, eyes locked with Jen in a wide shot, says, "I doubt it; this thief is ... very unusual.... And most likely smarter than a mere killer." As she speaks, she "accidentally" drops a covered teacup and saucer on Jen's side, and Lee uses an insertion shot to show Jen's "lightning fast" and "instinctive" catch, successfully done without her so much as looking down.[40] Luckily, the camera zooms back to show Te's and Mu Bai's arrival, so Jen can regain her composure and greet them formally. Still, Mu Bai studies her carefully and starts to unravel her disguises too—hence his wisdom in offering to teach the unschooled Jen, who may have deciphered the Wudan manual that Jade Fox could not but who still fails to understand the complex code of ethics that accompanies the moves she so deftly recreates.

As the film progresses and Jen asks Shu Lien to be her "sister," we realize the two need each other to learn how to achieve their desired destinies. Having such a wise "sister," Jen admits she needs "the power of sisterhood" to return to her rightful role in society, as Michelle A. Freeman claims le Fresne needs, again tying the film to its previously unstudied medieval romance influences.[41] Freeman argues that le Fresne needs other female characters to play surrogate mothers for her. Similarly, Jen surrounds herself with four surrogates who nurture and teach her: Shu Lien and Jade Fox, obviously, but also Mu Bai and Lo. Mu Bai, as stated, wants to be her "master" and take her to Wudan Mountain to train. This role of woman as tutor is found not only in the medieval world of le Fresne but also in the nineteenth-century world of wuxian lore in which *CTHD* is set.

Lo, meanwhile, cares for Jen in the desert; when she passes out from exhaustion, for instance, he hunts, cooks, and forces her to eat desert fowl, then makes her bathe and provides fresh clothes so she can feel clean again. Lo's nurturing side is plainly presented—a side rarely, if ever, seen in either medieval romance or HKAC male heroes. Later, Jen will renounce her ties of "sisterhood" with Shu Lien and Mu Bai when Shu Lien claims that Jen fails to appreciate all she and Mu Bai have done for

Jen (Zhang Ziyi) is the woman warrior in *Crouching Tiger, Hidden Dragon* (2000).

her. However, even that, Jen later realizes, is a mistake, one she eventually tries to amend, but without success, again showing that blending medieval European romance with the *wuxia* leads only to a pessimistic, forced ending unsatisfying for those expecting the usual outcome of either genre.

Because Jen does assert herself as a fighter and a dominator, her goal differs from that of a "normal" exiled and returning romance hero's, such as le Fresne's. For Jen is not an exiled aristocrat at all, but an exiled warrior-thief. Since the age of eight, we learn, she's taught herself Wudan moves deciphered from the manual that Jade Fox stole from Mu Bai's master, whom Jade Fox killed for his refusal to train women, treating them as "whores" instead. Hence, Jen grew up with sword in hand and Jade Fox disguised as her governess, and, although her aristocratic parents raised her and taught her all that a society lady must know, she has never accepted that as her station in life. Instead she has romanticized the Giang Hu lifestyle, taking the first opportunity to experience it firsthand in the desert with Lo. Hence, her return is not to the aristocratic station built for her by her parents, who remain aloof towards her, but instead to the Giang Hu lifestyle she has enjoyed briefly.

This reversal of the exile/return trope ultimately reveals the frustration Lee finds in working with these genres. For Jen *always* feels pulled

Jen with Green Destiny in *Crouching Tiger, Hidden Dragon* (2000).

by the two sides Shu Lien and Jade Fox represent; she is, I think, battling the tiger and dragon within herself,[42] slowly realizing that she is doomed no matter which path she chooses. She thinks she can succeed in abandoning her aristocracy, but she feels duty-bound to her parents and to following convention by marrying their choice of suitor for her, for example.[43] To go off with Lo, as she desires, would only shame her family, something with which she cannot quite come to terms. She also understands just how treacherous the Giang Hu path can be through witnessing Jade Fox's retaliation against her for bonding with Mu Bai and Shu Lien.[44] In the last sequence before the climactic ending, Jade Fox poisons her with sedating herbs and attacks Mu Bai with the *wuxian* equivalent of an AK-47, a multiholed weapon that shoots darts poisoned with deadly purple yin one after another, with the rapidity of today's automatic rifles.

Jade Fox feels betrayed by her former disciple, her only "family," for joining forces with the "enemy," Shu Lien and Mu Bai (who, unlike Jade Fox, use their fighting skills benevolently, not for anger or revenge, except for Mu Bai's honor-bound duty to avenge his master's death). Jade Fox means to kill Jen with purple yin, but Mu Bai gets in the way. He fights off most of the darts, sending them back to Jade Fox. However, he misses one, which lands in his neck. Heartbreakingly, Mu Bai knows that although he has met one goal by killing Jade Fox, he will never realize the other, a life with Shu Lien. Again, Lee pessimistically questions the *wuxia* and romance genres because, although the weakened Jen tries to assemble the antidote quickly enough to save him, she cannot; Mu Bai dies in Shu Lien's arms, but not before they share their first—and only—passionate embrace and kiss. Following chivalric codes thereby dooms them from ever fulfilling their desires, just as Jen's learned appreciation for honoring her familial ties condemns the young lovers.

Throughout *Crouching Tiger, Hidden Dragon*, Lee takes risks in making Jen the hero and also focusing the subplots on women's experiences. He tries, as Leung suggests, to feminize the *wuxia* genre. Yet he accomplishes much more, adeptly authoring a fiction from a combination of Hollywood love scenes and innovative martial arts sequences. However, in doing so, he overturns the very conventions of the two cinematic genres and cannot happily marry the two together, especially within the confines of medieval romance and *wuxia pian* tropes.

While the Hollywood love story and the Hong Kong action film beg for happy endings, Lee cannot produce one, even though many critics claim he does. Similarly, our hero can never meet her destiny, nor can she return from exile to reclaim her rightful place in society, as Jen, Wudan Warrior Princess. As the credits finally roll, we leave the theater having seen a powerful, mesmerizing, unforgettable film, but we realize that our expectations about its conclusion have been subverted. I find the pessimistic, ironic ending utterly satisfying, as I deplore the falsity that "happy endings" require. So for me, Lee has done exceptionally satisfying work here. Perhaps others agree, and this explains the film's success.

Notes

1. We learn this through an elaborate twenty-minute flashback scene.

2. This shot, when used in shot-reverse shot sequencing, is called "selective focus," wherein the two are sharing the same cinematic space, but one has more prominence. In this particular scene, Jen is prominent, while Lo is there merely to remind us to whom she speaks; focus almost naturally falls on Jen, as the "selection" emphasizes her.

3. Lee notes this in the DVD commentary, referring specifically to her as the *hero* rather than the heroine. This is strange, considering most awards for which she was nominated and/or won were as "supporting actress," except Hong Kong film awards and a few others. See www.magiclanternpr.com/films/crouching.html, the most comprehensive authority on the film.

4. According to Pauline Chen's review of the film in *Cineaste* 28.4 (2001): 71–9, "Jen" is shortened from her Chinese name, Yu Jiaolong, meaning "Winsome Dragon," while Lo's original name is Luo Xiaohu, or "Little Tiger." I argue

for a different meaning for the title herein, based on my comparison of the *wuxia* with medieval romances.

5. "Fat Boy" (his nickname) is probably the most famous Eastern action star in another HKAC genre, the "triad" film, such as *The Killer, Hard Boiled,* and *Bullet in the Head,* classic modern gangster films directed by John Woo; both actor and director have now "crossed over" into Hollywood success.

6. Yeoh, also known as Michelle Khan, is another contemporary icon of HKAC, and also is beginning to enjoy crossover success in American films, most notably as James Bond's capable (and sexy) sidekick in the 1997 *Tomorrow Never Dies.*

7. Pei Pei was one of the first female fighters in HKAC, considered the queen of sixties and seventies martial arts films.

8. One can tell that Jen is the main focus from watching the film on DVD, for, when the disc starts and the menu appears, the first swordplay between Jen and Shu Lien accompanies it; similarly, the lead-ins to other options (audio options, special features, language and subtitle choices) use fight scenes in which she figures prominently.

9. William Leung, "Crouching Sense, Hidden Sensibility," *Film Criticism* 26.1 (2001): 42–57, explains the liberal alterations Lee made in the film; my summary comes in part from his.

10. The little boy, Lo explains, has not died but rather "sailed away" to be free from his troubles. Though this is never stated, Lo could be that young boy, who then has to become a Giang Hu thief to survive. Perhaps this explains his acceptance of her jump.

11. "Worm's-eye view" means the camera is below the subject, looking up at it as though the camera were on the ground. Similarly, a camera capturing a "bird's-eye view" shows the perspective of a bird flying overhead.

12. See note 10. As I see it, the end is an easy way to escape reality and problems. The flashback scene occurs about 53 minutes into the film, and shows how the two met, her first struggle to prove herself a worthy warrior, and their subsequent romance based on mutual respect and love.

13. Unless otherwise noted, all explanations of the film come from Lee's DVD commentary track, in which James Schamus also participates.

14. Almost all the critiques I have found use the same information readily available at www.magiclanternpr.com/films/crouching.html, the commentary track on the DVD, and in the book, *Crouching Tiger, Hidden Dragon: A Portrait of the Ang Lee Film.* These include Chen's review and Leung's essay (although these two offer more than a genre comparison), as well as Gary Morris's "Beautiful Beast: Ang Lee's *Crouching Tiger, Hidden Dragon,* in *Bright Lights Film Journal* 1 (2001), available at www.brightlightsfilm.com/31/crouchingtiger.html; Oliver Wang's 2001 review, "Women Warriors," in *PopMatters,* available at www.pop matters.com/film/reviews/c/crouching-tiger.html; and Lucas Hilderbrand's "Girl-fight," www.popmatters.com/film/reviews/c/crouching-tiger2.html, among others too numerous to list.

15. All HKAC films owe their development to two of these genres, for the action scenes incorporate the values of an American Western, while the choreography of the action is fluid and seamlessly interwoven, as musicals purport to do with their dance scenes.

16. The term *wuxia* refers to poems, tales, and novels following this format; *pian* means "film." More of the history of this genre follows in the next few paragraphs. The genre's popularity declines year by year because audiences want

dazzling special effects, hi-tech weapons, and modern plots. Hong Kong cinema itself, due to the change in government from British to Chinese rule, now faces censorship so stifling that many of the key players in HKAC, such as Sammo Hung, Jet Li, and John Woo, have emigrated to the United States, while Jackie Chan splits his time between Hong Kong and Hollywood. Many of the Hong Kong artists involved in creating *CTHD* have entered the U.S. market as well, including Chow, Yeoh, and the film's choreographer, Yuen Wo-Ping, most famous in the U.S. for his fight choreography in 1999's *The Matrix* and the subsequent release of his 1991 *wuxia* film, *Iron Monkey*.

17. For more on this genre, see Bey Logan's *Hong Kong Action Cinema* (Woodstock, NY: Overlook Press, 1996) or Lisa Oldham Stokes and Michael Hoover's *City on Fire: Hong Kong Cinema* (New York: Verso, 1999), two very comprehensive anthologies/analyses of HKAC, its history and influences. Indeed, women can be equally as chivalric as men in HKAC; Cheung Pei Pei, for example, was an early fighting hero in films such as *That Fiery Girl, Lady of Steel,* and *Dragon Creek,* while Yeoh has had her share of leading roles; for instance, she was one of three powerful women in *The Heroic Trio* series and starred as the hero in *Wing Chun,* in which Pei Pei also appeared. Nevertheless many argue that this "gender-bending" comes at a great price, either objectifying powerful women, as Wendy Arons argues in "'If Her Stunning Beauty Doesn't Bring You to Your Knees, Her Deadly Drop Kick Will': Violent Women in the Hong Kong Kung Fu Film" in *Reel Knockouts: Violent Women in the Movies,* ed. Martha McCaughey and Neal King (Austin: University of Texas Press, 2001, pp. 27–51); or forcing them to repress sexual desires and emotions, which Lenuta Giukin claims happens, in "Boy-Girls: Gender, Body and Popular Culture in Hong Kong Action Movies" in *Ladies and Gentlemen, Boys and Girls: Gender in Film at the End of the Twentieth Century,* ed. Murray Pomerance (Albany, NY: SUNY Press, 2001, pp. 55–69). Though these are very interesting and, I think, viable examinations of women as heroes in HKAC, they have little relevance to my analysis of *CTHD,* especially since the camera and the women in love with Lo and Mu Bai objectify the two men as much as, if not more than, the camera does Jen, Shu Lien, or Jade Fox.

18. "Crouching Sense, Hidden Sensibility," *Film Criticism* 26.1 (2001): 42–57.

19. Leung, 51–4. I agree with him that Lee brings feminist politics to the fore, especially in the fight scenes between Jen and Shu Lien, which would never be given such prominence in a traditional *wuxia pian.* Also, Mu Bai, once a hero in his own right, here takes second stage to the women in the film, especially Jen. In fact, the flashback scene cuts off the importance of Mu Bai's attempts to leave the sword with Sir Te and retire from the life that he claims causes only bloodshed, violence, and woe.

20. I take this term and some of my examples from Jennifer Fellows's introduction to *Of Love and Chivalry: an Anthology of Medieval Romance,* ed. J. Fellows (London: J. M. Dent, 1993).

21. David Bordwell, "About Hong Kong Martial Arts Cinema," available at www.magiclanternpr.com/films/crouching.html.

22. This scenario is outlined in the beginning of *The East Is Red.* These films also feature a female hero, played by the androgynous Brigitte Lin Ching-Hsai.

23. "Introduction," in *Crouching Tiger, Hidden Dragon: A Portrait of the Ang Lee Film Including the Complete Screenplay* (New York: Newmarket Press, 2000), p. 7.

24. Perhaps the *wuxia* is somehow an influence on romances, but such an issue is outside the scope of this work.

25. Bordwell, "About *Wuxia Pian*," available at www.magiclanternpr.com/films/crouching.html. Unless otherwise noted, all information about this genre comes from this essay, part of which is reprinted in *Crouching Tiger, Hidden Dragon: A Portrait of the Ang Lee Film*—although as a fan of HKAC, I knew most of this already. My knowledge of medieval European romances stems from years of study; however, to investigate the genre further, good places to start are Erich Auerbach, "The Knight Sets Forth," in *Mimesis: The Representation of Reality in Western Literature*, tr. Willard R. Trask (Princeton: Princeton University Press, 1953), pp. 123–42; Rosalind Field, "Romance in England, 1066–1400," in *The Cambridge History of Medieval English Literature*, ed. David Wallace, (Cambridge: Cambridge University Press, 1999), pp. 152–76; and Stephen H. A. Shepherd, ed., *Middle English Romances: A Norton Critical Edition* (New York and London: Norton, 1995).

26. When a romantic scene ensues, the music becomes hopeful and uplifting, with lilting melodies; when a fight ensues, the music is faster, less melodic, more frenetic.

27. And women can be equally as chivalric as men; see notes 17 and 22.

28. A few exceptions exist: *Lai le Fresne* and *Lai le Freine*, mentioned above, center around a young woman's attempt to return from exile, while *Sir Launfal*, a Middle English translation of another of Marie's lays, *Lanval*, focuses on the *real* hero, Dame Tryamour, as I argue in my dissertation, "'As I Hafe Herde Telle': Collective Memory and Translation in Medieval English Romances," University of California, Riverside, 2002.

29. After the Black Death wiped out a large number of England's populace, more opportunities arose for less privileged classes, thus changing the once revered tripartite social structure and allowing social mobility to occur. The genre sought to appeal to audiences other than the noble classes, downplaying many of the noble virtues of heroes.

30. Not only does she fight with Lo for the comb, but she also fights her way out of a near gang-rape by other thieves marauding in the desert. I believe the escape from gang-rape is a trope in films based on medieval stories.

31. Lee claims that this is his first real "sex scene" in a film and his first nude scene, which he said he needed to do to blend the two genres coherently and show that a woman *can* be both a fighter and a lover.

32. To read more about the pentangle, see the standard edition of the romance, *Sir Gawain and the Green Knight*, edited by J. R. R. Tolkien and E. V. Cohen, 2nd ed. rev. Norman Davis (London: Oxford University Press, 1967), or its excellent, modern–English standard translation, Marie Borroff's *Sir Gawain and the Green Knight: A New Verse Translation* (New York and London: Norton, 1967).

33. Lee states that the sword needed a language all its own, consisting of eight to ten distinct sounds; that is why I see it as a character in its own right.

34. By this point in the film, Jen has donned her warrior attire, is mistaken for a male (as was Jade Fox earlier), and incites fear, then anger, in those she fights. In fact, after the fight, the stupid, comic relief warriors go to Mu Bai and Shu Lien to complain that they "politely asked for a friendly match" but were not respected, her "sword was too powerful," and she was too "uncivilized." Lee claims this sequence of scenes come straight out of the "kung fu comedy" genre for which Jackie Chan is so famous.

35. Because the fight scenes are explored in great detail in most of the critical work on the film, I pay less attention to them than I do to other scenes that

are neglected in most scholarship and are equally important for my argument. The examples I use prove that supreme fighting skills exist in the film, and to describe them as deeply as I would like to would require at least one more chapter in this book. Nevertheless, for those who have not seen the film, but have seen the trailers, the "bamboo" sequence takes place high in a grove of bamboo trees, with the two fighting each other on the limbs and branches. This scene required intense training and physical strength and stamina, which both actors were willing to endure. Using only wires to hold them up, they battle and move from tree to tree, eventually ending on one branch together. It cannot support them, so they leap off to safer ground.

36. When the bamboo-tree sequence ends, he taunts Jen by promising she can avoid becoming his disciple if she can take the Green Destiny from him in three moves or less, yet he takes it in one. However, he sees his offer to teach her means nothing to Jen. Then, feeling frustrated and angry at her futile stubbornness, he throws the sword into a deep, rapidly swirling river. Jen immediately dives for it and retrieves it, and is rescued from drowning by Jade Fox, who takes Jen away to her grotto hideaway.

37. That this first fight sequence starts sixteen minutes or so into the film provides one sign that Lee is indeed playing with genres, for in HKAC, usually considered "B-movies," stories focus on fight scenes and are often so "cheesy" (as Lee himself calls a lot of *CTHD* scenes) that they could not exist without the fighting. On the other hand, in many medieval romances, particularly non–Arthurian ones, fight scenes play secondary roles, used only to help prove a hero's worth.

38. This is known as a cutaway or insertion shot—we know the scene is still about Jen and Shu Lien, but we need a close-up of Jen's calligraphy skills to understand that Jen is an aristocrat.

39. Dollying, or tracking, occurs when the camera literally moves on a crane to produce a closer shot, as opposed to merely zooming in with its lens. This is an important distinction, for viewers feel more pulled into the action as a result.

40. This is the only scene in which I used the screenplay to quote dialogue or explain an action, for I found myself using the same adjectives Lee uses in his description of Jen's catch. In all other cases, I use my notes, which include shot-by-shot analyses not found in the screenplay.

41. Freeman, "The Power of Sisterhood: Marie de France's *Le Fresne*," *Women and Power in the Middle Ages*, ed. Mary Erler and Maryanne Kowaleski (Athens, GA: University of Georgia Press, 1988), pp. 250–64. Because of this power, says Freeman, "we notice the weak roles played by men ... [who are] less powerful than they first intimate" (p. 257). Susan Crane, in *Gender and Romance in Chaucer's Canterbury Tales* (Princeton, NJ: Princeton University Press, 1994) also argues that Marie's *lai* shows "the value of women's interrelations" (p. 200).

42. Hence the film's title. The title has, in fact, received much speculation. Some think it represents Shu Lien's and Mu Bai's struggle to reach their goal, to finally realize their love for each other, while others argue that it stands for Jen's and Lo's tumultuous affair. Lee seems torn about the issue (see note 4); however, in the DVD he and Schamus finally agree that it does ultimately signify Jen's internal struggles.

43. Hence when Lo shows up to reclaim her, she tells him to leave.

44. Shu Lien and Mu Bai promise to help her escape her forced marriage and join Lo, whom they have sent to Wudan Mountain to wait for her.

Works Cited

Arons, Wendy. "'If Her Stunning Beauty Doesn't Bring You to Your Knees, Her Deadly Drop Kick Will': Violent Women in the Hong Kong Kung Fu Film." In: *Reel Knockouts: Violent Women in the Movies*, ed. Martha McCaughey and Neal King. Austin, TX: University of Texas Press, 2001, pp. 27–51.

Auerbach, Erich. "The Knight Sets Forth." In: *Mimesis: The Representation of Reality in Western Literature*, tr. Willard R. Trask. Princeton, NJ: Princeton University Press, 1953, pp. 123–142.

Bordwell, David. "Films: *Crouching Tiger, Hidden Dragon*." "About Hong Kong Martial Arts Cinema." Magic Lantern, Inc., 2000. Available at http://www.magiclanternpr.com.films.crouching.html.

_____. "About *Wuxia Pian*." "Films: *Crouching Tiger, Hidden Dragon*." Magic Lantern, Inc., 2000. Available at http://www.magiclanternpr.com/films.crouching.html.

Borroff, Marie. *Sir Gawain and the Green Knight: A New Verse Translation*. New York and London: Norton, 1967.

Chen, Pauline. "*Crouching Tiger, Hidden Dragon*." *Cineaste* 26.4 (2001): 71–6.

Crane, Susan. *Gender and Romance in Chaucer's Canterbury Tales*. Princeton: Princeton University Press, 1994.

"*Crouching Tiger, Hidden Dragon*." 2000. Sony Pictures Classics Official Web site. Available at http://www.sonypictures.com/cthv/crouchingtiger/flash4.htm.

Fellows, Linda. "Introduction." In: *Of Love and Chivalry: An Anthology of Medieval Romance*, ed. Jennifer Fellows. London: J. M. Dent, 1993.

Field, Rosalind. "Romance in England, 1066–1400." In: *The Cambridge History of Medieval English Literature*, ed. David Wallace. Cambridge: Cambridge University Press, 1999, pp. 152–176.

Freeman, Michelle A. "The Power of Sisterhood: Marie de France's *Le Fresne*. In: *Women and Power in the Middle Ages*, ed. Mary Erler and Maryanne Kowaleski. Athens, GA: University of Georgia Press, 1988, pp. 250–264.

Giukin, Lenuta. "Boy-Girls: Gender, Body and Popular Culture in Hong Kong Action Movies." In: *Ladies and Gentlemen, Boys and Girls: Gender in Film at the End of the Twentieth Century*, ed. Murray Pomerance. Albany, NY: SUNY Press, 2001, pp. 55–69.

Hilderbrand, Lucas. "Girlfight." *PopMatters Magazine*. 2001. Available at http://www.popmatters.com/film/reviews/c/crouching-tiger2.html.

Lee, Ang, and James Schamus. *Crouching Tiger, Hidden Dragon: A Portrait of the Ang Lee Film including the Complete Screenplay*. New York: Newmarket Press, 2000.

Lee, Ang, and James Schamus. Commentary Track. *Crouching Tiger, Hidden Dragon*. d. Ang Lee. U.S.: United China Vision, 2000 DVD.

Leung, William. "Crouching Sense, Hidden Sensibility," *Film Criticism* 26.1 (2001): 42–57.

Logan, Bey. *Hong Kong Action Cinema*. Woodstock, NY: Overlook Press, 1996.

Morris, Gary. "Beautiful Beast: Ang Lee's *Crouching Tiger, Hidden Dragon*." *Bright Lights Film Journal* 1 (2001). Available at http://www.brightlightsfilm.com/31/crouchingtiger.html.

Mulvey, Laura. "Visual Pleasure and Narrative Cinema." In: *Feminisms: An Anthology of Literary Theory and Criticism*, ed. Robyn R. Warhol and Diane Price Herndl. New Brunswick, NJ: Rutgers University Press, 1991. First published in *Screen* 16.3 (1975).

Shepherd, Stephen H. A., ed. *Middle English Romances: A Norton Critical Edition.* New York and London: Norton, 1995.

Sir Gawain and the Green Knight, ed. J. R. R. Tolkien and E. V. Cohen. 2nd ed., rev. Norman Davis. London: Oxford University Press, 1967.

Slampyak, Diana E. "'As I Hafe Herde Telle': Collective Memory and Translation in Medieval English Romances." Ph.D. dissertation. University of California, Riverside, 2002.

Stokes, Lisa Oldham, and Michael Hoover. *City On Fire: Hong Kong Cinema.* New York: Verso, 1999.

Wang, Oliver. "Women Warriors." *PopMatters Magazine.* 2001. Available at http://www.popmatters.com/film/reviews/c/crouching-tiger.html.

Filmography

1966 *Dragon Creek,* d. King Hu, with Cheung Pei Pei. Hong Kong: Shaw Brothers.

That Fiery Girl, d. King Hu, with Cheung Pei Pei. Hong Kong: Shaw Brothers.

1967 *Lady of Steel,* d. King Hu, with Cheung Pei Pei. Hong Kong: Shaw Brothers.

1989 *The Killer,* d. John Woo, with Chow Yun-Fat. Hong Kong: Circle Releasing.

1990 *Bullet in the Head,* d. John Woo, with Chow Yun-Fat. Hong Kong: Gordon's Film.

1992 *Hard-Boiled,* d. John Woo, with Chow Yun-Fat. Hong Kong: Golden Princess.

The Heroic Trio, d. Johnny To Kei Fung, with Michelle Yeoh, Anita Mui, Maggie Cheung. Hong Kong: Universe.

Swordsman II, d. Chiang Siu-Tung and Stanley Tong, with Brigitte Lin Ching-Hsai, Jet Li. Hong Kong: Mei Ai.

1993 *The Heroic Trio II: Executioners,* d. Johnny To Kei Fung and Ching Siu Tung, with Michelle Yeoh, Anita Mui, Maggie Cheung. Hong Kong: Universe.

Iron Monkey, d. Yuen Wo-Ping. Hong Kong: Da Wai.

Swordsman III: The East Is Red, d. Chiang Siu-Tung and Stanley Tong, with Brigitte Lin Ching-Hsai. Hong Kong: Mei Ai.

1994 *Rumble in the Bronx,* d. Stanley Tong, with Jackie Chan. U.S./Hong Kong: Golden Harvest.

Wing Chun, d. Yuen Wo-Ping, with Michelle Yeoh, Cheung Pei Pei. Hong Kong: Guang Dong Tung Ah.

1995 *Sense and Sensibility,* d. Ang Lee, with Emma Thompson, Kate Winslet, Hugh Grant. U.S.: Mirage Productions/Columbia Tri-Star.

1997 *Tomorrow Never Dies,* d. Roger Spottiswoode, with Pierce Brosnan, Michelle Yeoh. U.S.: United Artists.

1999 *The Matrix,* d. Larry and Andy Wachowski, fight choreographer Yuen Wo-Ping, with Keanu Reeves, Laurence Fishburne. U.S.: Warner Bros.

2000 *Crouching Tiger, Hidden Dragon,* d. Ang Lee, with Zhang Ziyi, Chow Yun-Fat, Michelle Yeoh, Cheung Pei Pei, Chang Chen. U.S./Hong Kong/Taiwan: Sony Pictures Classics, Columbia Pictures Film Production Asia, and Good Machine International.

Not Your Typical Knight: The Emerging On-Screen Defender

SUSAN BUTVIN SAINATO

Sean Connery epitomizes the strong, handsome, aristocratic, athletic, valiant, and virtuous (almost picture-perfect) medieval knight of the movies whose nobility is shown in scene after scene. This hero is the gentle yet powerful leader who protects and helps those in need and, despite the great odds against him, wins because he represents justice. Over the last two decades or so, depictions of on-screen heroic medieval knights have shifted to include a variety of alternatives. These characterizations range from the aristocratic, almost pristine Lancelot of *Excalibur* (1981), to the disinherited Robin, his foreign friend Azeem, and, briefly, an armored Marian of *Robin Hood: Prince of Thieves* (1991), the mercenary Lancelot of *First Knight* (1995), William Thatcher, the peasant squire and would-be knight of *A Knight's Tale* (2002), an ogre, fighting princess, and talking donkey in the animated tale *Shrek* (2001), and finally the modern medieval "knights" Buffy, Giles, Xander, and Willow of the *Buffy the Vampire Slayer* television series (1997 through 2003). These changing portrayals of knights and heroes show us on-screen defenders who rarely fit the picture of traditional medieval knights and thus challenge our definitions of what constitutes a knight or hero.

The on-screen traditional medieval hero derives from heroes of medieval literature such as King Arthur, Sir Gawain, Sir Lancelot, and Sir Galahad. The medieval heroes are set apart from their enemies by their brawny physiques, their devotions to God, king, and lady, and their fighting abilities—which are used to promote justice. In *Excalibur*, King Arthur's and Sir Lancelot's good looks and actions define them as heroes.

133

(Mordred, although he is good-looking, wages an unjust war against his rightful king, murders knights, and murders his own mother, eliminating him from the hero category; heroes must at least try to behave righteously in addition to "looking good" in order to be true knights.) These heroes follow a chivalric code that echoes expectations expressed in medieval writings. Sir Thomas Malory's King Arthur requires his knights to take the following oath:

> Never to do outerage nothir mourthir, and allwayes to fle treson, and to gyff mercy unto hym that askith mercy ... and allwayes to do ladyes, damesels, and jantilwomen and wydowes socour: strength hem in hir ryghtes, and never to enforce them, uppon payne of dethe. Also, that no man take no batayles in a wrongfull quarell for no love no worldis goodis.[1]

Ideally, Arthur's knights are to be honorable, courageous, God-fearing, merciful, and just; they defend the weak and helpless and victoriously fight battle after battle for righteous causes. Traditionally, medieval knights are strong, courageous aristocratic men who have the natural abilities and equipment (armor, weapons, and horses) needed for battle and defense of the kingdom, the Church, and the weak—especially ladies. Their obligations to their lords, Church, and people to uphold justice help to control these powerful men as they maintain the standards of society.[2] Likewise, the medieval hero in the movies is the strong, silent type who also happens to be brave and handsome. Of course, this describes some of their enemies, as well. The quality that seems to separate the heroes from the villains is the heroes' determination to seek a larger justice.

The chivalric knight looks beyond his own interests to those of others, helping to solidify his society against lawlessness and evil. For example, near the end of *Excalibur*, Sir Perceval reminds King Arthur that his welfare is linked to the welfare of his kingdom, that the king and the land are one, giving Arthur strength to destroy the evil Mordred. This fight against anarchy and evil is articulated in themes found in many modern movies, including the *Star Wars*, *Lord of the Rings*, and *Harry Potter* film serials, as well as in medieval texts. As Richard Kaeuper observes, "Christine de Pisan, writing in the early fifteenth century, ... posited the creation of chivalry as one antidote to a world gone wrong."[3]

The heroes (some of them are knights) in the more modern adventure films are not necessarily perfect, but they, too, strive to make the world a better place, battle by battle. Our modern expectations of what "knights" or heroes should be are not as delineated as medieval notions of knighthood. Many of our heroes are not born into wealthy or noble families. (See, for example, the Lancelot of *First Knight* or William

Thatcher of *A Knight's Tale.*) Other heroes exhibit flaws or weaknesses. The beautiful Morgana of *Excalibur* easily manipulates Merlin; Shrek of *Shrek* allows his distrust of others and his impetuousness to govern him for a time. We may not expect our heroes to have perfect lineages or to behave ideally all the time; we do, however, expect nobility of heart, complete with a willingness to risk everything for a greater cause.

Perhaps this accepted fallibility in our modern heroes indicates an understanding of the human nature of all of us. Yet we still search for heroes—for people who enrich our lives through their abilities, their virtues, or their sacrifices. In an excerpt from *The Uses of Enchantment: The Meaning and Importance of Fairy Tales*, Bruno Bettelheim comments: "To find deeper meaning, one must become able to transcend the narrow confines of a self-centered existence and believe that one will make a significant contribution to life—if not right now, then at some future time."[4] Our modern heroes display this attribute of altruism more than they display physical perfection. Over the last twenty years, ever more modern characterizations show on-screen heroes as being superior while still having human failings. On the screen, in *Robin Hood: Prince of Thieves, First Knight, Shrek, The Knight's Tale,* and *Buffy the Vampire Slayer* (both the movie and the television series), concepts of heroes are constantly being reshaped.

Some films present traditional heroes while also suggesting that other representations are possible. For example, in *Robin Hood: Prince of Thieves*, while Kevin Costner's Robin of Locksley is a fairly typical hero (aristocratic, tall, strong, an able swordsman and archer, wise, and compassionate), Morgan Freeman's character Azeem (a tattooed foreigner, "Moor and Saracen") bends the definition of a knight. (He is not white, Christian, English, French, or aristocratic.) Even so, Azeem's noble bearing combined with his loyalty to Robin, and his knowledge and fighting prowess make him a valued fellow knight. The character of Marian, however briefly, demonstrates the emerging concept of a woman as a defender. A disguised Marian wears a suit of armor and battles Robin; he fights back, believing her to be a young man. For a short time, she mimics the fighting abilities found in agile young knights. However, she is not a knight but rather a lady, as Robin finds out when he has her cornered and forces her wrist over flames of a candle. An all-too-female scream explodes from the armored figure. Once her identity is unmasked, she seems to lose all ability to fight for herself. For the rest of the film, she relies on the men to protect and to rescue her; yet her short time as a defender foreshadows the emergence of other on-screen fighting females who do not lose their abilities to defend themselves and others.

Six years after *Robin Hood: The Prince of Thieves* demonstrated the potential fighting prowess of women, the movie *First Knight* returns physical combat to the male arena with its traditional gendered view of knights, as it plays up the premise that common men can shape themselves into knights. This retelling of the love triangle of King Arthur, Guinevere, and Lancelot removes Lancelot from his legendary (royal) lineage. Instead he is a mercenary. The film points out that his lack of family connections does not keep him from knightly pursuits, such as helping those in need. After one of his money-earning, sword-fighting exhibitions, Lancelot tells his defeated opponent that part of his strength is that Lancelot does not care whether he lives or dies. Of course, once he sees the beautiful young Guinevere, Lancelot begins to care about her and then about Arthur's Camelot. Protecting and defending Guinevere become his primary goals. Lancelot's daring rescues of Guinevere involve fighting scenes that emphasize his unorthodox approach to fighting. These moments imply that his ability to defeat his enemy is in part due to his constant "real-life" training. After being knighted by King Arthur (amid voiced concerns that the other knights know nothing about Lancelot's background), Lancelot demonstrates to the other knights of the Round Table his courage and fighting skills during battle. His battle prowess befits a knight, and so they accept him into their ranks. This medieval hero breaks through barriers of wealth and status.

Even though *First Knight* takes its knight-hero from a nonaristocratic background, Lancelot's focus in the film stays with knight-worthy tasks such as helping Guinevere and King Arthur. On the other hand, the film *A Knight's Tale* crafts its main hero as a disguised peasant whose goal is to win tournaments. This movie plays with the "fair unknown" motif often found in medieval romance literature. Generally, in medieval tales, the young knight (perhaps Perceval, Lancelot, or Gareth) rises from an obscure background to shine forth as a worthy knight. Knights in these medieval contexts are later shown to be worthy aristocrats, born of the blood royal. The knights who prove themselves through their noble actions are of aristocratic lineage.

In a thoroughly modern sense (in which a person's worth is not based on lineage), this film mocks many of the traditional medieval expectations, making the knight a son of a peasant instead of a noble. After William loses his livelihood because his former master (a knight) dies, he takes his master's armor and horse and begins a life of masquerade. He does this both because competing in tournaments is his dream and because winning at tournaments earns him (and his gambling friends) money.

In *A Knight's Tale*, the desire to excel is emphasized as a common link among "true knights," though contrary to the traditional on-screen knight, such as Lancelot or Gawain, William does not save any damsels in distress, regain a lord's kingdom, or destroy great evil. He wins tournaments. In one case, all the other combatants withdraw from battle when they learn that their opponent is Prince Edward, but William continues to joust. Near the end of the film, William's true parentage is exposed; he is identified as being the son of a commoner. William is arrested, punished, and put in the stocks for the public to ridicule. In a traditional tale, someone might have revealed that he is truly the son of a king or a prince—that he really has noble blood. William has no such ancestors. Instead, in this tale, the prince, his fellow jouster, elevates William's position in society. As he prepares to release William from the stocks, Prince Edward comments: "What a pair we make, eh. Both trying to hide who we are, both unable to do so. Your men love you; if I knew nothing else about you, that would be enough, but you also tilt when you should withdraw, and that is knightly, too." After the young man's release, Prince Edward's next action, after proclaiming (in an outright lie) William's aristocratic lineage, is to knight him. The ending of the movie merges the traditional expectations of rank for a knight (knights must have the proper lineage or be knighted by royalty) with the modern expectations of "knights" (anyone may follow a dream and succeed, if he or she tries hard enough).

The animated film *Shrek* may seem like an unlikely "medieval movie" after the previous examples of *Excalibur, Robin Hood: Prince of Thieves, First Knight,* and *A Knight's Tale;* nonetheless, this fairy tale plays to our traditional expectations of knights who will fight against all odds to succeed in their quests and ladies who need to be rescued; all the while, it requires us to see beyond appearances. This movie provides many twists and turns on concepts of the heroic. The main character, an ogre, agrees to take the mission to rescue the princess not to do what is "right" but to win back his swamp. He does, by the end of the movie, embrace a less egotistical attitude. When Donkey asks what his problem is, Shrek comments: "It's the world that seems to have a problem with me. People take one look at me and go 'Aaagh! Help! Run! A big, stupid, ugly ogre!' They judge me before they even know me."[5] His heartfelt comment points out that many people base their expectations of whether or not a character is a hero or a villain on his or her appearance, not on the many other qualities the character might have. Shrek almost allows this prejudice to keep him from being a hero, as he tries to maintain his antisocial behavior. He might look like a monster, but saving Princess Fiona ultimately becomes more important to him than avoiding others who may judge him.

In fact, none of the characters in *Shrek* fits the traditional recipe for "heroes." Donkey's willingness to help his newfound friend, even to the point of sneaking into a dragon's castle, is loyal and heroic. Donkey does not look like a "noble steed"; he faints at the sight of blood, and he is not the silent type. When the princess meets Donkey, she says, "It talks?" and Shrek replies, "Yeah, it's getting him to shut up that's the trick." While members in the audience may laugh, Donkey's human failings— not being strong (or more horselike), brave, or taciturn—place him outside the typical "hero" mode.

Princess Fiona does not represent the typical princess type either, no matter how much she seems to try to do so. Granted, she is beautiful and needs to be rescued from a fire-breathing dragon, but during her spare time she has learned martial arts. (Most fairy-tale princesses would have spent the time in more feminine pursuits, such as needlepoint.) Fiona lets out a loud belch in front of Shrek and Donkey just as Donkey corrects Shrek for his impolite behavior of belching in front of Princess Fiona. When a very annoying Robin Hood decides to save Fiona from Shrek, she punches and hits and kicks her way though Robin's Merry Men as if they are paper cutouts. (The choreography of this fight scene, with its lively, fast-paced, and artistically placed karate chops and kicks, visually alludes to similar fighting scenes found in the action movie *Charlie's Angels*, which also stars Cameron Diaz.) Just as Diaz's Angel character can defend herself from evil men and women, her Fiona is more than able to defend herself from an entire group of outlaws. Hence in *Shrek* the emerging heroes (a very large ogre, a donkey, and a princess who can fight) care enough about one another to fight against the oppression found in their society.

The hero-knights of *Excalibur*, with their aristocratic lineage, bravery, brawny physiques, and willingness to fight for justice, provide viewers with fairly clear-cut depictions of good and evil. However, the characterization of the emerging defender in more recent medieval movies encompasses other knights, as well, who are not as likely to be considered traditional. Whether they be foreigners, women, commoners, or ogres, the hero knights demonstrate fighting skills and a willingness to help others. This sense of sacrifice for society's good connects the traditional medieval knight to the many incarnations of the defending hero seen in various medieval movies over the past twenty years.

One out-of-the-ordinary example of a modern mythos that retains many elements of medieval movies is the on-screen world created by Joss Whedon in the *Buffy the Vampire Slayer* movie (1992) and television series (1997–2003). The knights or heroes in this world fight evil, defend, and aid those who need help, and become proficient in hand-to-hand combat, including fighting with swords and other medieval devices. In Whedon's work, the "chosen one" is not Sir Galahad or Sir Lancelot or Sir Perceval; the protector of the weak is Buffy. *Buffy the Vampire Slayer* transposes concepts of chivalry and knighthood from aristocratic and gendered definitions as this young woman and her friends

Buffy (Sarah Michelle Geller) confronts Spike (James Marsters) in *Buffy the Vampire Slayer* (1997–2003).

arm themselves night after night to make their town of Sunnydale a safer place.

While she might seem to be a fairly typical young woman, Buffy is the Slayer. She is the modern on-screen knight. She becomes the Slayer when the previous one dies. As the Slayer, "Though she has to work out to stay in shape, and trains with weapons, she possesses superhero strength, reflexes, and agility, and she heals faster than other human beings."[6] Her vocation is to fight evil, and she does so, always aware that as the Slayer, her vocation is framed by death. Throughout the series, she is unconventional, relies on others, and saves the world from multiple demon infestations and apocalypses. Her instincts and her "keen fashion sense" help her identify evil, dress well, and survive. She also saves her friends, the weak, and the downtrodden. As Farah Mendlesohn mentions, when Buffy rescues Willow, she "fulfills the role of shining knight without conflict, constantly reinforcing both the importance of her work and her sense of competence."[7] I would also argue that the rescues of her friends and of others echo the exploits of earlier film heroes and

The hero, in sequins and spaghetti straps, with Angel (David Boreanaz) in *Buffy the Vampire Slayer* (1997–2003).

place her within their realms as a chivalric defender and as a member of a tightly knit group that serves its community through sacrifice.

In the episode "Killed by Death," in Season Two, Buffy identifies herself as one of the good guys: "Grown-ups don't believe you, right? I do. There are real monsters, we both know that. But there're also real heroes, too, that fight monsters. That's me."[8] Rhonda V. Wilcox points out: "*Buffy* often manages an impressive convergence of realism with heroic romance. It is a rich text, with a humane and believable mixture of attitudes."[9] Characters react and respond to one another and circumstances in a variety of ways. In the series, characters grow, change, and even die.[10] Buffy displays knightly capabilities as she defends sick children against a demon; throughout the series she also demonstrates the virtues of bravery and self-sacrifice. Christopher Golden and Nancy Holder, in their book, *Buffy the Vampire Slayer, the Watcher's Guide,* Volume 1, comment that Buffy demonstrates a "courage that is rare in the human race, and it is even rarer for one so young to be mature enough to understand the nature of sacrifice."[11]

Buffy seems to be an unlikely hero: rather than being an aristocratic adult male, tall, and muscular, she is a girl, petite, and slight. She resembles a "damsel in distress" far more than the "knight in shining armor." And Buffy cult tradition has it that it is specifically this image that makes this hero so powerful. She should be the victim but instead becomes the hero: "Into every generation, a Slayer is born. One girl, in all the world, a Chosen One. One born with the strength and skill to hunt the vampires—to stop the spread of their evil...."[12] Her life mission is to protect others from evil. For many viewers, this depiction of strength in a young woman is heartening. Camille Bacon-Smith, in her foreword to the collection *Fighting the Forces: What's at Stake in Buffy the Vampire Slayer,* claims that Joss Whedon has "created" a "positive heroic role model for girls."[13] Buffy appears to be the underdog, a lightweight, and, quite frankly, often not very motivated. Despite her vocation as a Slayer, she is also human. In other words, she makes mistakes, allows her emotions to get the better of her, and even reacts in not-so-pleasant ways to circumstances, becoming moody, careless, angry, and sullen. While traditional medieval movies focus on the near-perfection of knights, the emerging knight of the modern medieval work is shown to be human. Such less-than-stellar reactions, mistakes, and emotions allow many viewers to relate to characters in *Buffy the Vampire Slayer.*

On the other hand, Buffy constantly shows herself to be crafted of the same material as medieval knights are. She, too, has trained with the quarterstaff, the sword, and the crossbow. Like Lancelot, her quests seem to be never-ending. In episode after episode, crisis after crisis, she rescues those who need help. (At her high school graduation she is given the title of "Class Protector" since, because of her actions, that graduation class has had the lowest mortality rate of any previous class in Sunnydale). Zoe-Jane Playden claims in her article "What You Are, What's to Come: Feminisms, Citizenship and the Divine" that Buffy should be placed "outside the mainstream of super-heroes."[14] As a woman who uses knowledge and skill, she does not fit into those categories of modern (male) fictional heroes (for example, Superman, Batman, Spider-Man). Instead, if one looks beyond her physical appearance and her personality, Buffy's constant defense of the weak, her leadership abilities, and her unorthodox approaches link her to the traditions of the medieval knight that we see in the emerging on-screen defender. She fights and protects, sometimes amazing even herself as she wins.

Joss Whedon's *Buffy the Vampire Slayer* mythos contains many champions, not just Buffy. They, too, are unlikely heroes: Willow, the extremely intelligent, sweet misfit; Xander, the foot-in-the-mouth jokester; and Giles, the British librarian (and Watcher). While these may not seem to be typical descriptions of heroes, Willow, Xander, and Giles constantly help Buffy in her fight against evil. These close connections for Buffy dilute the isolation that previous slayers have endured and force Buffy time and again to think beyond herself. She has her own, albeit small, brotherhood of knights. In the episode "Primeval" in Season Four, Giles, Willow, and Xander reinforce their unity with Buffy as they magically send their abilities into her, creating an even more powerful slayer. This episode overtly expresses the closeness of the group. Throughout the series, the loyalty and love these characters have for one another heighten their capabilities to defend one another and others. Buffy learns to use the strengths of her friends—their abilities to think, read, decipher, feel, care, use computers, problem-solve—often relying on them to provide her with what she needs so that she can fight.

One can argue that in many episodes of *Buffy the Vampire Slayer*, her friends and Watcher are actually braver than Buffy is; after all, they do not have the strength, agility, and healing abilities that she has, and yet they rush into the fray (knowing their own limitations and mortality) to help Buffy. Not only does this variety of character types as heroes promote diversity but it also changes the (modern) standard, allowing smart and caring people to become role models (instead of limiting the field to athletes, rock stars, and celebrities).

Intelligence becomes a desired characteristic for heroes; reading, researching, and learning are the components for success and survival. Most medieval movies have scholar/magician characters (Merlin, Gandalf, Dumbledore) that provide help, particularly in the form of knowledge, to the knights. The TV series stretches this notion to include heroes as users of the commodities of learning and knowledge. While the bookish Giles becomes the seeker of knowledge, the researcher who identifies the problem, providing Buffy with the knowledge she needs in order to defeat evil, the others, too—including Buffy—research and learn. As they fight evil, they gather knowledge.

Knowledge actually becomes one of the many weapons in the group's arsenal. Often the research involved takes effort from the characters. They have to work at obtaining the information they need; rarely does it appear without exertion. The task of spending hours looking through books or papers is not glamorous; research demands that the heroes forego other perhaps more entertaining activities. They sacrifice their time and energy to fight against evil. In *Buffy the Vampire Slayer*, viewers see the rewards of these endeavors as, time after time, some evil creature is defeated because the heroes were able to identify a weakness. A prime-time TV show actually encourages reading! Librarians and various associations have been quick to tie into this wave of encouragement. Christopher Golden and Nancy Holder note this phenomenon:

> Recognizing this enthusiasm [that viewers have for the TV series], the American Library Association has made *Buffy* the focus of its latest "READ" promotional poster. The poster includes the entire *Buffy* cast and the caption "Slay Ignorance at the Library."[15]

Books and the need for knowledge play a part in almost every episode of *Buffy the Vampire Slayer*. The heroes need knowledge to fight the good fight, to succeed, and to maintain their community against larger threats of isolation, ambiguity, and hopelessness. After all, they must continue to live their "regular lives" in the midst of slaying.

Language and learning become tools that all the heroes in *Buffy* wield. Even Buffy, who prefers physical combat to reading, comprehends the necessity of gathering information (see the episode "Teacher's Pet" in Season One). It is through her research that Buffy obtains the information she needs to save Xander from yet another monster that wishes to destroy him. Buffy explains to Giles that a bat is the natural enemy of the praying mantis: "Bats eat them—a praying mantis hears sonar, its whole nervous system goes kaplooie."[16] Armed with a tape of the sonar, Buffy and Giles go forth and save Xander from the deadly, larger-than-human-sized monster. Buffy, Giles, Willow, and Xander often spend hours going through the books, surfing the Internet, and discovering information to aid in the fight against evil.

While the big, strong knights in shining armor (so often played by Sean Connery) have become stereotypical on-screen medieval heroes, the emerging hero is quite different. The emerging on-screen defender may come in many shapes and sizes (and from various socioeconomic classes), but he or she still strives to make his or her world a better place in spite of the sacrifices he or she must make. The defender uses every type of information and knowledge he or she can gather to defeat evil and to protect others. The hero may be a tall, dark Saracen like Azeem, a peasant like William Thatcher, an ogre, a donkey, a princess expert in martial arts, a quiet young intellectual like Willow, a class clown (Xander), a petite young blonde (Buffy), or even a librarian (Giles). The emerging defender works in grays. Like issues in real life, circumstances, quests, and even monsters are not limited to the proverbial black and white. Our on-screen heroes, while they are heroes, are also fallible human beings with problems they need to overcome even as they continue the fight against ignorance and evil.

Notes

1. Sir Thomas Malory, *The Works of Sir Thomas Malory*, ed. Eugène Vinaver, 2nd ed. (Oxford: Oxford University Press Paperbacks, 1977), p. 75.

2. Richard Barber, *The Knight and Chivalry*, rev. ed. (Woodbridge, U.K.: Boydell Press, 2000), pp. 136–7.

3. Richard Kaeuper, "The Societal Role of Chivalry in Romance: North-western Europe," in *The Cambridge Companion to Medieval Romance*, ed. Roberta L. Krueger (Cambridge: Cambridge University Press, 2000), p. 107.

4. Bruno Bettelheim, "Introduction: The Struggle for Meaning," in *The Uses of Enchantment: The Meaning and Importance of Fairy Tales* (New York: Random House, 1989), pp. 3–4.

5. *Shrek*, animated film produced by Aron Warner, John H. Williams, Jeffrey Katzenberg, with Mike Myers, Eddie Murphy, Cameron Diaz, and John Lith-gow, VHS, (Universal City: DreamWorks Home Entertainment, 2001).

6. Nancy Holder, Jeff Mariotte, and Maryelizabeth Hart, *Buffy the Vampire Slayer: The Watcher's Guide*, Vol. 2 (New York: Pocket, 2000), p. 3.

7. Farah Mendlesohn, "Surpassing the Love of Vampires," in *Fighting the Forces: What's at Stake in Buffy the Vampire Slayer*, ed. Rhonda V. Wilcox and David Lavery (Lanham: Rowman & Littlefield Publishers, Inc., 2002), p. 52.

8. "Killed By Death," in *Buffy the Vampire Slayer: The Script Book, Season Two*, Vol. 4 (New York: Pocket, 2003), p. 34.

9. Rhonda V. Wilcox, "Who Died and Made Her the Boss?" in *Fighting the Forces*, p. 16.

10. Roz Kaveney, "She Saved the World, a Lot," in *Reading the Vampire Slayer*, ed. Roz Kaveney (New York: Tauris Parke Paperbacks, 2002), p. 2. Kaveney notes: "The show constantly tinkered with its own premises—important char-acters died or became evil."

11. Christopher Golden and Nancy Holder, *Buffy the Vampire Slayer: The Watcher's Guide*. Vol. 1, ed. Christopher Golden and Nancy Holder (New York: Pocket, 1998), p. 8.

12. "Welcome to the Hellmouth," in *Buffy the Vampire Slayer: The Script Book, Season One*, Vol. 1 (New York: Pocket, 2000), pp. 29–30.

13. Camille Bacon-Smith, "Foreword," in *Fighting the Forces*, p. xiii.

14. Zoe-Jane Playden, "What You Are, What's to Come: Feminisms, Citizen-ship and the Divine," in *Reading the Vampire Slayer*, p. 120.

15. Golden and Holder, *Buffy the Vampire Slayer*, pp. 34–35.

16. "Teacher's Pet," in *Buffy the Vampire Slayer: The Script Book, Season One*, Vol. 1 (New York: Pocket, 2000), p. 243.

Works Cited

Barber, Richard. *The Knight and Chivalry*, rev. ed. Woodbridge, U.K.: Boydell Press, 2000.

Bettelheim, Bruno. "Introduction: The Struggle for Meaning." In: *The Uses of Enchantment: The Meaning and Importance of Fairy Tales*. New York: Random House, 1989, pp. 3–4.

Buffy the Vampire Slayer: The Script Book, Season One, Vol. 1. New York: Pocket, 2000.

Buffy the Vampire Slayer: The Script Book, Season Two, Vol. 1. New York: Pocket, 2001.

Buffy the Vampire Slayer: The Script Book, Season Two, Vol. 3. New York: Pocket, 2001.

Buffy the Vampire Slayer: The Script Book, Season Two, Vol. 4. New York: Pocket, 2003.

Golden, Christopher, and Nancy Holder. *Buffy the Vampire Slayer: The Watcher's Guide*. Vol. 1. New York: Pocket, 1998.

Holder, Nancy, Jeff Mariotte, and Maryelizabeth Hart. *Buffy the Vampire Slayer: The Watcher's Guide*. Vol. 2. New York: Pocket, 2000.

Kaveney, Roz. *Reading the Vampire Slayer: An Unofficial Critical Companion to Buffy and Angel*. New York: Tauris Parke Paperbacks, 2002.

_____. "She Saved the World, a Lot." *Reading the Vampire Slayer: An Unofficial Critical Companion to Buffy and Angel*. New York: Tauris Parke Paperbacks, 2002, pp. 1–36.

Kaeuper, Richard. "The Societal Role of Chivalry in Romance." In: *The Cambridge Companion to Medieval Romance*, ed. Roberta L. Krueger. Cambridge: Cambridge University Press, 2000, pp. 97–114.

Llull, Raimon, tr. William Caxton. *The Book of the Order of Chyvalry*, ed. A.T.P. Byles. EETS OS 168. Woodbridge, U.K.: Boydell and Brewer, 1998.

Malory, Thomas. *The Works of Sir Thomas Malory*, ed. Eugène Vinaver, 2nd ed. Oxford: Oxford University Press Paperbacks, 1977.

Mendlesohn, Farah. "Surpassing the Love of Vampires." In: *Fighting the Forces: What's at Stake in Buffy the Vampire Slayer*, ed. Rhonda V. Wilcox and David Lavery. Lanham: Rowman & Littlefield Publishers, Inc., 2002, pp. 45–60.

Wilcox, Rhonda V., and David Lavery, eds. *Fighting the Forces: What's at Stake in Buffy the Vampire Slayer*. Lanham: Rowman and Littlefield Publishers, Inc., 2002.

Filmography

1981 *Excalibur*, d. John Boorman, with Nicol Williamson. U.S.: Orion.

1991 *Robin Hood: Prince of Thieves*, d. Kevin Reynolds, with Kevin Costner, Morgan Freeman. U.S.: Morgan Creek.

1992 *Buffy the Vampire Slayer*, d. Fran Rubel Kuzui, with Kristy Swanson, Donald Sutherland, Luke Perry, Rutger Hauer, Paul Reubens. U.S.: 20th Century–Fox.

1995 *First Knight*, d. Jerry Zucker, with Richard Gere, Julia Ormand, Sean Connery. U.S.: Zucker Brothers, Columbia.

2001 *Buffy the Vampire Slayer: The Complete First Season on DVD*, with Sarah Michelle Gellar, Nicholas Brendon, Anthony S. Head, Alyson Hannigan, Charisma Carpenter. U.S.: 20th Century–Fox.

A Knight's Tale, d. Brian Helgeland, with Heath Ledger. U.S.: Columbia, Escape Artists/Finestkind Prod.

Shrek, d. Andrew Adamson and Vicky Jenson, with the voices of Mike Myers, Eddie Murphy, Cameron Diaz, John Lithgow. U.S.: DreamWorks.

2002 *Buffy the Vampire Slayer: The Complete Second Season on DVD*, with Sarah Michelle Gellar, Nicholas Brendon, Anthony S. Head, Alyson Hannigan, Charisma Carpenter. U.S.: 20th Century–Fox.

2003 *Buffy the Vampire Slayer: The Complete Third Season on DVD*, with Sarah Michelle Gellar, Nicholas Brendon, Anthony S. Head, Alyson Hannigan, Charisma Carpenter. U.S.: 20th Century–Fox.

IV

Time Bandits

Contemporary Appropriations

SID RAY

On any given day, cable television will offer at least one and sometimes up to five films with medieval themes or settings. This should not
be surprising. As David John Williams has noted, "two or three films a
year depicting some sort of Middle Ages is no more than average ever
since the first Joan of Arc in 1898."[1] But over the years, the type of
medieval film being made has changed significantly. Until recently, most
medieval films were of what Williams calls the "serious" type, films
directed by European auteurs such as Ingmar Bergman, Lawrence
Olivier, Sergei Eisenstein, and Roberto Rossellini.[2] Today's television
and film listings give us films directed by such crowd-pleasers as Mel
Brooks, Mel Gibson, and Brian Helgeland whose work appeals to a much
larger demographic. Though Hollywood produced a sprinkling of comic
and camp classics between the 1930s and 1970s— *The Adventures of Robin
Hood* (1938), *The Court Jester* (1955), and *Camelot* (1967) to name a
few—the watershed may well have been 1975 when Terry Gilliam and
Terry Jones released *Monty Python and the Holy Grail*. This film changed
everything; not only did medieval films begin regularly to appeal to large
audiences, they also became self-consciously self-referential and a site at
which filmmakers could both mock and celebrate "serious" medieval
film. *Monty Python and the Holy Grail* engages a vastly different cohort
than the one excited by Bergman and Rossellini. It is a film quoted as
often (and as accurately) by college fraternity brothers as it is by college
professors. As the authors in this section demonstrate, the self-referentiality and intertextuality of post–Python medieval film involve the appropriation of aspects of medieval narrative and medieval film that attract
mass audiences.

Appropriations of the Middle Ages in other media have also gained
in popularity. Over the last several years, the *New York Times* has listed
children's books with medieval themes as among the nation's bestsellers.
Though it has become the standard-bearer, the *Harry Potter* series does

not account for all of these listings. *The Magic Tree House* book series, for example, now at thirty books, features a benevolent character named Morgan Le Fay who travels through time from the Middle Ages and recruits two children from contemporary America to serve as "Master Librarians and Magicians of Everyday Magic." The author makes Morgan a kind old lady who only wants to augment the library at Camelot. Other "chapter book" bestsellers include novelized versions of the *Star Wars* movies, and *Eragon*, a book about a boy and a dragon by Christopher Paolini, which promises to be the first in another "medieval" book series. In adult fiction, there has also been a resurgence of the medieval. The *Da Vinci Code*, a grail narrative by Dan Brown, was popular summer reading in 2003, and the J.R.R. Tolkien books came back strongly in the midst of Peter Jackson's release of *The Lord of the Rings* films. Stephen King has followed the trend. His *Dark Tower* series of books focuses on a questing hero named Roland and involves towers, wizards, and waste lands. In keeping with the success of Dungeons & Dragons' conversion to the computer screen, computer games continue to have medieval themes. Top-selling games of 2003–2004 inspired by medieval romance include the Myst Trilogy, Dark Age of Camelot: Trials of Atlantis, and Star Wars Jedi Knight: Jedi Academy.

The underside of this appropriation and revision of the Middle Ages is, of course, that monetary gain appears to be the primary motivation. In many ways, medieval film accumulates more capital than culture from its appropriation of the Middle Ages.[3] J.K. Rowling, by some accounts, has now surpassed the Queen of England as the wealthiest woman in the United Kingdom.[4] It is difficult to begrudge Rowling's financial success; a struggling single mother who writes updated medieval fantasies for children and strikes it rich can hardly be faulted. Nobody, after all, has done more to promote children's reading since J.R.R. Tolkien. But many appropriations of the Middle Ages do come at a cost. As Carl James Grindley suggests, filmmakers have caught on to one *topos* of the Middle Ages that appeals to the rather large section of the American population fascinated by weaponry, and thus such violent medieval films as *Excalibur* (1981), *Conan the Barbarian* (1982), and *The 13th Warrior* (1999). have been very successful at the box office. In fact, these types of medieval films can be found much more regularly in cable television listings than the "serious" ones.

In medieval film, we must cope then with a commodified Middle Ages that has been expropriated of its history, its treatment of narrative, and its very culture. Michael A. Torregrossa examines the many on-screen Merlins and demonstrates the ways in which they have become homogenized by filmic self-referentiality. But, as Torregrossa suggests, such replication and revision are not necessarily bad; though appropri-

Robin Hood (Errol Flynn) displays his derring-do in *The Adventures of Robin Hood* **(1938).**

ating the Middle Ages radically revises medieval narratives, in doing so, these stories—and film versions of them—are creating a generation of fledgling medievalists, students who already have a taste for costume drama, action-adventure, and even allegory. As Elizabeth S. Sklar writes, "as long as Arthur sells, his legend is alive and well."[5] Moreover, while the politics of gender and class have sometimes found expression in medieval movies, race is now also being addressed, at least nominally, as the essay by Caroline Jewers demonstrates. Consequently, when female characters such as Morgan Le Fay are redeemed from villainy as in the *Magic Tree House* series, and when heroines Hermione Granger and Buffy the Vampire Slayer are both bookish and brave, and when black characters are inserted into medieval contexts where none existed before, such as in *Robin Hood: Prince of Thieves* and *Black Knight*, popular medieval films may encourage our fledgling medievalists to comprise a more diverse group than generally seen in the medieval academy: male and female, old and young, white and nonwhite. Such a change is coming, if it is not here already.

Notes

1. David John Williams, "Looking at the Middle Ages in the Cinema: An Overview," *Film & History* 29. 1 (1999): 9.
2. Williams: 9.
3. The term "cultural capital" was coined by Pierre Bourdieu and refers to the symbolic capital gained through the process of appropriation, the calculated poaching of aspects of culture that may then be reapplied against the source. See Bourdieu, *Distinction: A Social Critique of the Judgment of Taste*, tr. R. Nice (Cambridge, MA: Harvard University Press, 1984).
4. See http://news.bbc.co.uk/1/hi/entertainment/arts/3004760.stm.
5. Elizabeth S. Sklar, "Marketing Arthur: The Commodification of Arthurian Legend," in *King Arthur in Popular Culture*, ed. Elizabeth S. Sklar and Donald L. Hoffman (Jefferson, NC: McFarland, 2002), p. 21.

The Hagiography of Steel: The Hero's Weapon and Its Place in Pop Culture

CARL JAMES GRINDLEY

It is a given that mainstream contemporary film and television are fascinated by weapons, the people who wield them, and the complicated mythologies that always seem to proliferate around a well-crafted sword, spear, shield, or sharp metal whatnot. But since a weapon's story, told through its physical description or provenance, can appear anywhere from the credits of an Arnold Schwarzenegger movie to the text of *Beowulf*, it is evident not only that this hagiography of steel is an ancient *topos* but that it must serve some overarching function that transcends any particularized exegesis. In its purest form, the weapon's tale is an encomium that sings the praises of arms and armor that, for the most part, contribute little to the overall narrative structure of a text but contain a concentrated symbolic functionality. Interestingly enough, the realized symbolism of the applied *topos* is nowhere near as compelling as the shifting battle for meaning that lurks behind its seeming ubiquity.

Although there are many early appearances of weapons' encomiums in Western literature, the gold standard is in the works of Homer. The arms of Achilleus—the topic of most of Book 18 of the *Iliad*—are described in a manner that far outweighs their usefulness to the epic's central narrative. Homer's text focuses on the divine manufacture of Achilleus' shield, but the poet dedicates more lines to describing the elaborate engravings than he ever spends showing us the thing in action. The shield and its golden text have a definite symbolic functionality, but given that the opening lines of Book 19 of the *Iliad* assert that among mortals only Achilleus had the courage to view the object directly, the reception of its story is necessarily limited to Achilleus, the gods, and Homer's audience. The shield of Achilleus is a private object that we may share in but which can never truly enter the fictional human discourse created by Homer. Over the years, many readings of the shield's engravings have been offered, but the true importance of the passage is that it exists at all.

Homer's text, regardless of interpretation, represents the birth of a long campaign to define the hero by making fetish objects of his or her artifacts, whether through the creation of literal or figurative pedigrees or through an appeal to the distinctness or specialty of the item's use. The hero's item functions like a medal; it is the public recognition of perceived ability, even in an entirely nonreadable form such as the shield of Achilleus, which is particular to an individual and for the most part nontransferable. Although the weapon gets a story, the subtext always relates to its rightful owner. Homer presents another such encomium when he describes Achilleus' spear. In Richmond Lattimore's translation, Book 19, lines 387 and following read:

> Next [Achilleus] pulled out from its standing place the spear of his father,
> Huge, heavy, thick, which no one else of all the Achaeans
> Could handle, but Achilleus alone knew how to wield it,
> The Pelian ash spear which Cheiron had brought to his father
> From high on Pelion, to be the death for fighters in battle.[1]

Cheiron was a centaur, so, as with the great shield forged by Hephaistos, an implied otherworldliness adds to the power of the spear, whose ownership is passed through the mechanism of patriarchal descent and which is unusable by anyone outside the bloodline. The spear is a potent symbol, in any conceivable context, of the might of its possessor. Again, the symbolism of the weapon, although amusingly phallic—its hard shaft penetrates a variety of hapless Trojans until it ends up stuck in Hektor's throat—is unimportant. What is important is that the spear's functionality is limited. Like the shield, with its unreadable narrative, the spear, as mighty as it is, is unusable by anyone other than Achilleus. It is a symbol of his greatness and is worthless to any other character. A similar situation exists in the *Odyssey*, which stresses the importance of the great bow of Odysseus. It carries significantly more narrative importance than either Achilleus' shield or his spear and is the agency of revelation in the *Odyssey*. Since no one but Odysseus is capable of drawing the bow, anyone who can use the bow must be Odysseus returned:

> You thought I never would return from Troy;
> And so—you dogs—you sacked my house, you forced
> My women servants to your will and wooed
> My wife in secret while I was alive.

> You had no fear of the undying gods,
> Whose home is spacious heaven, and no fear
> Of men's revenge, your fate in days to come.
> Now all of you are trapped in death's tight thongs.[2]

This feature of solitary effectiveness is reinforced in the *Iliad* when Patroklos "borrows" the original armor of Achilleus and ends up dead. Regardless of how the scene is manipulated, the point is made that Patroklos is not Achilleus, and although some "power" may remain in an item when it becomes removed from its original context, it loses most of its meaning. Ultimately, the armor of Achilleus without its rightful owner becomes the cause of insanity and discord. The fetish item loses its status of medal and becomes a mere badge that at the most provides a surety of the pedigree of its possessor and at the least serves as an arbitrarily or nepotistically ordained recognition of apparent inherent worth.

This condition of the hero's weapon being particular to the hero, a statement of his or her inherent worth, persisted well into the Common Era. Consider, for example, the way that the *Beowulf* poet treats Hrunting, the mighty sword given to Beowulf, at lines 1455 and following of the Anglo-Saxon epic:

> Another item lent by Unferth
> At that moment of need was of no small importance:
> The brehon handed him a hilted weapon,
> A rare and ancient sword named Hrunting.
> The iron blade with its ill-boding patterns
> Had been tempered in blood. It had never failed
> The hand of anyone who hefted it in battle,
> Anyone who had fought and faced the worst
> In the gap of danger. This was not the first time
> It had been called to perform heroic feats.[3]

Beowulf, in the process of arming for his encounter with Grendel's mother, receives a variety of gifts from his kinsmen and allies. As is well known, this particular blade refuses to cut into Grendel's mother's head. Regardless of current or historical interpretation, lurking below all layers of meaning is the simple message that Beowulf is no Unferth, and Unferth is no Beowulf, a truism confirmed when Beowulf abandons Hrunting and comes across a giant's sword:

> Then he saw a blade that boded well,
> A sword in her armory, an ancient heirloom
> From the days of the giants, an ideal weapon,
> One that any warrior would envy,
> But so huge and heavy of itself
> Only Beowulf could wield it in a battle.[4]

Instantly, there is a return to the situation that exists between Patroklos and Achilleus and between Odysseus and Penelope's suitors. Identity matters. The ownership of such an object does not always guarantee performance; there must also exist a unique claim to its symbolism. And again, the true import of the giant's sword is without universal internally received meaning; no one who lives sees Beowulf wield the giant's sword in battle, and the blade dissolves in Grendel's mother's blood before its grandeur can be witnessed by any of the poem's other characters. Certainly, Hrothgar is privy to a partial narrative, but one that gets filtered through Beowulf and without the text of the sword's original appearance; by the time Hrothgar hears the story, the sword has been reduced to its hilt. The giant's sword's full narrative is for Beowulf, the *Beowulf* poet, and his audience alone. Indeed, no sword is the match for Beowulf; no object can symbolize his worth.

In the later Middle Ages, the weapon's encomium makes a number of important appearances, and in some of these appearances we learn that texts will sometimes present false encomiums that merely expose the inadequacies of a character. In Malory's *Morte Darthur*, for example, a lot of text is dedicated to King Arthur's various swords, but instead of pointing to Arthur's worth, they illustrate his failings. The sword in the stone, for example, appears to be an object unique to Arthur that functions as a badge indicating his right to kingship, but it delivers a mixed message. Certainly, it can be drawn from the stone only by him, a feat he performs about a dozen times or so in nearly as few lines of text, but no one is able instantly to recognize its message.[5] Ownership of the sword is particular to Arthur, but that is due wholly to patriarchal association; Arthur has done nothing that warrants possession of the sword in the stone beyond the accident of his birth. The repetition of the ritual of drawing the sword from the stone merely highlights the inability of the peripheral characters to read the scene. The sword is not a symbol of what Arthur is, only of who he is.

The various appearances of Excalibur underscore the narrative's low opinion of Arthur. If Excalibur and its scabbard are possessed, their powers are obtained, so in Book 4, chapters 8, 9, and 10 of Malory's text, Sir Accolon of Gaul wields Excalibur, using its magic against Arthur, who "so sore be-bled he was dismayed, and then he deemed treason that his sword was changed; for his sword bit not steel as it was wont to do, therefore he dreaded him sore to be dead."[6] Arthur, quite correctly, surmises, that "the sword in Accolon's hand was Excalibur, for at every stroke that Accolon struck he drew blood."[7] Until it bites into his body, Arthur is unable to recognize any inherent worth in Excalibur's appearance; the situation is quite at odds with the presentation of Odysseus' bow, which Homer depicts as clearly being the weapon of a hero, or

Achilleus' shield, which cannot even be glanced upon by the unworthy.

In the case of *Sir Gawain and the Green Knight*, the Green Knight's ax receives a lengthy description:

> Þe hede of an elnȝerde þe large lenkþe hade,
> Þe grayn al of grene stele and of golde hewen
> Þe bit burnyst bryȝt, with a brod egge
> As wel schapen to schere as scharp rasores.
> Þe stele of a stif staf þe sturne hit bi grypte,
> Þat watz woundedn wyth yrn to þe wandez ende
> And al bigrauen with grene in gracios werkes;
> A lace lapped aboute þat louked at þe hede
> And so after þe halme halched ful ofte,
> Wyth tried tasselez þerto tacched innoghe
> On botounz of þe bryȝt grene brayden ful ryche.[8]

Once the ax has been described as an item of special status and is used by Gawain to behead the Green Knight, its function abruptly vanishes. Arthur suggests that the ax should be hung up on the wall, "Þer alle men for meruayl myȝt on hit loke/And bi trwe tytel þerof to telle þe wonder" (ll. 479–480). The ax then vanishes for the duration of Gawain's quest. Arthur uses the ax and its instant mythology to demonstrate Gawain's apparent worthiness, but after the ax becomes an emblem of Gawain's heroic qualities, it ceases to have a place in the text it helps to create. Likewise, Gawain's wonderful shield, whose description provides a major weapon's encomium, is an empty object as far as the poem's plot is concerned. Although the descriptive poetry is compelling, the shield is raised only once in the text, and even then, its functionality is aborted. As it turns out, Gawain's heroic development is incomplete, and only at the end of his quest does his character develop enough to earn everlasting fame. Unfortunately, although Gawain returns as a true knight, when he produces the green lace belt and tells his tale, his symbolic heroism is co-opted by the entirety of the royal court all of whom continue to put their faith in the simple contrivance of the object. The position of the object in *Sir Gawain and the Green Knight* is problematized; on one hand, the green sash and the ax are medals of Gawain's heroism, but on the other, they are unfairly co-opted and deliberately misinterpreted by those at the court of King Arthur, who see the objects as badges that convey status to all who participate—even through the oblique nonparticipation of a passive viewer—in Gawain's quest.

It is this background, running from Homer to the late Middle Ages, that informs the fictions of the present day, and contemporary cinema uses much the same division between viewing the hero's weapon as a medal and viewing it as a badge. The current attitude to the weapon's encomium might best be exemplified by the classic fetish weapon of modern cinema:

"Make my day!" Dirty Harry Callahan (Clint Eastwood) brandishes his weapon in *Magnum Force* (1973)

HARRY
This is the .44 magnum, the most powerful handgun in the world, and it could blow your head clean off. Do you feel lucky?[9]

This is the opening voice-over from the 1973 film *Magnum Force*, the sequel to 1972's *Dirty Harry*, and it serves to introduce police detective Dirty Harry Callahan's .44 magnum handgun. This gun is probably the most famous modern fetish weapon. Everyone knows that Dirty Harry carries it; everyone knows that no one else does. At first glance, the .44 magnum has all of the symbolism inherent in Achilleus' spear or Odysseus' bow. But the .44 magnum is not what it seems, and the opening of *Magnum Force* did not appear spontaneously. Consider this final moment from the first Dirty Harry movie, itself a reprise of an earlier scene, repeated like a litany:

> HARRY
> Ah Ah, I know what you're thinking. Did he fire six shots or only five? Well, to tell you the truth, in all this excitement, I've kinda lost track myself. But being as this is a .44 Magnum, the most powerful handgun in the world, and will blow your head clean off, you've got to ask yourself one question: 'Do I feel lucky?' Well, do ya, punk?[10]

The movie closes with this speech, which follows Harry's final showdown with the bad guy. The two have an extended gun battle, and when Harry asks his question, the audience has to answer in all honesty that it does not feel lucky. The villain is doomed through the agency of the gun. But during the course of *Dirty Harry* and its sequel, the .44 magnum's meaning is both externally and internally subverted; the object itself is not as important as it originally seems. The two scenes were added in the fourth draft of the shooting script by John Milius.[11] The .44 magnum was chosen by Eastwood himself; it was not an original part of the script. The Smith and Wesson model 29 .44 magnum with a six-and-a-half-inch barrel was not even being manufactured in the early seventies, and Dirty Harry's gun had to be assembled from parts.[12] To the other characters in the film's narrative as well as the film's readers, the weapon was unavailable, but not because it was unique in any way; it was a relatively ordinary object out of commercial production. In addition, the gun was so powerful that Eastwood had special blanks produced just to be able to keep its recoil under control.[13] In *Magnum Force*, Eastwood's character even tells the other characters that he uses depowered rounds—which are cartridges loaded with less gunpowder.[14]

So we also have a situation where the hero himself is unable to use the weapon to its full potential; it is as if Achilleus, although entitled to own his great spear, were not strong enough to use it. And although no other character carries or can carry a .44 magnum, other characters are just as adept as Harry is at using it. In *Magnum Force*, in the firing range scene, one of the movie's young villains is allowed to use Harry's revolver, and does so with great gusto and nearly as much accuracy as the film's hero. The audience is even informed that this particular character is not

Conan the Barbarian (Arnold Schwarzenegger) seeks vengeance in *Conan the Barbarian* (1982).

even considered by his peers to be the best shot, merely average for the group.

Although a minor point, it should be noted that Harry, while not an Achilleus, would not be out of place in the Anglo-Saxon milieu of "The Wanderer," "The Seafarer," or, indeed, *Beowulf* or "The Battle of Maldon." Like the anonymous, defeated narrator of "The Wanderer," Harry is stoic and uncomplaining, easily confused by unexpected changes in the hierarchy or challenges to the linear structure of the society he inhabits. When the system fails, Harry is reduced to either lethargy or senseless violence. He understands the need for controlled and managed revenge and values a consistent rule of law over chaos. Harry is unemotional, hides his stresses behind the sheen of alcohol, and although his public manner is taciturn at the best of times, he actually seems incapable of existing outside of his homosocial warrior context.

Regardless of the interesting facets of Harry's character, when John Milius wrote the script for *Magnum Force*, the gun was an object that was most highly prized. Milius was paid $35,000 for his work and was allowed to keep the prop .44 magnum; that object, just like Judy Garland's ruby slippers or the Maltese Falcon, has transcended the world of fictional fetish and attained the realm of the real.[15]

In *Dirty Harry* and *Magnum Force*, the simple weapon's encomium is transcended and the text of *Magnum Force*, with minor revisions, is catapulted into the real world as a sort of motto. The film is important because it single-handedly moved the motion picture catchphrase into the political arena, culminating with Ronald Reagan using a Dirty Harry quip, "make my day," in a presidential debate. Obviously no longer mere dialogue, Dirty Harry's catchphrase became the most instantly recognized sound bite of the election, a rallying call for America.

John Milius's interest in weaponry did not end with the two Clint Eastwood movies; Milius continued with a major foray into the sword-and-sorcery genre. Reworking an original screenplay by Oliver Stone, Milius directed the 1982 *Conan the Barbarian*. In this film, Conan's adult life centers around a quest to recover a finely crafted sword that was made by his father and was stolen when Conan's parents were killed and their village destroyed. The opening credit sequence is constructed around the forging of this sword, and the movie's first scene shows Conan's father instilling in his son "the riddle of steel," telling his young son to put his trust in a good sword.[16]

Great liberties were taken with the opening sequence of *Conan the Barbarian*, and the film's master sword-maker, Jody Samson, readily confesses that the process as depicted would result in a broken sword with a shattered blade; the story of the sword's creation is unreliable, and the item itself as it exists is unusable outside the world created by the film. At 6.5 pounds, Conan's father's sword is too heavy for use in actual combat. This weapon, incidentally, contains its own secret motto, which cannot be read through either the movie or the screenplay. Further, the sword is engraved with the (pseudo-archaic and ungrammatical) English inscription: "suffer no guilt ye who wields this in the name of Crom."

Another of *Conan the Barbarian*'s early scenes shows Arnold

Schwartzenegger's character acquiring his own sword, the so-called Atlantean sword, the weapon of a nine-foot tall giant, which he finds in the tomb of a long-dead general from the dead kingdom of Atlantis. Conan keeps this weapon for the remainder of the film, but like Beowulf's experience with the giant's sword, no one except Conan is ever privy to the story of his sword's origins, and indeed, the item itself is entirely unreadable, even to Conan. According to Jody Samson, the motto engraved on the Atlantean sword comprises a sequence of meaningless symbols.[17] Like the father's sword, the Atlantean sword is also too heavy for real use, weighing nearly 9 pounds, whereas a usable sword would weigh no more than 2.5 pounds.[18]

At the climax of *Conan the Barbarian,* when Conan encounters the people responsible for his father's death, he also rediscovers his father's sword, which he must face in battle. In a key moment, Conan breaks his father's sword with his own weapon, not only fulfilling a snickering spectrum of Oedipal conjecture but also asserting the view put forward by Homer, that the sword does not make the hero, but the hero makes the sword.

In 1976, *Beowulf* was transformed into Michael Crichton's book *Eaters of the Dead,* which was in turn made into the film *The 13th Warrior.* Crichton's version of *Beowulf,* told through the agency of an Arabian ambassador named Ibn Fadlan, includes the sword Hrunting, but, simplifying its function, Crichton removes it from the court of Hrothgar and instead casts the sword as Beowulf's own ancestral weapon; in Crichton's book, Beowulf is renamed Buliwyf and Hrunting is called Runding:

> I saw by their faces that all the other earls, nobles and warriors were happy as Buliwyf himself. I asked Herger why this was so.
> "Buliwyf is our chief, and we are happy for him, and for the power that he will soon have."
> I inquired what was this power of which he spoke.
> "The power of Runding," Herger answered me.[19]

Unfortunately, Crichton's Neanderthal Grendel equivalents have already destroyed Beowulf's homeland, but the warrior is able to rescue his birthright:

> Now this happened: Buliwyf entered one smoking ruined house and returned to our company bearing a sword. This sword was very large and heavy, and so heated by the fire that he carried it with a cloth wrapped around the handle. Verily I say it was the largest sword I have ever seen. It was as long as my own body and the blade was flat and broad as the palms

of two men's hands set side by side. It was so large and heavy
that even Buliwyf grunted at the carrying of it. I asked Herger
what was the sword, and he said, 'That is Runding.'[20]

Crichton's treatment of Hrunting strays from the Anglo-Saxon original; in his book, the sword is a stunningly effective weapon, which gives
it an aura of importance that seems at odds with the portrayal of Buliwyf as a hero in his own right. When William Wisher and Warren Lewis
drafted the screenplay for John McTiernan's film (later rejected by test
audiences and partially reshot by Michael Crichton himself), all mention of Buliwyf's sword was removed from the text.[21] Instead, the film's
narrator, Fadlan, is given a Viking sword that he reworks into the approx-
imate shape of a scimitar. Fadlan has so supplanted Buliwyf as the film's
hero, that he has to be identified by a particular object, and Buliwyf's
sword must vanish. At some level, the film shows discomfort with the
idea of Fadlan achieving centrality, and the script almost rebels; although
Fadlan's sword is a particular item to him, it is also the topic of ridicule
when one of the Vikings asks "when you die, can I give that to my daughter?"[22] Certainly, Fadlan has been singled out by his weapon, whose text
he creates himself but which is utterly dismissed by the narrative's active
agents; Fadlan, for all of his posturing, remains an ineffective warrior,
by far the least able of his compatriots.

Pop culture has a similarly complicated stance on the subject of
Arthurian mythos. Consider John Boorman's film *Excalibur*. In a pivotal
scene, Merlin introduces Excalibur, which is in the possession of Uther
Pendragon and which is supposed to terrify his enemies. In the filmed
version, Merlin introduces the sword by saying:

MERLIN
Behold the sword of power, Excalibur,
Forged when the world was young and bird
And beast and flower was one with man and
Death was but a dream.[23]

In Boorman's film, which cheekily credits Malory as the screenplay's ultimate source, Arthurian legend is not only drastically simplified but
reworked to move the focus slightly away from the Arthurian court, away
from Lancelot or any of the other knights, away from the Holy Grail.
Instead, the movie centers on and indeed titles itself after Excalibur,
which takes central importance. But as one would expect, in an attempt
to refocus the story around an iron totem, the original script did not
quite go as expected. In one of the early scripts, for example, the previous scene read:

> MERLIN
> Behold the sword of power, Excalibur. Before Uther, it
> belonged to Lud, before Lud, to Beowulf, before Beowulf to
> Baldur the Good, before Baldur to Thor himself and that was
> when the world was young and there were more than seven
> colors in the rainbow.[24]

Boorman must have recognized that there were certain philosophi-
cal problems with the mélange of Viking, Celtic, and Christian symbolism, or (and as conceded by the film's internal logic) he understood that
the Arthurian mythos traditionally predates *Beowulf* by a few hundred
years. Regardless of why the script changed, there must have been an
originating impulse, however misdirected, to provide a more and more
elaborate pedigree for Excalibur, as if the loss of symbolic meaning could
be counteracted only by an increased appeal to genealogy. The effort
landed the script squarely in the waters of unintentional parody, and the
filmmakers had to retreat. The script wavered too close to Monty
Python's treatment of a similar scene:

> WOMAN
> Well, how did you become king then?

> ARTHUR
> The Lady of the Lake, her arm clad in the purest shimmering
> samite, held aloft Excalibur from the bosom of the water sig-
> nifying by Divine Providence that I, Arthur, was to carry
> Excalibur. That is why I am your king!

> DENNIS
> Listen, strange women lying in ponds distributing swords is
> no basis for a system of government. Supreme executive power
> derives from a mandate from the masses, not from some far-
> cical aquatic ceremony.[25]

Dennis the Peasant's reaction to Arthur's pedigree via his sword
problematizes the system of hero identification through weapon possession. Dennis does not question the identity or powers of Excalibur;
instead the item is simply dismissed. In a reaction similar to the Vikings'
dismissal of Fadlan's scimitar, Dennis has refused to read the weapon's
encomium as presented, and so its power is lost. Most hagiographies are
laughable lunacy to the committed atheist.

Perhaps the most interesting modern treatment of the weapon's
encomium, complete with a knightly motto, occurs in the otherwise
limited genre of the low-budget comedy/horror film. In 1993, Sam
Raimi's film *Army of Darkness* contained a sly reference to Excalibur and
featured a weapon's encomium unlike any other. In this scene, the film's
hero, Ash, has been transported back in time to the world of King Arthur

Arthur (Nigel Terry) with the famous sword in *Excalibur* (1981).

and has inadvertently stumbled into British politics and managed to offend Arthur:

ARTHUR
Sword boy! For that arrogance I shall see you dead.
(BOOM) <ARTHUR'S sword is broken by a shotgun blast>

ASH
Yeah. Alright you primitive screwheads, listen up. See this? This is my boomstick! It's a twelve-gauge double-barreled Remington, S-Mart's top-of-the-line. You can find this in the sporting goods department. That's right, this sweet baby was made in Grand Rapids, Michigan. Retails for about a hundred and nine dollars and ninety-five cents. It's got a walnut stock, cobalt-blue steel and a hair trigger. That's right. Shop Smart. Shop S-Mart. Ya got that?! Now I swear, the next one of you primates even touches me.... Ya! (BOOM) (BOOM).[26]

When Ash, a modern-day Connecticut Yankee, destroys Excalibur and then holds up his shotgun and declares its pedigree, it becomes clear

that writing partners Sam and Ivan Raimi have provided a very sophisticated reply to nearly three thousand years of weapons' encomiums.

At first glance, Ash's weapon has a quite ordinary story, but although
he claims that the shotgun can be possessed by anyone with $110, in con-
text Ash's speech is entirely unintelligible. There are no S-Marts in Ash's
immediate present; the name "Remington" is meaningless; Grand Rapids
does not exist; and twelve-gauge is an empty measurement. Even if any
of the above could have been understood by Ash's on-screen audience,
his story is fabricated; Remington shotguns are not made in Michigan,
and according to the film's director, the Michigan reference was there to
point to the cast and crew's hometown.[27]

Ash's shotgun, therefore, becomes a mystical device, and its story,
even when told in a fabricated, mutually understandable English, is
denied to the greater audience, much like the golden tale inscribed on
the shield of Achilleus; but this particular text is controlled by one of
horror's most picaresque of characters. Ash lacks nearly every single conceivable heroic quality; he is a braggart, a coward, an unreliable and
frankly stupid antihero for the postmodern age. In the director's commentary a few more details are exposed, including the fact that the shotgun is a rubber prop.[28] Furthermore, *Army of Darkness* is the second
sequel to Raimi's movie *The Evil Dead*, but through the course of the
three films, continuity errors have transformed Ash's shotgun from a sin-
gle-barreled break-action weapon to a sawn-off double-barreled break
action weapon to a full-sized double-barreled pump-action weapon.[29] In
its final incarnation, the gun appears to be a Remington model 870, but
even that is hard to determine. The nature of Ash's shotgun is that it is
his; it does not make him important, nor is it a particularly fearsome
weapon in its own right, but it does aggressively signal Ash's inherent
worth as a hero.

With Achilleus' armor and weaponry, with Odysseus' bow, and with
Beowulf's swords, it is seen that a hero's weapon derives its importance
from the hero, not the reverse. Hrunting's story does not matter; this is
why the stories that weapons tell are so often unintelligible or are told to
partial or absent audiences. Beowulf is the essential element of the text,
and the *Beowulf* poet himself stresses that point in the well-known aside
regarding his hero's luck with edged weapons; no sword is Beowulf's
equal.[30] Similarly so in popular culture: Dirty Harry's magnum revolver
is important and useful only in the context of Dirty Harry; Conan's
sword is meaningful only through Conan; Ash's shotgun through Ash,
and so on. The *topos* has remained relatively consistent for nearly three
thousand years.

Notes

1. *The Iliad of Homer*, tr. Richmond Lattimore (Chicago: University of Chicago Press, 1962), p. 402.
2. *The Odyssey of Homer*, tr. Allen Mandelbaum (Berkeley, CA: University of California Press, 1990), p. 446.
3. *Beowulf*, tr. Seamus Heaney (London: W.W. Norton, 2000), ll. 1455–64.
4. *Beowulf*, ll. 1557–62.
5. Thomas Malory, *Le Morte D'Arthur*, in *The Works of Sir Thomas Malory*, ed. Eugene Vinaver, 2nd ed. (Oxford: Oxford University Press, 1977), Bk I, chap. 5–6.
6. Malory, Bk IV, chap. 9.
7. Malory, Bk IV, chap. 9.
8. *Sir Gawain and the Green Knight*, tr. Casey Finch, ed. Malcolm Andrew, Ronald Waldron, and Clifford Peterson (Berkeley, CA: University of California Press, 1993) p. 218, ll. 210–220.
9. Ted Post, *Magnum Force*, Warner Bros., Hollywood, 1973.
10. Don Siegel, *Dirty Harry*, Warner Bros., Hollywood, 1972.
11. Cited on http://www.the-dirtiest.com/magnum.htm.
12. Cited on http://www.the-dirtiest.com/44magnum.htm.
13. DVD Extras on Don Siegel, *Dirty Harry*, Warner Bros., Hollywood, 1972.
14. DVD Extras on Ted Post, *Magnum Force*, Warner Bros., Hollywood, 1973.
15. DVD Extras on Ted Post, *Magnum Force*.
16. John Milius, *Conan the Barbarian*, Universal, Hollywood, 1982.
17. Interview with Jody Samson, on http://www.jodysamson.com/interview.htm.
18. Interview with Jody Samson.
19. Michael Crichton, *Eaters of Dead* (New York: Ballantine, 1988), pp. 67–8.
20. Crichton, p. 69.
21. Cited on http://us.imdb.com/Trivia?0120657.
22. John McTiernan, *The 13th Warrior*, Touchstone, Hollywood, 1999.
23. John Boorman, *Excalibur*, Orion, Hollywood, 1981.
24. Early draft script on http://dandalf.com/dandalf/ExcaliburScript.html.
25. Film transcript on http://www.montypython.net/grailmm.php.
26. Sam Raimi, *The Army of Darkness*, Renaissance Pictures, Hollywood, 1993.
27. Cited on http://www.remington.com/aboutus/companyinfo.htm; director's commentary on DVD, Sam Raimi, *The Army of Darkness*, Renaissance Pictures, Hollywood, 1993.
28. Director's commentary on DVD, Sam Raimi, *The Army of Darkness*.
29. Director's commentary on DVD of Sam Raimi, *The Evil Dead*, Renaissance Pictures, Hollywood, 1983; Director's commentary on DVD of Sam Raimi, *The Evil Dead II*, Renaissance Pictures, Hollywood, 1987.
30. *Beowulf*, ll. 680–88.

Works Cited

Beowulf, trans. Seamus Heaney. London: W. W. Norton, 2000.
Crichton, Michael. *Eaters of the Dead*. New York: Ballantine, 1988.

The Iliad of Homer, trans. Richmond Lattimore. Chicago: University of Chicago Press, 1962.

Malory, Thomas. *The Works of Sir Thomas Malory,* ed. by Eugene Vinaver, 2nd ed. Oxford: Oxford University Press Paperbacks, 1977.

The Odyssey of Homer, tr. Allen Mandelbaum. Berkeley: University of California, 1990.

Sir Gawain and the Green Knight, tr. Casey Finch, ed. Malcolm Andrew, Ronald Waldron, and Clifford Peterson. Berkeley, CA: University of California Press, 1993.

Filmography

1972 *Dirty Harry,* d. Don Siegel, with Clint Eastwood. U.S.: Warner Bros.

1973 *Magnum Force,* d. Ted Post, with Clint Eastwood. U.S.: Warner Bros.

1975 *Monty Python and the Holy Grail,* d. Terry Jones and Terry Gilliam, with Terry Jones, Terry Gilliam, Graham Chapman, John Cleese, Eric Idle, Michael Palin. U.K.: Python (Monty) Pictures.

1981 *Excalibur,* d. John Boorman, with Nichol Williamson. U.S.: Orion.

1982 *Conan the Barbarian,* d. John Milius, with Arnold Schwarzenegger. U.S.: Universal.

1983 *The Evil Dead,* d. Sam Raimi, with Bruce Campbell. U.S.: Renaissance Pictures.

1987 *The Evil Dead II,* d. Sam Raimi, with Bruce Campbell. U.S.: Renaissance Pictures.

1993 *Army of Darkness,* d. Sam Raimi, with Bruce Campbell. U.S.: Renaissance Pictures.

1999 *The 13th Warrior,* d. John McTiernan and Michael Crichton, with Antonio Banderas. U.S.: Touchstone.

The Way of the Wizard: Reflections of Merlin on Film

MICHAEL A. TORREGROSSA

Although the Middle Ages are often considered part of the distant past, medieval subjects nevertheless remain common themes in our contemporary culture, a fact that has led Umberto Eco to observe, "it seems that people like the Middle Ages."[1] Episodes and elements from medieval (particularly Arthurian) romance have served for centuries as the inspiration for creative artists working in a variety of media from stone to canvas and print to film, and stock character types featured in the romances, such as the questing knight, the damsel in distress, and the magic-wielding wizard, have long been a familiar part of our imaginative world. Unfortunately, the Medieval Studies of academics and the medievalism of the masses often remain separate, and proponents of each are largely unaware that they share similar interests.[2] However, the "reel" Middle Ages envisioned by filmmakers allow enthusiasts of the medieval period to bridge the gap between serious study and entertainment, because, as Martha W. Driver notes, "in a culture that values the visual over the printed page, film keeps medieval history and heroes alive, topical, and under discussion, sometimes heated discussion."[3]

As a contribution to furthering this work on the reception of the medieval in film, the present essay focuses on the treatment of wizards—here restricted to male magic-users—in American and British films and television productions. An investigation into modern wizards complements the other essays in this volume on medieval heroes in film, since wizards are most often found in the presence of heroes, such as King Arthur, Luke Skywalker, Frodo Baggins, John Sheridan and Harry Potter. The wizard is a multifaceted being engaged in a variety of narrative roles in the works in which he appears, but, for the purposes of the current study, I will limit my discussion to how representations of one of the best-known enchanters in Western culture, the character of Merlin from the Arthurian tradition whom Peter H. Goodrich has dubbed "the archetype of the Western wizard," appears to have influenced the conventions of depicting his brethren in popular culture.[4]

As E. M. Butler explains in her seminal study *The Myth of the Magus* (1948), the idea of the wizard has been a feature of human culture for millennia; nonetheless, the figure is at present undergoing something of a renaissance. Of course, Merlin remains the most prevalent and best-known member of his order, and it is no surprise to enthusiasts of the Arthurian legend that Merlin continues to be featured each year in a number of new works, including films, novels, and comics.[5] In her *Merlin: A Thousand Heroes with One Face* (1994), Charlotte Spivack claims that "Merlin is the touchstone of any age, for each age has its own versions of the medieval sage," but she also observes that each age also has "its own derivatives" of Merlin.[6] This formula holds especially true in the twentieth and twenty-first centuries, in which Merlin has had to share the spotlight with modern wizards, such as J. R. R. Tolkien's "Odinic wanderer,"[7] Gandalf, introduced in *The Hobbit* (1937), and George Lucas's Obi-Wan Kenobi, who made his debut in *Star Wars, Episode IV: A New Hope* (1977).

Besides these veteran wizards, other additions to the fraternity have also received media attention in recent years. Most notably, the popularity of the wizard has increased exponentially, as readers around the globe have succumbed to the phenomenon surrounding the first five *Harry Potter* novels of writer J. K. Rowling and have become entranced by their interplay between the enchanted demesne of wizards and witches and the mundane realm of nonmagical Muggles. The world has also turned its attention to film wizards through the intense promotion of director Peter Jackson's film trilogy based on Tolkien's classic *The Lord of the Rings* (1954–1955) and Chris Columbus's film adaptations of Rowling's *Harry Potter and the Philosopher's Stone* (1997) and *Harry Potter and the Chamber of Secrets* (1998). In addition to these works, Rowling has promised two more volumes to conclude her *Harry Potter* series, and Warner Bros. appears committed to adapt all seven of her books to film, with the third and fourth installments set to appear in 2004 and 2005 respectively. Based on these few examples, it looks as though fans of wizards will have much to be entertained by before the conclusion of the first decade of the twenty-first century.

The enduring presence of wizards in mythology and popular culture and their continued prominence in popular texts such as Rowling's novels and Jackson's films attest to the fact that the figure of the wizard has long been a favorite character for creative artists. As the most prominent representative of this character type, Merlin and his legend have been appropriated in a seemingly endless number of works in the modern era; one such work appeared in 1995, when writer Deepak Chopra published *The Return of Merlin: A Novel*, in which he proposes that readers could "awaken the Merlin inside" themselves.[8] No doubt many would consider Chopra's suggestion that aspects of the archmage of the Arthurian legend live within them to be absurd. Yet his theorizing of a Merlin within has some merit in analyzing popular texts, and we can profitably apply this idea to reading fictional and film characters that possess attributes of Merlin and his legend.

In Tolkien's *The Fellowship of the Ring* (1954), we are warned, "Do not meddle in the affairs of wizards," yet one cannot resist for long the appeal of these magic-users who continue to fascinate modern audiences and consequently appear in a startling variety of texts.[9] As both an admirer of these stories and a scholar as well, I am especially interested in how new works of medievalism make use of older stories and images such as the figure and legend of Merlin as creative artists—here specifically directors, screen writers, and conceptual artists—reshape this material into innovative forms. Although the texts discussed in this essay span almost a century, each mage participates in what might best be called the "way of the wizard."[10] In "Merlin: The Figure of the Wizard," Goodrich submits that "Merlin has become tacit in our very conceptions of the wizard in any art or science," and I would suggest that these figures serve as reflections of Merlin in contemporary popular culture both in their use of the iconography traditionally associated with Merlin (specifically, the image of an aged and bearded figure) and in their shared roles as guides or mentors in their respective narratives.[11]

"Elderly fellow, big gray beard, pointed hat": The Iconography of the Wizard

Goodrich has remarked that "there are (and must be) many Merlins—each drawing upon the wizard's tradition in different ways expressive of genre, periodization, and authorial imagination."[12] Despite the variety in narrative representations of Merlin in modern Arthuriana, creative artists are more limited when it comes to Merlin's physical appearance. Some elements of his iconography, such as clothes resembling robes or clerical garb, are traditional and not evidence, as some have suggested, of Merlin's identity as a "crossgendered figure who wears a dress."[13] However, although our modern conception of Merlin as an aged man with a long flowing beard has become the stereotype for both the

Arthurian mage and wizards in general, this image of the character is a relatively late addition to the Arthurian tradition.[14]

Advanced age and a preference for facial hair do not appear to have become fixed features of Merlin's iconography until at least the second half of the nineteenth century.[15] As attested by Goodrich, Adelaide Marie Weiss, and other researchers into the modern history of Merlin, poets and other creative artists of the period, including American Ralph Waldo Emerson, were drawn to Merlin and his perceived link to bardic tradition. Therefore it appears likely that the nineteenth-century envisioning of Merlin as a sagacious figure may have been inspired by late-eighteenth- and nineteenth-century ideas about and illustrations depicting the bards and druids of classical antiquity.

A few artists of the period, such as Aubrey Beardsley in his illustrations for an edition of Thomas Malory's *Le Morte Darthur* entitled *The Birth, Life and Acts of King Arthur* (1893–1894) and Edward Burne-Jones in his paintings *Merlin and Nimue* (1861) and *The Beguiling of Merlin* (1872–1877), ignored the newly developing trend and represented the mage as a clean-shaven adult. But the majority of depictions of Merlin, including Daniel Carter Beard's illustrations for Mark Twain's *A Connecticut Yankee in King Arthur's Court* (1889) as well as Julia Margaret Cameron's photographs and Gustav Doré's woodcuts for separate editions of Alfred Tennyson's *Idylls of the King,* presented an older, unshaven version of the character.[16] By the early part of the twentieth century, the Merlin of the latter group of artists had become the new standard, as found, for example, in versions of the Arthurian legend illustrated by H. J. Ford, Howard Pyle, Louis Rhead, and N. C. Wyeth.[17] Mature and hirsute Merlins also found their way into film, beginning with William V. Mong's portrayal of the aged enchanter in director Emmett J. Flynn's *A Connecticut Yankee at King Arthur's Court* (1921), the first in a long line of film adaptations of Twain's novel.

In the early decades of the twentieth century, the convention of portraying Merlin as an aged figure appears to have incorporated other imagery associated with wizards in general, such as the pointed hat and magic wand, and many enthusiasts of the Arthurian legend—especially those who discovered the legend as children—were introduced to this revised version of Merlin in T. H. White's *The Sword in the Stone* (1938). Updated for the twentieth century and incorporating elements from a variety of magical traditions, White's depiction of Merlyn as an "old gentleman ... dressed in a flowing gown with fur tippets which had the signs of the zodiac embroidered all over it, together with various cabalistic signs" and with "a long white beard and long white mustaches which hung down on either side of it" has become the new standard for representing Merlin.[18] In 1963, animators at the Walt Disney studio offered

Merlin (Nicol Williamson) aids Uther Pendragon (Gabriel Byrne) in *Excalibur* (1981).

an interpretation of White's Merlyn in their film adaptation of *The Sword in the Stone*, which helped crystallize in the public's mind the visage of the elderly Merlin in robes and a pointed hat as the "official" version of the mage.

With the image of the aged Merlin now firmly ensconced in popular culture, creative artists appear reluctant to deviate from tradition, and it is a rare depiction of Merlin that does not present the character with his flowing white hair and beard and costumed in long robes, often depicting arcane astrological formulae, as in White. For example, this is the Merlin discovered by readers of Thomas Berger's *Arthur Rex: A Legendary Novel* (1978), where he is described as "a man with a long white beard and wearing the raiment of a wizard, which is say a long gown and a tall hat in the shape of a cone, both dark as the sky at midnight with here and there twinkling stars and a hornèd moon."[19] It is also the Merlin perpetuated by most film versions of the legend, such as *Knights of the Round Table* (1953), *Excalibur* (1981), and the animated *Quest for Camelot* (1998), or cartoon series with Arthurian themes, like *King Arthur and the Knights of Justice* (1992 and 1994). Moreover, the image of the aged, bearded Merlin is also the expected version of the character in the new millennium, as attested by the direct-to-video film *The Sorcerer's Apprentice* (2001) and Anna-Marie Ferguson's illustrations for a new edition of Malory's *Morte Darthur* published in 2000. With very few exceptions, the older and bewhiskered Merlin has become the stereotype for representing the character—as well as his brother wizards—in popular works, and in fact facial hair has become so much associated with Merlin that Rowling does not need to clarify her introduction of the phrase "Merlin's beard" as an exclamation in *Harry Potter and the Goblet of Fire* (2000).

Moving from Merlin to his successors in the way of the wizard, we turn first to some of the descendants of Merlin in works of literature and other print media.[20] Most recently, Rowling introduces the modern-day wizard Albus Dumbledore in *Harry Potter and the Philosopher's Stone* as being "tall, thin, and very old, judging by the silver of his hair and beard, which were both long enough to tuck into his belt. He was wearing long robes, a purple cloak which swept the ground, and high-heeled, buckled boots."[21] With his long beard, this portrait of Dumbledore recalls modern representations of Merlin as the grandfatherly mage. Some literary wizards who precede Dumbledore include the wizard Shazam, a three-thousand-year-old mage with a long white beard introduced in 1940 by comic-book artist C. C. Beck and writer Bill Parker, and Mabruk, an elderly magician appearing in Peter S. Beagle's *The Last Unicorn* (1969). Earlier in Beagle's novel, a character comments, "A magician without a beard is no magician at all," so it should be no surprise to learn that

Mabruk, who is introduced as being "a magician's magician," is represented as "An old man in a dark, spangled gown and a pointed, spangled hat" and whose "beard and brows were white."[22] C. S. Lewis includes two wizards in his *The Voyage of the Dawn Treader* (1952), one of his *Chronicles of Narnia*, and both Coriakin and Ramandu, two former stars, according to Lewis, appear with the long beards and aged appearance required of their current occupations as enchanters.

Besides these mages, other wizards, such as Tolkien's Gandalf the Grey and Saruman the White, are more familiar to today's readers. Gandalf appeared first in *The Hobbit*, where (prefiguring Dumbledore and his boots) he is presented as "a little old man with a tall pointed blue hat, a long grey cloak, a silver scarf over which his long white beard hung down below his waist, and immense black boots"; a character in Jackson's *The Lord of the Rings: The Fellowship of the Rings* (2001) offers a shorthand version of this recitation and sums up Gandalf as "Elderly fellow, big gray beard, pointed hat."[23] Tolkien devotes more attention to Gandalf and Saruman, the chief of his order of wizards, in *Lord of the Rings*, where he describes them as coming into Middle-earth "in the shape of Men, though they were never young and aged only slowly."[24] All seven of these wizards have made an easy transition from print to film, and Dumbledore, Shazam, Mabruk, Coriakin, Ramandu, Gandalf, and Saruman have all turned up in generally accurate representations of their original physical appearance on either the silver screen or the smaller screens of our home entertainment systems (and sometimes on both).

Like their literary brothers, wizards native to film have also displayed a preference for the unshaven look. For many, Lucas's Kenobi is the most recognizable of these mages, but the Jedi Knight has other company in the world of motion pictures. Notable bearded wizards appearing in films with medieval settings include Tim the Enchanter from the cult classic *Monty Python and the Holy Grail* (1975) and Ulrich (played by screen veteran Ralph Richardson) from *Dragonslayer* (1981).[25]

Additional mages who fit this model feature in fantasy films, where we find Yen Sid (Disney spelt backwards) in "The Sorcerer's Apprentice" segment of *Fantasia* (1950); the dwarfish Avatar and his evil brother, the mutant Blackwolf, in *Wizards* (1977); the unfortunately named High Aldwin, played by little person Billy Barty, in *Willow* (1988); the eponymous mage in *The Pagemaster* (1994), and newcomer Mimir from the made-for-TV movie *Mr. St. Nick* (2002). *The Secret of NIMH* (1982), an animated film based on Robert C. O'Brien's children's novel *Mrs. Frisby and the Rats of NIMH* (1971), provides further evidence of the wizard's stamina in modern media through the reenvisioning of two ordinary-looking animals from the novel, an owl and Nicodemus, the leader of the rats of Nimh. Transformed by the magic of the film's conceptual artists and animators, both become anthropomorphic characters of advanced age in *Secret of NIMH*; the owl, transmogrified into the Great Owl (voiced by John Carradine), has a long gray moustache and a dark-gray beard, while the filmic Nicodemus (Derek Jacobi) wears a wizard's robe and grows the elongated beard and moustache required of his new guise. Additionally, a few evil mages in fantasy films have also appropriated the appearance of their more benevolent cousins. Their roster includes the shapeshifting Merlock from *Duck Tales: The Movie—Treasure of the Lost Lamp* (1990) and the Winter Warlock from *Santa Claus Is Coming to Town* (1970), a classic television Christmas special.

Finally, as attested by the presence of Kenobi in the *Star Wars* films, medieval and fantasy films are not the only genres to include wizards, and important bearded mages also star in works of science fiction. J. Michael Straczynski's *Babylon 5* television series (1994–1998) introduces a bearded alien named Lorien, self-described as the first of the First Ones, who fulfills many functions of a traditional wizard in the final two seasons of the series. Likewise, in Lucas's *Star Wars* films, which Kevin J. Harty classifies as examples of "pseudo-medieval film," human-looking Jedi Knights engaged in teaching (either in the past or present) are always unshaven, as illustrated by the facial hair found on Kenobi's master Qui-Gon Ginn in *Star Wars, Episode I: The Phantom Menace* (1999) and Ginn's former master Count Dooku in *Star Wars, Episode II: Attack of the Clones* (2002).[26] Interestingly, Kenobi himself is clean-shaven in *Phantom Menace*, where he is still Ginn's student, but, once the Jedi has become a master to young Anakin Skywalker, Kenobi, too, grows a beard. Like the mature Kenobi, the majority of the bearded wizards noted above derive other qualities from Merlin besides their physical appearance, and they also imitate the primary narrative role of Merlin in the Arthurian tradition and serve as guides or mentors to the protagonists of the film or text in which they exist.

Appropriating the Role of Merlin: The Wizard as Guide and Mentor

As I noted in my "Merlin Goes to the Movies: The Changing Role of Merlin in Cinema Arthuriana," two of Merlin's most important roles in the Arthurian tradition are that of teacher and kingmaker. I would now suggest that these functions of the character should be subsumed into his larger role as guide and mentor, occupations that other wizards appear to have inherited from Merlin. From medieval to modern texts, Merlin's primary purpose in most versions of the Arthurian legend is to assure

Mrs. Jonathan Brisby meets the re-envisioned Nicodemus (voiced by Derek Jacobi) in *The Secret of NIMH* (1982).

the betterment of the country (whichever it may be) and to assist the king (or his surrogate) and the members of his court in achieving their destinies. The mage first performs these tasks in Geoffrey of Monmouth's *Historia Regum Britanniae* (c. 1136–1138), where he aids a succession of British kings, including the uncle and father of a future King Arthur, and Merlin's final act in the narrative is to make possible the conception of Arthur, who will lead the British people into a golden age.

In later works, Merlin has a more direct role in the life of Arthur, and writers such as Robert de Boron and his continuators, who composed the various components of the great cycle romances of the High Middle Ages, extended Merlin's narrative life span beyond the genesis of Arthur. As in Geoffrey's text, the Merlin of the Arthurian romances serves as advisor to the kings who precede Arthur, but he now also functions within the reign of Arthur himself. It is during this previously untouched period of Merlin's life that the mage displays a newfound ability to multitask, as he subdivides his accustomed roles as guide and mentor into those of teacher, strategist, advisor, and counselor for a variety of kings and their knights, who in turn become, as Goodrich suggests, "'sorcerer's apprentices'—though they are learning not the wizard's craft but the secret forces governing proper conduct on their own."[27]

Beyond the medieval period, Merlin continues to serve as guide or mentor in new Arthurian texts. Similar to works from the Middle Ages, the majority of pre-twentieth-century texts featuring Merlin are oracular in nature, and it is as prophet that Merlin continues to shepherd the destinies of heroes and nations. A smaller number of these manifestations of Arthuriana, such as Edmund Spenser's *The Faerie Queen* (1579–1596), John Dryden's *King Arthur, The British Worthy* (1691), and Thomas Love Peacock's *The Round Table; or, King Arthur's Feast* (1817), revisit Merlin's role as wizard and advisor to kings, but the greatest number of narratives employing Merlin in these professions appeared in the twentieth century, where, inspired by White's novel and its film adaptation, the representation of Merlin as an educative force in the Arthurian world reigns supreme.

In relation to the way of the wizard, the legend of Merlin appears to offer three models for modern wizards willing to adopt the vocation of guide or mentor. The first two groups of sorcerers limit their presence in the life of their charges, as Merlin does in director Steve Barron's miniseries *Merlin* (1998), where the mage has too much on his mind to worry about the affairs of Arthur. Like Barron's representation of Merlin, many modern wizards maintain less active roles in their respective narratives, although this representation of the wizard is antithetical to the richer tradition of Merlin as a proactive educator, as found in White's *The Sword in the Stone*, his later *The Once and Future King* (1958), and film adaptations of his work, such as *The Sword in the Stone*. Ignoring the paradigm established by White, these wizards either appear only to provide indispensable aid or disappear almost entirely from the narrative to allow their students to develop on their own with relatively little guidance from the master mage.

Like some versions of Merlin, this first set of wizards serves as *deus ex machina* figures, who surface only when required to provide the needed advice or necessary bit of magic to set things right. Gandalf acts this way in *The Hobbit*, as when he arrives at the most opportune moment to save Bilbo Baggins and the Dwarves from their adversaries (these are some of the most memorable scenes from the Rankin-Bass telefilm), and on occasions in *Lord of the Rings*, but Dumbledore is a better example of this type of wizard. Rowling's mage is largely absent in the life of Harry Potter and turns up mostly to offer the boy guidance, as in *Harry Potter and the Philosopher's Stone,* or to provide a clue essential for completing the latest adventure, as in *Harry Potter and the Prisoner of Azkaban* (1999). In *Dragonslayer,* the wizard Ulrich performs similar service for

From *The Sword in the Stone* (1963), Merlin instructs Arthur in modern geography.

his apprentice Galen Bradwardyn when he returns from the dead to put an end to the fire-breathing dragon Vermithrax Perjorative. Another version of this type of mage appears in *Santa Claus Is Coming to Town*, where a reformed Winter Warlock provides magical assistance to a young Kris Kringle.

In a complementary mode, a number of wizards are adept at using a disembodied voice to provide support when things look bleak, as when, in the climax to *Harry Potter and the Goblet of Fire*, young Potter hears the voice of Dumbledore encouraging him during his struggle with Voldemort. Although Merlin has a penchant for speaking from beyond the grave in some medieval texts, the majority of modern wizards display this power while still alive, and the model appears to be Gandalf, who, as Verlyn Flieger has noted, often "out–Merlins Merlin," rather than the Arthurian mage.[28] In *The Fellowship of the Ring*, Frodo Baggins hears Gandalf shouting, "*Take it off! Take it off! Fool, take it off! Take off the Ring*," as he struggles between his Hobbit common sense and the will of the Dark Lord Sauron that threatens to overpower him.[29]

A more familiar example of the disembodied voice occurs in *A New*

Yen Sid and Mickey Mouse at the end of "The Sorcerer's Apprentice," from *Fantasia* **(1940).**

Hope, when the presumed deceased Kenobi suddenly speaks to Luke Skywalker and instructs him, "Run, Luke! Run!" Although at one point linked to Merlin, another alien, Kosh, echoes the urgency of Gandalf and Kenobi when the voice of the deceased Vorlon Ambassador enjoins Captain John Sheridan to "Jump! Jump now!" in the finale to Season Three of *Babylon 5.* In addition, the Pagemaster also employs a disembodied voice to relay information to ten-year-old Richard Tyler, compelling him near the climax of *The Pagemaster* to "Look to the books!" for aid. Lastly, *The Secret of NIMH* also makes use of the motif when the voice of the recently murdered Nicodemus (who, as noted, has been recreated by the filmmakers to fit the model of wizard) reminds Mrs. Brisby that "*Courage of the heart is rare*" and that her amulet "*has a power when it is there.*" As in other films, the wizard's words provide Brisby with the impetus necessary to fulfill the task set before her.

Besides these few representatives of the brotherhood of wizards, the majority of mages adopt a hands-off strategy to aiding those under their care, allowing them to learn without their direct guidance. Sometimes the wizard's absence is unintentional. For instance, in many works, Merlin is removed from the narrative by his paramour or a rival sorcerer, and similar circumstances repeat in the lives of many wizards. Gandalf is imprisoned for a while by Saruman and later killed in battle with the Balrog at Khazad-dûm, as recounted in Tolkien's *Fellowship of the Ring* and shown in the films directed by Bakshi and Jackson; Kenobi, Ulrich, and Nicodemus in *Secret of NIMH* are struck down by foes less powerful than they are. Other wizards arrive at their predetermined ends soon after instructing their pupils, as is the case with Shazam, while the wizened Yoda simply dies of old age in *Star Wars, Episode VI: Return of the Jedi* (1983).

More often, the wizard makes a conscious choice to be absent and approaches the supervision of his charge as a type of challenge setting various tasks before him. Both the High Aldwin in *Willow* and the Pagemaster follow this pattern. Although appearing wise and all-powerful, the magic of the High Aldwin is not quite what it appears to be (rather like that of the Wizard of Oz), and he uses the chance appearance of a Daikini child in the Nelwyn village to send his would-be apprentice Willow Ufgood, who, the Aldwin had earlier assessed, lacked faith in himself, on a life-altering adventure. Likewise, in a story similar to the animated special *Puff the Magic Dragon* (1978), the Pagemaster uses young Tyler's unexpected visit to the local library to transform the paranoid and phobic child into a courageous and imaginative one. A variant of this type of story occurs in the "Sorcerer's Apprentice" from *Fantasia*, where the wizard Yen Sid tests the mettle of Mickey Mouse.

In contrast to these examples, a third group of wizards shares similarities to the Merlin of medieval romance and certain modern versions of the character (such as in the telefilm *Arthur the King* [1982]), choosing to be more active participants in the world in which those under their supervision exist. However, this expansion of the wizard's activities often has dire consequences, as in *Monty Python and the Holy Grail*, where the help provided by Tim the Enchanter leads to the death of many Knights of the Round Table (though unfortunately not "brave" Sir Robin) at the Cave of Caerbannog because Arthur fails to heed his warning that "death awaits you all with nasty big pointy teeth." Introduced as "An Illuminating history bearing on the everlasting struggle for world supremacy fought between the powers of Technology and Magic," *Wizards* offers another variant of this motif at the climax of the film. At this point, the hero Avatar, who had earlier spouted such slogans as "They have weapons and technology. We just have love" and "No more wars, you fool. Scorch can be beautiful too," appears to betray his ideals when, to prevent a second atomic holocaust, he pulls a gun on his wicked brother Blackwolf, a twisted parody of humanity who has resurrected the Nazi war machine in his desire to conquer the world, and shoots him.

Beagle's *The Last Unicorn* (both in its print and film versions) is another story in which the wizard's actions cause death, but here the tragedy is short-lived. In the final climatic battle with the supernatural entity known as the Red Bull, Prince Lir asks the unbearded mage Schmendrick, "What use is wizardry if it cannot save a unicorn?" The mage replies, "That's what heroes are for," and, resigned to his fate, Lir realizes, "Yes, of course. That is exactly what heroes are for. Wizards make no difference, so they say that nothing does, but heroes are meant to die for unicorns."[30] Lir then leaps into the path of the Red Bull and is trampled; his sacrifice motivates the last unicorn of the title into action, and she later restores her champion to life. Lastly, although unintentionally, the advice of Oswald, the Merlin analogue in *First Knight*, also proves disastrous when he urges young Guinevere to wed the much older King Arthur (played by Sean Connery). Of course, at the time, none of the three was aware of the existence of Lancelot or the effect the young man would have on Guinevere.[31]

In still other narratives featuring the presence of dynamic wizards, the allies of the wizards become pawns in the larger schemes of the mages and their opponents, as is also the case with Merlin in, for example, novelist Susan Cooper's *The Dark Is Rising* series (1965–1977). There is a hint of this theme in *Babylon 5*, where the seemingly good Vorlons attempt to manipulate Sheridan and his "army of light" into continuing their age-old struggle with a Lovecraftian race of aliens known as the Shadows. A similar situation seems to be developing in the *Star Wars* prequel films, where the Dark Lords of the Sith are engaged in a covert war against the Jedi Knights and Senator (later Emperor) Palpatine manipulates young Anakin Skywalker into betraying his Jedi code of ethics. Of course, viewers know that young Anakin is fated to become Darth Vader, who, as Kenobi notes in *A New Hope*, "helped the Empire hunt down and destroy the Jedi Knights."

As attested by his "Merlin: The Figure of the Wizard," Goodrich notes that "Comics ... [are] a medium in which the figure of the wizard is very much alive under other names."[32] Although not discussed by Goodrich, the comics also feature more authentic wizards, such as Shazam, who appears in both comics and film. Although Merlin-like in appearance like the worldly Tim the Enchanter, Avatar, and Oswald, Shazam serves as a variant of this class of sorcerer, since, unlike the others, he fails to maintain an active role in the life of his champion. Shazam emerges first on the comics page in *Whiz Comics* No. 2 (February 1940) to transform the young orphan Billy Batson into his successor, the super-powered adult known as Captain Marvel, charged "to defend the poor and helpless, right wrongs and crush evil everywhere."[33] By uttering the name Shazam, the unwitting newsboy and later radio reporter begins a pursuit of evildoers that still continues today, over sixty years later. Both Shazam and a more mature Batson feature in the *Adventures of Captain Marvel* serial (1941), where the wizard empowers the reporter to "see that the curse of the Scorpion is not visited upon innocent people" for "so long as the golden Scorpion [a weapon of mass destruction] may fall into the hands of selfish men, it is the duty of Captain Marvel to protect the innocent from its use." Unlike the four-color Captain Marvel appearing in the comics, the career of this version of the hero ends at the conclusion of the serial when he destroys the scorpion idol and the disembodied voice of Shazam transforms him back into Batson a final time.

Perhaps illustrating his mastery of the way of the wizard, Tolkien provides the most developed examples of the active wizard in his *Lord of the Rings*, with Saruman's plotting against the designs of the White Council and Gandalf's various activities in Middle-earth. As explained in "Appendix B: The Tale of Years (Chronology of the Westlands)," Gandalf and Saruman "came out of the Far West and were messengers sent to contest the power of Sauron, and to unite all those who had the will to resist him; but they were forbidden to match his power with power, or to seek to dominate Elves or Men by force and fear."[34] In his letters and other works published posthumously, Tolkien elucidates that the Valar, the angelic guardians of the created world, sent wizards, who, Tolkien states, are supernatural entities, as emissaries into Middle-earth.[35] In his desire for power and, later, to acquire the one Ring for himself, Saruman fails in his appointed duty, but Gandalf, largely through his efforts to inspire the free people of Middle-earth against Sauron, fulfills his assignment, as he explains to Aragorn near the conclusion of *The Return of the King* (1955): "The Third Age of the world is ended, and the new age is begun; and it is your task to order its beginning and to preserve what may be preserved.... The Third Age was my age. I was the Enemy of Sauron; and my work is finished. I shall go soon. The burden must lie now upon you and your kindred."[36]

In order to achieve his goal, Gandalf allies with members of all the races of Middle-earth, from Eagles, Elves, and Ents to Dwarves, Men, and Hobbits, but as with many of his fraternity, his aid often comes with a price, as when Gandalf himself perishes (albeit temporarily) in the Mines of Moria in *Fellowship of the Ring*. More permanent harm is done, for example, to Théoden, King of Rohan, who meets his death in one of the wars against Sauron's forces, and to the Hobbits Bilbo and Frodo Baggins, who become emotionally scarred after serving as Ringbearers for Gandalf and must pass into the West for healing at the conclusion of *Return of the King*. Clearly, the admonition at the beginning of *The Lord of the Rings* to "not meddle in the affairs of wizards" is one that should have been heeded.

Conclusion

Many scholars have noted the interrelationships between Merlin and his fellow wizards, but Goodrich offers one of the most interesting sound bites. In a turn of phrase inspired by Joseph Campbell, he proposes that Merlin is "the wizard with a thousand faces" because the character and legend of Merlin are "in public domain. He has long since entered that nonverbal space of consciousness which is the spawning ground of new fictional creations in archetypal modes."[37] The preceding discussion has provided illustration for the veracity of Goodrich's statement and has shown that the medieval legend of Merlin and its modern adaptations still have an enormous influence on how creative artists choose to represent the idea of the wizard in popular texts.

As noted, the majority of wizards and wizard-like figures (like the film versions of the Great Owl and Nicodemus) are influenced by the legend of Merlin at the most basic level of shared iconography and, like the now-standard depiction of Merlin as an aged man, they too display flowing white beards and often wear the long robes and pointed hats associated with Merlin's characteristic attire. More importantly, some wizards and their analogues in popular texts, such as Kosh from *Babylon 5* and Oswald in *First Knight*, attest to the further vitality of the legend of Merlin and its influence on the representation of his brother wizards in their similar purposes in their respective narratives. Like Merlin in Arthurian works produced from the Middle Ages to the present day, these wizards serve their protégés in the pivotal role of guide and mentor, either aiding or inspiring their charges as they fulfill their predestined tasks. Displaying an incredible vigor for a character-type thousands of years old, wizards are protean figures morphing under the guidance of creative artists into new forms to fulfill this vital narrative role. As both magic-users and magical beings, they bring some of this mutability to any text they appear in, thus transforming the story into something memorable.

Acknowledgments

The ideas behind this essay originated with my undergraduate honors project at Rhode Island College, which was undertaken under the direction of Professors Meradith T. McMunn and Mary Alice Grellner. I am grateful to them as well as to Professors Martha Driver, Kevin J. Harty, and Charlotte T. Wulf for their support and continued interest in my research; I also wish to thank Professor Kathy Jambeck for inviting me these past two years to speak to her classes about the legend of Merlin. Lastly, I am appreciative of my fellow graduate students at the University of Connecticut, particularly Elizabeth Passmore, M. Wendy Hennequinn, Amy Mendoza, Michael Mendoza, Daniela Sovea, and Kisha Tracy, for their suggestions at various stages as I refined my thoughts on wizards.

Notes

1. Umberto Eco, "Dreaming of the Middle Ages," in *Travels in Hyperreality*, tr. William Weaver (San Diego, CA: Harcourt Brace and Co., 1986), p. 61.

2. The term "medievalism" was adopted by the late Leslie J. Workman in the 1970s to classify, as he defines it in a more recent essay, "any aspect of the postmedieval response to the Middle Ages," in Workman, "Medievalism and Romanticism," *Poetica* (Tokyo) 39–40 (1993): 15.

3. Martha Driver, "Writing about Medieval Movies: Authenticity and History," *Film & History* 29.1-2 (1999): 5. Lee Tobin McLain anticipates her sentiments both in "Contemporary Medievalism as a Teaching Tool" and in "Introducing Medieval Romance via Popular Films," where she comments that film "can provide an enjoyable and useful entryway into studies of medieval romance. Enjoyable because we live in a media-driven age, because today's students are more visually than textually oriented, and because film grips most students more quickly than a difficult medieval text. Useful because the familiar element of film links students' own world to the less familiar medieval world" (Tobin McClain, "Introducing Medieval Romance via Popular Films: Bringing the Other Closer," *Studies in Medieval and Renaissance Teaching* 5.2 (Fall 1997): 59. I have adopted the idea of the "reel" Middle Ages from Kevin J. Harty's comprehensive *The Reel Middle Ages: America, Western and Eastern European, Middle Eastern and Asian Films about Medieval Europe* (Jefferson, NC: McFarland, 1999).

4. Peter H. Goodrich, "Merlin: The Figure of the Wizard in English Fiction," Diss. University of Michigan, 1983, vol. 2, pp. 435–436.

5. Useful surveys of the representation of Merlin from the Middle Ages to the modern era include the studies by Christopher Dean, Peter H. Goodrich, and Charlotte Spivack noted below.

6. Charlotte Spivack, *Merlin: A Thousand Heroes with One Face* (Lewiston, NY: Edwin Mellen, 1994), p. 2.

7. J.R.R Tolkien, *The Letters of J.R.R. Tolkien*, ed. Humphrey Carpenter and Christopher Tolkien (Boston: Houghton Mifflin, 1981), p. 119.

8. The quotation here appears on the third unnumbered page of Chopra's introduction to the novel, *The Return of Merlin: A Novel* (New York: Harmony Books, 1995).

9. J.R.R. Tolkien, *The Fellowship of the Ring*, rev ed. 1965 (New York: Ballantine Books, 1986), p. 123. *Fellowship of the Ring* is the first third of Tolkien's *Lord of the Rings*, which he originally published in three parts as *The Fellowship of the Ring* (1954), *The Two Towers* (1954) and *The Return of the King* (1955).

10. While the alliterative phrasing for the "way of the wizard" is borrowed from the title of Chopra's *The Way of the Wizard* (New York: Harmony Books,

1995), the rationale behind it is related to E.M. Butler's formation of "the myth of the magus," a term she uses to refer to ten characteristics associated with magic-users in myth and literature; see Butler, *The Myth of the Magus* (New York: Cambridge University Press, 1979), pp. 2–3; and to Spivack's description of a "monomyth of the wizard" focused on Merlin, who, she argues, is "actually a thousand heroes with one face, that of the wise old man" (Spivak, p. vi). Even though we are often privy to only a limited amount of information on their lives, recent texts featuring modern wizards replicate many of the narrative traits Butler describes, as Miriam Youngerman Miller notes in "J. R. R. Tolkien's Merlin— An Old Man with a Staff: Gandalf and the Magus Tradition," in *The Figure of Merlin in the Nineteenth and Twentieth Centuries*, ed. Jeanie Watson and Maureen Fries (Lewiston, NY: Edwin Mellen, 1988). In the present discussion, the way of the wizard refers to qualities of the magus not addressed specifically by Butler but nevertheless highlighted by modern texts. Likewise, although again developed independently, Barbara D. Miller's approach to wizards and wizard-like figures in "'Cinemagicians': Movie Merlins of the 1980s and 1990s," *King Arthur on Film: New Essays on Arthurian Cinema*, ed. Kevin J. Harty (Jefferson, NC: McFarland, 1999) is similar to my own, and she looks at Arthurian film for "Merlin sighting[s]" and notes his presence in other characters through their role as a "bearded guide" or when "A filmic Merlin may cryptically animate the personage of a quest hero or communicate his message through a disembodied voice" (p. 161). Lastly, what I refer to here as "reflections" of Merlin, have recently been termed "adaptations" of the character by Goodrich, whose final chapter of his dissertation is concerned with modern analogues of Merlin. He defines these as forms of Merlin that "assume an independent identity related to the Arthurian mage only by a metaphorical pattern of association"; see Goodrich, "Merlin in the Twenty-First Century," *New Directions in Arthurian Studies*, ed. Alan Lupack (Cambridge, U.K.: D.S. Brewer, 2002), p. 158, while Spivack names some of the same characters as "Avatars of Merlin." Other studies devoted to analogues of Merlin include Frongia's "Good Wizard/Bad Wizard: Merlin and Faust Archetypes in Contemporary Children's Literature," *Merlin versus Faust: Contending Archetypes in Western Culture*, ed. Charlotte Spivack (Lewiston, NY: Edwin Mellen, 1992) and Zacharias P. Thundy's "Merlin in the Indo-European Tradition," *Comparative Studies in Merlin from the Vedas to C.G. Jung*, ed. James Gollnick (Lewiston, NY: Edwin Mellen, 1991).

    11. Goodrich, "Merlin: The Figure of the Wizard in English Fiction," vol. 2, p. 402.

    12. Goodrich, "Merlin: The Figure of the Wizard in English Fiction," vol. 2, p. 430.

    13. Joanne Moliver Neff, "Translating Malory into Film: Misogyny in Boorman's *Excalibur*," "*A Ful Noble Knyght*": *A Newsletter Devoted to the Life and Art of Sir Thomas Malory* 1.3 (Fall 1999): 1.

    14. There is at present no comprehensive study of Merlin in the visual arts, but the following works have been helpful here: Donald L. Hoffman, "Seeing the Seer: Images of Merlin in the Middle Ages and Beyond," in *Word and Image in Arthurian Literature*, ed. Keith Busby (New York: Garland, 1996); Linda K. Hughes, "Illusion and Relation: Merlin as Image of the Artist in Tennyson, Doré, Burne-Jones, and Beardsley," in *The Figure of Merlin in the Nineteenth and Twentieth Centuries*, ed. Jeanie Watson and Maureen Fries (Lewiston, NY: Edwin Mellen, 1988, rpt. in *Merlin: A Casebook*, ed. Peter Goodrich and Raymond Thompson (New York: Routledge, 2003). Roger Sherman Loomis and Laura

Hibbard Loomis, *Arthurian Legends in Medieval Art* (New York: Modern Language Association of America, 1938); Debra N. Mancoff, *The Arthurian Revival in Victorian Art* (New York: Garland, 1990) and *The Return of King Arthur: The Legend through Victorian Eyes* (New York: Abrams, 1995); Stuart Piggott, *The Druids* (New York: Thames and Hudson, 1996); Christine Poulson, *The Quest for the Grail: Arthurian Legend in British Art 1840–1920* (New York: Manchester University Press, 1999); Roger Simpson, *Camelot Regained: The Arthurian Revival and Tennyson, 1800–1849* (Cambridge, U.K.: D.S. Brewer, 1990); and Muriel Whitaker, *The Legends of King Arthur in Art* (Cambridge, U.K.: D.S. Brewer, 1990). Given the evidence provided by these works, it appears safe to state that the character of Merlin is never old in the Middle Ages. Instead, the medieval Merlin was at first something of a child prodigy (as in Geoffrey of Monmouth's *Historia Regum Britanniae* and illustrated in British Library, MS Cotton Claudius B.VII Art. 15, fol. 224, and in British Library, MS Cotton Julius A.V, fol. 53v) and later a wise youth or young adult who never seems to grow much older than the kings and the knights whom he counsels (as in British Library, MS Royal 20.A.II, fol. 3v, and British Library, MS Add. 10292, discussed by Hoffman). However, as a shape-shifter, Merlin does at times assume the appearance of an older man, such as in the *Estoire de Merlin*, the *Roman de Silence*, and Malory's *Le Morte Darthur*, but he always reverts to his true form upon completion of whatever task required that particular shape. Only Geoffrey of Monmouth's *Vita Merlini*, where an older Merlin features, proves an exception to the rule, but the text is based on Welsh traditions of the "original" Merlin and has little relevance to the mainstream tradition of the character. However, the romance tradition may offer a possible origin for Merlin's beard, since the Merlin of medieval romance was said to be excessively hairy, a trait derived from his demonic sire.

15. It is possible that the trend of depicting Merlin as an older man may have begun earlier in the century (see Roger Simpson "Arthurian Legend in Fine and Applied Art of the Nineteenth and Early Twentieth Centuries," *Arthurian Literature* 11 (1992): 83, and Roger Simpson, *Camelot Regained: The Arthurian Revival and Tennyson, 1800–1849* (Cambridge, U.K.: D.S. Brewer, 1990), pp. 145, 170, plates 2b, 6b, and 15), but additional work is still needed on this period to assess whether or not this was the dominant image of Merlin in the first half of the nineteenth century.

16. Discussions of these artists occur in the works of Hoffman, Hughes, Mancoff, Poulson, and Whitaker.

17. Ford's work appears in Lang's *King Arthur: The Tales of the Round Table,* illus. H.J. Ford (New York: Longmans, Green and Co., 1902, rpt. Mineola, NY: Dover Publications, 2002*),* Pyle's in his *The Story of King Arthur and His Knights* (New York: Charles Scribner's Sons, 1903, rpt. New York: Dover Publications, 1965), Rhead's in Knowles's *King Arthur and His Knights,* illus. Louis Rhead (New York: Harper and Brothers, 1923, rpt. New York: Random House, 1998), and Wyeth's in Sidney Lanier's *The Boy's King Arthur,* illus. N.C. Wyeth (New York: Charles Scribner's Sons, 1917, rpt. New York: Atheneum Books for Young Readers-Simon & Schuster Children's Publishing Division, 1989).

18. T. H. White, *The Sword in the Stone* (New York: Dell Publishing, 1963), pp. 31–32. White's spelling of the wizard's name is unique. Although I have yet to confirm his statement, Goodrich claims that "The popular image of the mage in heavy robes and conical hat emblazoned with astrological symbols" derives from the accouterments of both medieval and early modern astrologers and

alchemists ("The Alchemical Merlin," in *Comparative Studies in Merlin from the Vedas to C.G. Jung*, pp. 92, 102).

19. Thomas Berger, *Arthur Rex: A Legendary Novel*, 1978 (Boston: Little, Brown and Co., 1990), p. 3.

20. Although the text is outside the scope of this essay, both Frongia (pp. 67–75) and Spivack (pp. 88–91) address additional analogues to Merlin in Ursula K. Le Guin's *A Wizard of Earthsea* (Berkeley, CA: Parnassus Press, 1968).

21. J.K. Rowling, *Harry Potter and the Philosopher's Stone* (London: Bloomsbury, 1997), p. 12.

22. Peter S. Beagle, *The Last Unicorn*, 1969 (New York: Ballantine Books, 1975), pp. 110, 138, 139. Voiced by Kennan Wynn, the short, hunched Mabruk of the animated version of *The Last Unicorn* seems a darker, slightly sinister version of the character.

23. The text of the original edition is reconstructed by Douglas Anderson in *The Annotated Hobbit, Revised and Expanded Edition* (Boston: Houghton Mifflin 2002, pp. 32 and 36 n. 13). After the appearance of *The Lord of the Rings*, Tolkien revised the description of Gandalf and reintroduced the wizard as "an old man with a staff" (*Annotated Hobbit*, p. 32), but the remainder of the passage was unchanged. Many studies have suggested that Gandalf owes his appearance to the Norse god Odin. See Marjorie Burns, "Gandalf and Odin," *Tolkien's Legendarium: Essays on the History of Middle Earth*," ed. Verlyn Flieger and Carl F. Hostetter (Westport, CT: Greenwood, 2000) for details and Miriam Youngerman Miller for some words of caution about this linkage. Anderson makes some important comments in *Annotated Hobbit* on the inspiration for Gandalf (pp. 36–39 n. 17); Tolkien's own drawings of Gandalf are reproduced in Wayne G. Hammond and Christina Scull, *J.R.R. Tolkien: Artist and Illustrator* (Boston: Houghton Mifflin, 1995), figs. 91, 100. Also of interest is that there exists at least one precedent for a Gandalf-like Merlin independent of these works, and the Arthurian mage appears in a wide-brimmed hat and cloak in M. L. Kirk's illustrations for Inez N. McFee's *The Story of Idylls of the King Adapted from Tennyson*, illus. M.L. Kirk (New York: Frederick A. Stokes Co., 1912).

24. J.R.R. Tolkien, *The Return of the King*, rev. ed. 1965 (New York: Ballantine Books, 1986), p. 455.

25. In addition to these characters, Barbara Miller suggests a third analogue to Merlin in the character of Oswald (played by the late John Gielgud) in *First Knight* (1995), who, although nonmagical, is both aged and bearded (pp. 157–161).

26. Harty, p. 5.

27. Goodrich, "Merlin: The Figure of the Wizard," vol. 2, p. 324.

28. Verlyn Flieger, "J.R.R. Tolkien and the Matter of Britain," *Mythlore* 87 (Summer-Fall 2000), p. 50.

29. Tolkien, *The Fellowship of the Ring*, p. 519 (emphasis in original).

30. Beagle, pp. 222–23. The exchange is the same in the film.

31. My comments on Oswald are indebted to Barbara Miller's discussion of his role in the film (pp. 157–161).

32. Goodrich, "Merlin: The Figure of the Wizard," vol. 2, p. 421.

33. Captain Marvel's origin story is reprinted in C.C. Beck, *The Shazam! Archives: Volume One* (New York: DC Comics, 1992), where this passage is reproduced on p. 24.

34. Tolkien, *The Return of the King*, p. 455.

35. Important information on Tolkien's wizards appears in Tolkien, *Letters*, pp. 180, 200–207, 236–237; and Tolkien, *Unfinished Tales*, pp. 405–420.

36. Tolkien, *The Return of the King*, pp. 307–08.
37. Goodrich, "The Metamorphosis of the Mage," *Avalon to Camelot* 2.4 (1987): 4.

Works Cited

Beagle, Peter S. *The Last Unicorn*. 1969. New York: Ballantine Books, 1975.
Beck, C. C. *The Shazam! Archives: Volume One*. New York: DC Comics, 1992.
Berger, Thomas. *Arthur Rex: A Legendary Novel*. 1978. Boston: Little, Brown and Co., 1990.
Burns, Marjorie. "Gandalf and Odin." In *Tolkien's Legendarium: Essays on the History of Middle-earth*, ed. Verlyn Flieger and Carl F. Hostetter. Westport, CT: Greenwood, 2000.
Butler, E. M. *The Myth of the Magus*. 1948. New York: Cambridge University Press, 1979.
Chopra, Deepak. *The Return of Merlin: A Novel*. New York: Harmony Books, 1995.
_____. *The Way of the Wizard*. New York: Harmony Books, 1995.
Dean, Christopher. *A Study of Merlin in English Literature from the Middle Ages to the Present Day*. Lewiston, NY: Edwin Mellen, 1992.
Driver, Martha. "Writing about Medieval Movies: Authenticity and History." *Film and History* 29.1-2 (1999): 5–7.
Eco, Umberto. "Dreaming of the Middle Ages." In Eco, *Travels in Hyperreality*, tr. William Weaver. San Diego, CA: Harcourt Brace and Co., 1986.
Flieger, Verlyn. "J. R. R. Tolkien and the Matter of Britain." *Mythlore* 87 (Summer-Fall 2000): 47–58.
Frongia, Terri. "Good Wizard/Bad Wizard: Merlin and Faust Archetypes in Contemporary Children's Literature." In *Merlin versus Faust: Contending Archetypes in Western Culture*, ed. Charlotte Spivack. Lewiston, NY: Edwin Mellen, 1992.
Goodrich, Peter H. "The Alchemical Merlin." In *Comparative Studies in Merlin from the Vedas to C.G. Jung*, ed. James Gollnick. Lewiston, NY: Edwin Mellen, 1991.
_____. "Introduction." In *Merlin: A Casebook*, ed. Peter Goodrich and Raymond H. Thompson. New York: Routledge, 2003.
_____. "Merlin in the Twenty-First Century." In *New Directions in Arthurian Studies*, ed. Alan Lupack. Cambridge, U.K.: D. S. Brewer, 2002.
_____. "Merlin: The Figure of the Wizard in English Fiction." 2 vols. Diss. University of Michigan, 1983.
_____. "The Metamorphosis of a Mage." *Avalon to Camelot* 2.4 (1987): 4–8.
_____. "Modern Merlins: An Aerial Survey." In *The Figure of Merlin in the Nineteenth and Twentieth Centuries*, ed. Jeanie Watson and Maureen Fries. Lewiston, NY: Edwin Mellen, 1988.
Hammond, Wayne G., and Christina Scull. *J. R. R. Tolkien: Artist and Illustrator*. Boston: Houghton Mifflin, 1995.
Harty, Kevin J. *The Reel Middle Ages: America, Western and Eastern European, Middle Eastern and Asian Films about Medieval Europe*. Jefferson, NC: McFarland, 1999.

Hoffman, Donald L. "Seeing the Seer: Images of Merlin in the Middle Ages and Beyond." In *Word and Image in Arthurian Literature*, ed. Keith Busby. New York: Garland, 1996.

Hughes, Linda K. "Illusion and Relation: Merlin as Image of the Artist in Tennyson, Doré, Burne-Jones, and Beardsley." In *The Figure of Merlin in the Nineteenth and Twentieth Centuries*, ed. Jeanie Watson and Maureen Fries. Lewiston, NY: Edwin Mellen, 1988, rpt. in *Merlin: A Casebook*, ed. Peter Goodrich and Raymond H. Thompson. New York: Routledge, 2003.

Knowles, James. *King Arthur and His Knights*, illus. Louis Rhead. New York: Harper and Brothers, 1923, rpt. New York: Random House, 1998.

Lang, Andrew. *King Arthur: The Tales of the Round Table*, illus. H. J. Ford. New York: Longmans, Green and Co., 1902, rpt. Mineola, NY: Dover Publications, 2002.

Lanier, Sidney. *The Boy's King Arthur*, illus. N. C. Wyeth. New York: Charles Scribner's Sons, 1917, rpt. New York: Atheneum Books for Young Readers—Simon & Schuster Children's Publishing Division, 1989.

Lewis, C. S. *The Voyage of the Dawn Treader*, illus. Pauline Baynes. 1952. *The Chronicles of Narnia*. 4. New York: Collier Books, 1970.

Loomis, Roger Sherman, and Laura Hibbard Loomis. *Arthurian Legends in Medieval Art*. New York: Modern Language Association of America, 1938.

Malory, Thomas. *Le Morte D'Arthur: Complete, Unabridged, New Illustrated Edition*, ed. John Matthews, illus. Anna-Marie Ferguson. London: Cassell and Co., 2000.

Mancoff, Debra N. *The Arthurian Revival in Victorian Art*. New York: Garland, 1990.

_____. *The Return of King Arthur: The Legend through Victorian Eyes*. New York: Abrams, 1995.

McFee, Inez. *The Story of Idylls of the King Adapted from Tennyson*, illus. M. L. Kirk. New York: Frederick A. Stokes Co., 1912.

Miller, Barbara D. "'Cinemagicians': Movie Merlins of the 1980s and 1990s." In *King Arthur on Film: New Essays on Arthurian Cinema*, ed. Kevin J. Harty. Jefferson, NC: McFarland, 1999.

Miller, Miriam Youngerman. "J. R. R. Tolkien's Merlin—An Old Man with a Staff: Gandalf and the Magus Tradition." In *The Figure of Merlin in the Nineteenth and Twentieth Centuries*, ed. Jeanie Watson and Maureen Fries. Lewiston, NY: Edwin Mellen, 1988.

Moliver Neff, Joanne. "Translating Malory into Film: Misogyny in Boorman's *Excalibur*." *"A Ful Noble Knyght": A Newsletter Devoted to the Life and Art of Sir Thomas Malory* 1.3 (Fall 1999): 1–4.

O'Brien, Robert C. *Mrs. Frisby and the Rats of NIMH*, illus. Zena Bernstein. New York, Atheneum, 1971.

Piggot, Stuart. *The Druids*. 1985. New York: Thames and Hudson, 1996.

Poulson, Christine. *The Quest for the Grail: Arthurian Legend in British Art 1840–1920*. New York: Manchester University Press, 1999.

Pyle, Howard. *The Story of King Arthur and His Knights*. New York: Charles Scribner's Sons, 1903, rpt. New York: Dover Publications, 1965.

Rowling, J. K. *Harry Potter and the Chamber of Secrets*. London: Bloomsbury, 1998.

_____. *Harry Potter and the Goblet of Fire*. London: Bloomsbury, 2000.

_____. *Harry Potter and the Philosopher's Stone*. London: Bloomsbury, 1997.

_____. *Harry Potter and the Prisoner of Azkaban*. London: Bloomsbury, 1999.

Simpson, Roger. "Arthurian Legend in Fine and Applied Art of the Nineteenth and Early Twentieth Centuries." *Arthurian Literature* 11 (1992): 81–96.

_____. *Camelot Regained: The Arthurian Revival and Tennyson, 1800–1849.* Cambridge, U.K.: D. S. Brewer, 1990.

Spivack, Charlotte. *Merlin: A Thousand Heroes with One Face.* Lewiston, NY: Edwin Mellen, 1994.

Thundy, Zacharias P. "Merlin in the Indo-European Tradition." In *Comparative Studies in Merlin from the Vedas to C. G. Jung,* ed. James Gollnick. Lewiston, NY: Edwin Mellen, 1991.

Tobin McClain, Lee [née Lee Ann Tobin]. "Contemporary Medievalism as a Teaching Tool." *Studies in Medieval and Renaissance Teaching* 1.2 (Fall 1990): 13–19.

_____. "Introducing Medieval Romance via Popular Films: Bringing the Other Closer." *Studies in Medieval and Renaissance Teaching* 5.2 (Fall 1997): 59–63.

Tolkien, J. R. R. *The Annotated Hobbit, Revised and Expanded Edition,* ed. Douglas Anderson. Boston: Houghton Mifflin, 2002.

_____. *The Fellowship of the Ring, Being the First Part of The Lord of the Rings,* rev. ed. 1965. New York: Ballantine Books, 1986.

_____. *The Letters of J. R. R. Tolkien,* ed. Humphrey Carpenter and Christopher Tolkien. Boston: Houghton Mifflin, 1981.

_____. *The Return of the King, Being the Third Part of The Lord of the Rings,* rev. ed. 1965. New York: Ballantine Books, 1986.

_____. *Unfinished Tales of Númenor and Middle-earth,* ed. with intro. and commentary by Christopher Tolkien. 1980. New York: Ballantine Books, 1988.

Torregrossa, Michael A. "Merlin Goes to the Movies: The Changing Role of Merlin in Cinema Arthuriana." *Film & History* 29.3-4 (1999): 54–65.

Weiss, Adelaide Marie. *Merlin in German Literature: A Study of the Merlin Legend in German Literature from Medieval Beginnings to the End of Romanticism.* Washington, DC: Catholic University of America Press, 1933.

Whitaker, Muriel. *The Legends of King Arthur in Art.* Cambridge, U.K.: D.S. Brewer, 1990.

White, T. H. *The Sword in the Stone.* 1938. New York: Dell Publishing, 1963.

Workman, Leslie J. "Medievalism and Romanticism." *Poetica* (Tokyo) 39–40 (1993): 1–44.

Filmography

1920 *A Connecticut Yankee at King Arthur's Court,* d. Emmett J. Flynn. U.S.: Fox.

1940 *Fantasia,* d. Ben Sharpsteen. U.S.: RKO Pictures.

1941 *Adventures of Captain Marvel,* d. William Witney and John English. U.S.: Republic Pictures.

1953 *Knights of the Round Table,* d. Richard Thorpe, with Robert Taylor, Mel Ferrer, Ava Gardner. U.S.: MGM.

1963 *The Sword in the Stone,* d. Wolfgang Reitherman, with the voices of Sebastian Cabot, Ricky Sorenson. U.S.: Walt Disney Productions.

1970 *Santa Claus Is Coming to Town,* d. Jules Bass and Arthur Rankin, Jr. U.S.: Rankin-Bass.

1975 *Monty Python and the Holy Grail,* d. Terry Jones and Terry Gilliam, with

Terry Jones, Terry Gilliam, Graham Chapman, John Cleese, Eric Idle, Michael Palin. U.K.: Python (Monty) Pictures.

1977 *The Hobbit,* d. Jules Bass and Arthur Rankin, Jr. U.S.: Rankin-Bass.

Star Wars, Episode IV: A New Hope, d. George Lucas, with Mark Hamill, Harrison Ford, Carrie Fisher. U.S.: 20th Century–Fox.

Wizards d. Ralph Bakshi, with the voices of Bob Holt, Jesse Wells. U.S.: 20th Century–Fox.

1978 *The Lord of the Rings,* d. Ralph Bakshi, with the voices of Christopher Guard, John Hurt. U.S.: United Artists.

Puff the Magic Dragon, prod. Romeo Muller and Peter Yarrow. U.S.: CBS-TV.

1979 *The Return of the King,* d. Arthur Rankin, Jr., and Jules Bass. Rankin-Bass/Toei Animation.

1981 *Dragonslayer,* d. Matthew Robbins, with Peter McNichol. U.S.: Disney/Paramount.

Excalibur, d. John Boorman, with Nicol Williamson. U.S.: Orion.

1982 *The Last Unicorn,* d. Arthur Rankin, Jr. and Jules Bass, with the voices of Mia Farrow, Jeff Bridges. U.K.: ITC Films.

The Secret of NIMH, dir. Don Bluth. U.S.: MGM/United Artists.

1983 *Star Wars, Episode VI: Return of the Jedi,* d. Richard Marquand, with Mark Hamill, Harrison Ford, Carrie Fisher. U.S.: 20th Century–Fox.

1985 *Arthur the King* (a.k.a. *Merlin and the Sword*), d. Clive Donner. U.S.: Martin Poll Productions/Comworld Films.

1988 *Willow,* d. Ron Howard, with Val Kilmer, Warwick Davis. U.S.: MGM.

1989 *Prince Caspian and the Voyage of the Dawn Treader,* d. Alex Kirby. U.K.: BBC.

1990 *Duck Tales: The Movie—Treasure of the Lost Lamp,* d. Bob Hathcock, with the voices of Alan Young, Christopher Lloyd. U.S.: Buena Vista.

1992 *King Arthur and the Knights of Justice,* d. Xavier Picard. France: Bohbot Entertainment Worldwide.

1994–1998 *Babylon 5.* Created by J. Michael Straczynski. U.S.: Warner Bros.

1994 *The Pagemaster,* d. Joe Johnston (of live action) and Maurice Hunt (of animation). U.S.: 20th Century–Fox.

1995 *First Knight,* d. Jerry Zucker, with Richard Gere, Julia Ormond, Sean Connery. U.S.: Zucker Brothers, Columbia.

1998 *Merlin,* d. Steve Barron, with Sam Neill, Helena Bonham-Carter. U.S.: Hallmark Entertainment.

Quest for Camelot, d. Frederick Du Chau, with the voices of Cary Elwes, Eric Idle, Jane Seymour. U.S.: Warner Bros.

1999 *Star Wars, Episode I: The Phantom Menace,* d. George Lucas, with Liam Neeson, Ewan McGregor, Natalie Portman. U.S.: 20th Century–Fox.

2001 *Harry Potter and the Sorcerer's Stone,* d. Chris Columbus, with Daniel Radcliffe. U.S.: Warner Bros.

The Lord of the Rings: The Fellowship of the Ring, d. Peter Jackson, with Elijah Wood, Ian McKellen, Viggo Mortensen, Cate Blanchett. U.S.: New Line Productions.

The Sorcerer's Apprentice, d. David Lister. U.S.: Peakviewing Transatlantic.

2002 *Harry Potter and the Chamber of Secrets,* d. Chris Columbus, with Daniel Radcliffe. U.S.: Warner Bros.

The Lord of the Rings: The Two Towers, d. Peter Jackson, with Elijah Wood, Ian McKellen, Viggo Mortensen, Cate Blanchett. U.S.: New Line Productions.

2002 *Mr. St. Nick*, d. Craig Zisk. U.S.: ABC-TV.

Star Wars, Episode II: Attack of the Clones, d. George Lucas, with Ewan McGregor, Natalie Portman, Hayden Christensen. U.S.: 20th Century–Fox.

Hard Day's Knights:
First Knight, A Knight's Tale, and *Black Knight*

CAROLINE JEWERS

> That is the heart of Camelot.... Not these stones, timbers, towers, and palaces. Burn them all, and Camelot lives on, because Camelot lives in us, it is a belief we hold in our hearts.
>
> ...You've probably read my book—*The Book of the Duchess?* Fine, well, it was allegorical....
>
> Well, we won't hold that against you. That's for each man to decide for himself.[1]

My purpose here is to consider briefly how the Middle Ages has found mediation in Hollywood films and look at some recent knights' tales—*First Knight, A Knight's Tale,* and *Black Knight*—in order to analyze political and politicizing aspects of their function in popular culture and the nature of the dialogue they engage with the literary past. To do so is to scrutinize how the medieval hero on film has become not just a figure laden with predictable symbolic resonances but also a vehicle for the scripting of contemporary values and mores. *First Knight* will be symptomatic of how this process of knightly accommodation functions, and *A Knight's Tale* and *Black Knight* will serve as examples of specific ways in which this recasting manifests itself.

The relationship of the modern Hollywood Middle Ages to literary history is always already at one remove, since the medieval has been reduced to a recognizable, Technicolor paradigm by a semi-distant filmic past that swiftly encodes a visual grammar of adventure, wooing, jousting, and rebelling. We "read" medieval-themed films not only through the filter of what we know of the past but also via what we have seen on the screen already, generating a sort of double-fictionalizing process along the way.[2] The Middle Ages has become its own formulaic shorthand, which might account for the difficulty in film translation of producing something either "old" and somehow authentic, or new, innovative, and redemptive of tired clichés. Trapped in its short-circuit-like self-referentiality and therefore predictability, the expression of the medieval world is doomed to an uneasy alterity, characterized by wooden dialogue and Renaissance-festival/theme-park settings.

However, if the first charges we level at the movies are for creating an artificial backdrop that says more about contemporary than medieval times and for positing a worldview in which a few loaded concepts and scenarios recirculate according to established narrative mechanisms, then medieval authors are as guilty as Hollywood of period reductionism. Both movies and romances share a double movement: the same formulae that produce predictability also reiterate the very inflections of adventure that perpetuate popular appeal, and their potential for failure is thus linked to their potential success. It is also beyond dispute that the nebulous Celtic twilight has always allowed for the concoction of something that smacked of historical specificity in a referentially broad and imprecise way. Jacqueline Jenkins, Susan Aronstein, and Nancy Coiner have variously shown how Arthur's court is an experimental space for idealizing and modelling modernity in noble and fantastic garb, spinning off new interpretive possibilities and narrative declensions.[3]

While chivalric romances are generally better written than even the best film script, many texts we could think of as "B" romances are less satisfying in the verbally and visually leaden way that films can be. At the same time, filmic and written genres are equally revealing of the values and fashions that produced them and no less valuable as commentaries on the spirit of the day. Chivalric romances obviously promote a literature of personal, material aspiration, turning the dysfunctional aspects of feudalism into ordered social mobility and integration. For equally materialistic and upwardly mobile modern times, where boundaries of class, race, and gender have become blurred, the romance model offers a simple, positive paradigm of ascension and a dialectic in which gender roles retain a fundamental conservatism that has an appeal in an age where such roles—and indeed sexuality itself—float more freely. In our version of the Middle Ages as well as the feudal order of romance, men are manly, women feisty but ultimately doubly adherent to traditional roles; good and bad are easily distinguished; a structured meritocracy encourages individual entrepreneurship and instant rewards without anything resembling really hard work or education, just an emblematized struggle. The typical medieval hero's maverick behavior

194 IV. Time Bandits: Contemporary Appropriations

temporarily alters the status quo, and the net result is reversion to comfortable conservatism.

In essence, evoking the medieval performs and reperforms a socially prelapsarian and preindustrial setting in which the battle of the sexes has not begun in earnest, and the world is bounded only by the politics of personal desires and ambition, *seemingly* exclusive of other forms of political reality and yet not—and this is a vital part of the illusion. Dressing, masking, or cloaking the present in the drapery of the past can enhance, neutralize, or disguise, and this fact is no more lost on medieval authors than on Hollywood screenwriters. On a larger scale, every historical resurrection of Arthur including his twelfth-century rebirth has had some broader sociopolitical context and message to be decoded. The virtual reality of the Arthurian twilight cannot escape the weight of the Zeitgeist, be it the propaganda of Norman kings, the inner turmoil of the Wars of the Roses, the social idealism of those dismayed by the industrial revolution of the nineteenth century, the glorification of the ideals of king, queen, and country, the Cold War, Reaganomics, and the "war on terrorism" in more recent times.[4] The most recent latter-day knights' tales are similarly imbued with *fin de vingtième siècle* cultural politics and the values of a new millennium. *First Knight*, *A Knight's Tale*, and *Black Knight* create a trio of unlikely *laboratores* who become *bellatores* in spite of themselves and through the codes of the past articulate the culture of the present.

First Knight *and the New World Order*

Not inaccurately dubbed "Les très riches heures de Jerry Zucker,"[5] the film follows sword-slinger Richard Gere as Lancelot and Julia Ormond as Guinevere. She plays a mean center-forward, but unfortunately for her land of Leonesse, her skill in midfield cannot match the evil Malagant's attacking strategies in the surrounding countryside, and she is left with no defense but to marry a much older Arthur in the form of Sean Connery. Lancelot retains his usual valency as the flawed individual with the capacity for change so that he can struggle with human weaknesses, and triumph in spite of the baggage of sin and guilt he carries. Zucker's beefy yet sensitive Lancelot is also a man with a troubled past: he suffers from an alienating sort of survivor's guilt following the burning of his family, and we are meant to understand him as the product of a symbolic, ideological holocaust that he must exorcise in order to embrace a new, redeemed self. Trials, kisses, and tribulations ensue until, eschewing the customary lack of closure in the Arthurian cycle, Zucker has Arthur die, consigning him to a flaming, floating pyre in a sunset *son et lumière* that dampens any expectation of the return of a future king or sequel. As such, the film both perpetuates the Arthurian myth and inevitably destroys it by uniting the lovers with Arthur's blessing. This is heresy to traditionalists but at the same time delivers the resolution that medieval audiences probably eagerly anticipated, as their sensibilities were probably just as geared toward the happy resolution of human drama as are modern ones.

Whatever its compositional utility as a catalyst for the creation of vast cycles, narrative open-endedness is perhaps more beloved of postmodernist critics and authors than appreciated by consumers of culture, although, with series like *Star Wars* and *The Lord of the Rings*, modern audiences find themselves similarly unwilling to let go of beloved created worlds of proving and adventure. My own conflict about *First Knight*'s adaptation of the Arthurian world led me to contact William Nicholson, who was brought in to dramatize the story by Lorne Cameron and David Hoselton when many elements of the production were already in place.[6] Nicholson saw an opportunity not to be constrained by textual tradition, and "to focus on the eternal triangle":

> I was primarily interested in the interlocking relationships, Arthur and Lancelot (father/son), Arthur and Guinevere (father/daughter/lovers), and Lancelot and Guinevere (lovers). My object was to set up a situation in which three good and honourable people are caught in a trap of duty and emotion, and must hurt those they love in order to escape the trap. For me, story construction is all about setting up moments of great emotional power, and letting them play out in front of our eyes. This has little to do with the Arthur legend.

Ironically, what Nicholson says about his borrowed narrative dynamics describes Chrétien de Troyes's approach to the *Chevalier de la Charrette*, whose borrowed matter and eternal triangle remained unresolved perhaps because the only two possible solutions (the union or separation of the lovers) were problematic, and Nicholson is in fact closer to the spirit of the original than he might think. Many endings to Zucker's film were discussed before they reached the final decision to have Lancelot and Guinevere inherit Camelot, another favorite being the one with Richard Gere riding away like the samurai with no name. This simplified Camelot dispenses with all the customary additional ritualistic accoutrements, like jousting and magic, but according to Nicholson, the conscious distancing from medieval context allowed the addition of more contemporary symbolism:

> it's much more to do with our take on present-day conflicts (individual freedom v. duty to the community, law v. love etc.)

> than with the legend. I invented the motto of Camelot, "In serving each other we become free," to express the attitude to life which I think is fast becoming incomprehensible to most people, and devised the story so that the great opponent of this approach, Lancelot, comes round to believe in it at the end.

Again, I am not sure these aims differ wildly from those of medieval French *romanciers*, who constantly complain that the good old days are over and use the solitary knight as a remedy to present chaos through the rediscovery and revalorization of a nostalgic chivalric code. Like modern movie directors, they specialize in creating maverick loners whose unilateral action conveniently results in the common good. Chivalric fiction, good or bad, always pits the individual against the collective, and desire against duty, and tests the system of trial and reward.

While some primary concerns of Zucker's film lie with the timeless internal workings of the myth, there is no denying the time-specific extradiegetic possibilities inherent in his Camelot. Jacqueline Jenkins's reading constructs a convincing argument for *First Knight* as a modern theater of masculinity and discusses the film within the framework of the men's movement and American individualism, with "the new order of freedom that it represents."[7] Aronstein and Coiner illustrate how medieval spaces have been translated into contemporary expressions of American society: "What Disney has done is to turn the Americanized Arthurian romance into medievalized American romance. In this way, he creates an American Middle Ages."[8] In the reappropriation of the knightly hero and Arthur's court there is strong evidence that the whole ethos has been subject to a sort of mercantile "democratization." I think we can extend this notion further in different ways when interpreting *First Knight*'s reconstruction of one Arthurian frame and indeed its use in other films, including *A Knight's Tale*.

While Camelot as a seat of fairness and justice for all is a distinct part of literary tradition, feudalism real or imaginary never looked quite like *First Knight*, where it is a virtual democracy. Shown the Round Table, composed of fetching blue/grey slate, Arthur reaffirms that it has: "No head, no foot, everyone equal. Even the King." Mutual service by its members assures liberty for all. The empty chair that Arthur offers Richard Gere once belonged to Malagant, Arthur's original "first knight," and is a direct borrowing from Chrétien's text. The renegade Malagant proposes to Arthur that Leonesse be divided, such that "the lesser gives way to the greater." Arthur resists this temptation as it would not be democratic: "And where is it written that beyond Camelot live lesser people, people too weak to protect themselves, [so] let them die?" To which Malagant retorts: "Other people live by other laws, Arthur. Or is the law of Camelot to rule the entire world?"

The choice between liberty and democracy, tyranny, and chaos is a clear one. Arthur gives the basic tenets by which his utopic world lives: "There are laws that enslave man, and laws that set them free. Either what we hold to be right, and good, and true is right, and good, and true for all mankind under God, or we are just another robbers' tribe?" Later, Malagant declares that: "Men don't want brotherhood. They want leadership." The whole setup that pits paternalistic, strong government by assent against tyranny is highly suggestive; the only thing keeping Leonesse, an archetypal small country in crisis, from being invaded and occupied by morally unsound terrorists is the pale-blue peacekeeping force commanded by Arthur. Certainly the civic responsibility of Zucker's Camelot follows the tenets of the American way, but could it be that we have here more than a post–Kennedy Camelot, a Camelot of the New World Order, an Arthur for the United Nations, bent on enlightened globalization? The Round Table is more a body of peacekeepers than a select group of noble peers, a United Nations on the West's terms.

H. Niogret deems *First Knight*: "A project without ambition—or constantly worn down by the demands of an insidious, globalizing kind of commerce—that wishes to draw everyone together, but ends up by touching nobody on account of its compromises. And after having eliminated all originality, *Lancelot* [the French title] peters out without enchantment."[9] One can only concur with the way in which this review hints at the global-political angle inherent in *First Knight* and the problematic way in which it seeks to create community. And yet, although it misses the mark, the fact that it articulates these ideas is a departure from the usual significance of Camelot and a broadening of what it signifies politically. At the same time, looking at the modern helps us to see that strange medieval Arthurian geography in a different, globalizing, totalizing light; just as modern filmic Camelots stand in somehow for the West and its ideological outlook, so the medieval Camelot did, too.

While his fellow knights remain suspicious of this low-class Lancelot until he has proven himself in battle, their motto is: "Brother to brother, yours in life and death." Arthur and Lancelot exemplify a democratic, noninterventionist-but-get-tough-if-we-have-to attitude to foreign policy and set themselves up against the enemies of democracy and free will. Somewhat illogically offering despotism as a relief from what he terms Arthur's "tyrannical dream," law and God, Malagant stages what would have been the final battle within the walls of Camelot itself. Both he and Arthur will die as a result, but Camelot will go on—or at least sort of, in the form of a democratic principle, a wish-fulfillment ideology, expressed via a simple vehicle that pares down the psychological complexity of the Arthurian model to a minimum. Rebecca and Samuel Umland are correct in suggesting that in the absence of the Grail, Camelot has displaced it as the ultimate goal of the quest.

The color values of Zucker's Arthurian world have rightly attracted comment. Jacqueline Jenkins sees the natural tones of Lancelot as designed to be more individual and distinct from the more uniform Camelot, which is predominantly rich, muted, blue, grey, and silver. In fact, most of the costumes of the court are variations on those tonal themes. Janet Maslin seethes: "*First Knight* is distinguished from other, better retellings of the Arthurian legend by its conviction that Camelot was ruled by someone much more powerful than a mere king: a decorator. How else to explain blue rooftops that match the blue Round Table, on which the knights clank down their swords in perfect symmetry?"[10] True, the Disneyfied Middle Ages as presented here are an extreme version of what Viollet-le-Duc intended as he went round "restoring" ancient monuments, creating a romantic, overembellished, and somewhat inaccurate version of what they would have been. Perhaps, though, it can be seen as supporting iconographical evidence for the new, democratic UN/Camelot; Zucker gives us *casques bleus* as *cuirasses bleues*.

Moreover, beyond the blue tones of the costumes there is heavy use of symbols suggesting peace: olive branches woven into fabric, Guinevere's wedding dress with bird appliqués, as well as recurring images of doves. It is not that the filmmakers were conscious of this latent political level of *First Knight*. If Indiana Jones was Reagan's knight, perhaps Richard Gere's Lancelot embodies a latter-day American political ideology in a Camelot that seeks, however problematically, to exist in a political environment that has changed forever, one that must look anxiously beyond its own borders to find other ways of expressing and imposing its cultural ideology.

Whatever its weaknesses, *First Knight* is a useful illustration of how modern renderings of Arthur's court continue to inspire metafictional readings and how the medieval hero continues to emblematize the mediating, liminal figure that negotiates the space between the individualistic and the collective, the personal and political. *First Knight* channels popular culture and shows how the medieval backdrop can function as a versatile template for narratives that resonate on several levels in a way accessible to modern audiences. Beyond its encoded ideology of peace and justice, it is also the story of how Richard Gere's Lancelot journeys from the obscure margins to become Arthur's new first knight, and is typical of the ascensionist pattern of modern medieval knighthood, one that finds a different yet no less note- or critique-worthy expression in *A Knight's Tale*.

Golden Years: A Knight's Tale

As Sir William Thatcher leans over Count Adhemar of Anjou after he has unhorsed him in the World Championships of jousting, he announces: "Welcome to the new world. God save you, if it is right that he should do so." *First Knight* eliminates the joust, and aside from the literal and figurative gauntlet run by Lancelot that reduces knightly proving to a speedy test of agility and skill, it proposes an Arthurian world in which conflict is all too earnest, even in its EuroDisney setting. *A Knight's Tale* excludes all *but* this ludic aspect of chivalry to show a costumed sports movie, a *tour de France* (and London) of tournaments that features a peasant-born central character keen to "change his stars" by overcoming a cavalcade of noble opponents, illustrating that nobility of heart is a fine substitute for pedigree. It fits perfectly the proving ground of masculinity described by Jenkins, imbued with the spirit of the Las Vegas-style Excalibur, as described by Aronstein and Coiner.

Although some medieval knights also changed their stars by rising through the ranks, one cannot imagine a period in which names and rank mattered more, and this most recent knight's tale is a transposed fourteenth-century Camelot for Generations X and Y, an arena for the personal triumph of a new world over the old order, and the older generation, a Camelot for MTV, for video-gamers and aspiring dot.communists. Visiting the *aknightstale.com* Web site confirms as much, for while it offers information about the medieval past and tournaments, it is filtered through present-day analogies like football and NASCAR. It is a revalorization, a popularizing *translatio studii* where tournament grounds are now stadiums and the mud resulting from strings of combats and their "collateral damage" can be a "mosh pit" for those viewers whose point of reference is more Woodstock than Agincourt. The site also features a virtual jousting league that draws its inspiration from the popular fad for extreme sports. As if to remind us that this is a newly forged forgery of medieval times, in tongue-in-cheek style the material culture of medieval romance is reduced to product placement in the film, as Kate the farrier etches a couple of Nike "swooshes" onto William's state-of-the-art armor. The motto underpinning the movie's premise and poses is thus "Just Do It." In this incongruous world of mixed registers and semiotics, there are even drunken soccer chants ("He's blond,/ He's pissed,/ He'll see you in the lists, /Lichtenstein, Lichtenstein... He's blond,/ He's tanned,/ He comes from Gelderland... he comes from Gelderland").

In short, *A Knight's Tale* is the most advanced concoction yet of a brash, medieval youth culture restyled for a new millennium and yet aimed not just at young men. It tilts too at ultramodern young women in a postfeminist age through the liberated (yet annoyingly conventional) Jocelyn, who is William's love interest, and the widowed blacksmith Kate, who can make it in a man's world and still remain feminine, though she remains significantly manless, perhaps because she chooses to do so. Played by Shannyn Sossamon, Jocelyn retains some characteristics of Chrétien's Guinevere in the scene where she demands that William lose a series of jousts at the tournament in Paris in order to prove his love for her, just as Lancelot does at the tournament of the *Dame de Noauz* in the *Chevalier de la Charrette*. Her reasoning hearkens back to the code of courtly love and the total submission of the lover to the beloved but at the same time adds a modern spin to it that overlays the ethos of the imperious courtly lady. Throughout the film she is underwhelmed by her suitors' declarations that they will win tournaments for her, as it does not constitute a real proof of love since they are competing for their own glory anyway and dedicating their triumphs to her is no sacrifice. Realizing her status as an object of love, and that the knightly code is clearly a masculinist one, Jocelyn sees how gender is polarized and constructed, and, temporarily at least resists it. She asks William, "Why must everything be run on a man's schedule?" while Roland quizzes Kate: "Are you a woman, or a blacksmith?" To this she replies: "Sometimes both...."

The anachronism is, of course, striking, but here again, modern filmmakers adapt and convert the medieval model of individual aspiration into an American/Western capitalist dream, one that had and has young, dispossessed males (the new *iuvenes*) as a target audience and flatters the ambitions and vanity of women in its interrogation of gender values. One (at least I) cannot help but like *A Knight's Tale*; perhaps we can accord a partial pardon to its anachronistic sins because it so blatantly and boisterously flouts conventions without any pretension to achieve much, if any, narrative depth. However much we like or dislike what the film's director, Brian Helgeland, makes of the Middle Ages, even at one or two removes the film should remind us of the freshness and youthful energy that imbues medieval romances, an energy that has dissipated over time, its effects worn down by familiarity, the repetition of formulae, and their academic elevation to high art. The reduction of knightly proving to a series of sporting competitions crystallizes the pattern of the *Bildungsroman*, but it is not this feature alone that recalls the narrative structure of classic romances and the ways in which modernity reinscribes and reperforms them to its own ideologically reflective ends.

A secondary aspect that challenges and seduces our reading of the film is the use of a modern sound track.[11] The set piece is David Bowie's *Golden Years*, originally released in 1975 and featured on *StationtoStation* (1976), a song he helped integrate into the central medieval banquet

"He's blond,/ He's tanned,/ He comes from Gelderland": William Thatcher (Heath Ledger) disguised as a nobleman in *A Knight's Tale* (2001).

scene. While rock songs might jar medievalist sensibilities, they add an intertextual dimension and layer of internal commentary just as the many self-conscious lyric inserts do in hybrid romances such as the *Roman de Flamenca*, and *Le Roman de la rose, ou de Guillaume de Dole*. We assume that in such texts the lyrics (though often truncated or subject to the briefest allusions) similarly create an atmosphere, adding a layer of signs for interpretation as well as a parallel verbal sound track and internal commentary of their own.

For the references to be effective in colluding with a romance audience, their inclusion must reflect songs well-known at the time of composition. While their melodies are not so easily evoked, they play their part in creating a suggestive accompaniment to the action. So it is in *A Knight's Tale*, where the featured songs belong not to the early twenty-first century but, significantly, to the seventies and eighties. The music is already part of a nostalgia movement from the standpoint of the target audience of *A Knight's Tale*. These are energetic, aspirational rock songs that chart ascendance from the working class to something better via the conduits of personal idealism, innate cool, and sweaty travail.

The chosen songs work harmoniously to propel the simple plotline, especially "Golden Years": "Don't let me hear you say life's taking you nowhere, angel / Look at that sky, life's begun, / Nights are warm and the days are young...." While most of the songs operate as an overlay to the action, this song and the initial, testosterone-charged and prophetic "We Will Rock You" are experienced by the characters and woven directly into the narrative, the former being the choreographic centerpiece danced by the main characters at the banquet, and the latter, the stadium chant in which the extras filling the stands join in with the sound track. Just as in *First Knight*, music and action coincide to underscore moments of intensity, but in *A Knight's Tale* the moments are of a different nature, seeking on a simpler, metanarrative level to capture the beauty and narcissistic confidence and invincibility of youth and the timelessness of falling in love.

The banquet dance begins as a formal period piece performed by a group of minstrels and ends as an unstructured "knight club," surely a cipher for the movie as a whole. In its way, this film recasts courtly love for a contemporary audience and turns the materialistic past into a materialistic, competitive present, dominated by action, bright colors, fashion, and dancing; for all that it assaults our sense of the Middle Ages, there is an overlap in the way that cultural essence finds visual articulation. The film's self-referentiality and its parodic consciousness of itself as artifice through the juxtaposition of medieval and modern conspire to make a fun virtue of what could easily be a vice.

The controversial inclusion of Geoffrey Chaucer as few of us have imagined him, first appearing as a naked, penniless gambler and itinerant jobbing author collecting material for the future *Canterbury Tales*, is another illustration of this jocular attitude towards the Middle Ages as high culture and its displacement by the cult of youth. Helgeland states in the production notes that the film's Chaucer is intended as: "[n]ot a dead poet, but a brilliant, if scattered, combination sports manager/press agent/ring announcer."[12] Before we even get to the character of Chaucer, there is an echo of the *Canterbury Tales* in the film's title: a knight obviously replaces *the* knight, and in addition, the foregrounding of Wat and Roland (William's squires) alludes to—or perhaps "samples"—another of the *Tales*. Moreover, the character Chaucer is on the run from his creditors, who turn out to be a mockingly allusive summoner and a pardoner, condemned in the film as in literature to an eternity of ridicule. This MTV-generation Chaucer is a streetwise bohemian, an opportunistic showman, and more show-off than poet. The literary Middle Ages presented here is the equivalent of the day-residue of a college education, just enough to collude with a young audience and be an effective enough in-joke to take the unwary viewer by amused surprise. It is also perhaps the scene-stealing, extrovert quality of Paul Bettany's performance that allows an unlikely spoofing of Geoffrey Chaucer to work.

A political reading of the kind one could make of *First Knight* does not suggest itself as readily in this case. However, it is arguably successful in its ability daringly to channel the pop culture of the present through the past and project contemporary values through the lens of earlier, more symbolic times. Like *First Knight*, it uses the unlikely model of feudalism to underscore that lineage and birth are not important in the modern tournament of life or in the "winner takes all" vision of society peddled to the young and impressionable within and without the United States, those spectators who, like the sports fans Chaucer addresses in the tournament arena, "are not sitting on a cushion" but someday hope to do so. As William says, "How did nobles become nobles in the first place? They took it...."

In contemporary cultural politics, Sir Ulrich von Lichtenstein is a barrow boy made good, a knightly day-trader who puts it all on the line, and in this fantasy of a fantasy, he is doubly bound to win. Umland and Umland rightly say of *First Knight* that it is full of transgressions and collapsing borders, and the dissolving of boundaries can be seen on many levels;[13] *A Knight's Tale* gives us a more intensified version of this deregulated world of risk and reward, with a particular emphasis on class and youth, and the New World Order it portrays. The film's appeal relies on our suspension of disbelief and ability to overcome its digitally enhanced, exhibitionist sense of its own anachronism, but these considerations aside, it stands or falls on our willingness to be charmed by Heath Ledger as Sir Ulrich and be drawn in once again, as romance readers were, by the seduction of the genre and its central hero as a sublimation of life as we wish it would be.

Brother to Brother:
Knight/Hood and Black Knight

As if scripting the politics of globalization and the credo of personal opportunism were not enough, the most recent knight's tale to emerge from Hollywood goes as far as using the medieval hero redux as a way of introducing the issue of race. Literary posterity and previous films have paraded a number of black knights, but being an apologist for Gil Junger's *Black Knight*, a vehicle for Martin Lawrence's comedic talents, is a harder challenge than most. It recycles stereotypes and clichés about black urban society and the Middle Ages in a way that risks oversimplifying and rendering a disservice to both. "Who be ye?" quizzes a guard, puzzled at his own unconvincing grammar, at the gate of the fourteenth-century castle where Martin Lawrence's Jamal lands from his time travel. "I be stomping yo' ass, if you put your hand on me one mo' again!" Clearly, in the ghetto style of underworld King Arthur/Marsellus Wallace in *Pulp Fiction* (1994), Lawrence too intends to "git medieval" and, again, in this context it is played for easy laughs.[14] A simplistic venture and a one horse-power comedy, *Black Knight* still merits consideration as a site where, in addition to giving us a formulaic tale of personal achievement, themes of race and civil rights find expression, however superficially.

Here is medieval England filtered through Mark Twain's *A Connecticut Yankee* (1889) as "Medieval World," a "family fun center" representing old-fashioned values as embodied by the owner, Mrs. Bostick.[15] We confront the now familiar medieval theme park, a façade without substance: history is there to allude to lost community, pride, and humanity, all exchanged for a bigger, more alienating world where cold self-interest destroys the ties that bind. At the same time, while the male-bonding, gender-conformist patriarchy celebrated in *First Knight* and *A Knight's Tale* continues to prevail, it has become nominally at least matriarchal in orientation, since Medieval World is run by the determined Mrs. Bostick. She is cast as the park's threatened black queen who will find her opposite number in medieval England, a white queen equally imperiled since she has been driven from her throne into exile. Both are saved by Jamal Walker, a fast-talking Angelino from the intersection of Florence and Normandie, who is propelled back to the Middle Ages when he tries to retrieve a medallion from a trash-filled moat.

He thinks he is about to pluck a valuable piece of hip ghetto-wear from the water; it is rather fate, in the form of a medieval-style fantastic device, that he grasps. It pulls him under until he surfaces in a lake, close to a castle somewhere in England that looks as much like a set as Medieval World does. In an echo of the familiar romance motif of water as a barrier to be crossed to the Otherworld, Jamal makes the abrupt transition from modern California to Olde Englande and quite literally becomes a medieval brother from another planet. As the medieval is layered over urban black culture, inevitable linguistic and mechanistic comedy results: booty, for example, no longer refers to the spoils of war, and so forth. The location of Florence and Normandie is evocative not just generically of the richness of the past but also of the epicenter of the Los Angeles riots. As old and new worlds overlap, there is identification here with a medieval world subject to uncertainty and repression, defined by a culture of fear, and once again in need of salvation from a strong hero.

Saving Mrs. Bostick's castle means resisting a takeover by the rival, corporate Castle World, while aiding a general revolt against King Leo will set the unnamed white queen back on her throne. Still a Middle Ages as testing ground for male prowess and posturing, this is also a redemptive wasteland waiting not for some grail but for a Black Knight who can start a civil rights movement and create community by overcoming his selfishness and embracing the waning codes of courage and honor that are part of the unjust feudal world to which he has been sent. King Leo's cruel castle is full of incongruity: in fourteenth-century England we are led to believe that a Norman looked exotic, that Normans had a reputation as great dancers, and that Martin Lawrence's supposed Frenchness is a bigger exotic surprise than his blackness. Or rather, no one cares that we do not believe it. Mistaken for a ducal messenger, when King Leo asks what the news is from Normandy, Jamal replies: "a couple of drive-bys."

Aside from exploiting linguistic incongruity to its fullest extent, Jamal is made to stumble through some of the biggest clichés of the theme-park medieval world: smelly privies and smell in general, bad breath, gory executions, large animals (and nature, to which Jamal seems almost allergic), lusty maidens, unhygienic banquets without flatware, leeches, and music that has no beat. Jamal remedies this last defect by coaxing a group of medieval musicians and banquet guests to recreate spontaneously Sly and the Family Stone's "Dance to the Music" (1967), and provides a scene comparable to, though much less successful than *A Knight's Tale*'s "Golden Years."[16] Sly and the Family Stone invoke more in this context than their song "I Want to Take You Higher" (1967) does as a part of the upbeat sound track in *A Knight's Tale*. Against the backdrop of black/white culture, they recall the sixties, Lyndon Johnson, Vietnam, the War on Poverty, and the growth of civic and racial consciousness. As well as embodying black funk in its militant years, they were also one of the first interracial bands, making them a suitable choice for the black-and-white fantasy world of *Black Knight*.

In a bland plot that increases in banality as it limps along, Jamal plays the Moor to his love interest Victoria's Nubian damsel and gets caught up in a plot to overthrow wicked King Leo through a series of mishaps, during which he wins and loses the king's favor and earns the enmity of the dastardly Sir Percival (Vince Regan). When he finds success and a fiefdom, the best thing he can think of to do is to plan a ride-through frappucino franchise; when his star wanes, he eventually has no choice but to get in touch with his altruistic side, fight back, and become a hero. Along with Victoria, whose principles of equality and justice make her a superficially more modern character, he is aided by a former knight, Sir Knolte of Marlborough (Tom Wilkinson as a parodic medieval Marlboro man), who has sunk low since the exile of his queen. Knolte is patterned after the good-hearted Western gunslinger who has lost one kind of battle to discover another, needing only the stimulus of a just cause to bring him out of retirement and alcoholic stupor. He is the first person Jamal sees after he surfaces in the Middle Ages, and Jamal mistakes him for a homeless person, encouraging him to get help from welfare and ask for food stamps.

Jamal has no relationship to the Middle Ages as a meaningful cultural referent, but the film constructs his connection to the other characters through using the setting not as an aspirational, ascendant paradigm but more as a simple model of social dissent and descent constructed of oppressors and oppressed. The ascensional world is not one he relates to or even aspires to join. *Black Knight*'s England is an expression of white culture that Jamal can relate to, as a theater of the downtrodden, a place where most people live in conditions equivalent to or worse than the ghetto. Here, white people (or at least the peasants) are essentially black in spirit, if not in body. Jamal is comparatively better off, more educated and enlightened, and certainly more empowered to enact lasting change that will better the common lot than any of the characters around him, regardless of their class. As proof, one of the other great film clichés *Black Knight* exploits is the Robin Hood forest-speech scene familiar from both *The Adventures of Robin Hood* (1938) and *Robin Hood: Prince of Thieves* (1991). When the Queen's declamatory rhetoric fails (a feeble "England... England..."), Jamal offers "to give it the ol' Al Sharpton." He then evokes another king, Rodney King (whose most eloquent words he cites as "... ow... ow!"), and makes a plea for action and self-respect, urging his band of peasants and misfits to fight for improved social conditions and overthrow injustice.

Jamal's speech inspires the attack that finally transforms him into the Black Knight of the title, whom we meet first as a figure in a puppet show. Lawrence/Jamal in turn becomes a predictable savior figure, overcoming evil as he swaps his trainers for the weapons and accoutrements of knighthood. Not understanding the import of what he is saying to those who will never ascend to the landowning class, he borrows Kennedy's famous speech, exhorting them: "Ask not what your fiefdom could do for you, but what you could do for your fiefdom!" He is unaware of the fact that these dispossessed peasants will never have a fiefdom, and that if they win, they will still be living in the same huts, dreaming of a chicken in every pot and a horse in every stable. Of course, in this rootless Middle Ages, this has ceased to matter, as what is scripted is about us and not them. In helping others he finds himself, much as Richard Gere's Lancelot is supposed to, and is in the process of being knighted when he awakens to find paramedics trying to resuscitate him. As the constructed world of the castle recedes in a dreamscape, the closing images return to Medieval World, which is soon reborn in the spirit of altruism learned by Jamal and where values traditional to the black community have become one with those expressed in the film's rudimentary Technicolor code of chivalry. Here the medieval dreamscape becomes an I-have-a-dreamscape.

These three films are symptomatic of what Hollywood is making of the past, of the ever more obvious move towards encoding contemporary cultural politics in its films, and of what we as readers and spectators are making and assimilating of this old world in the new. Unsurprisingly, we meet it on our terms, not on its own. At the same time, when modernity appropriates the wooing and jousting ethos of the romance, it is guilty not so much of completely falsifying it or the medieval world it has sublimated, but merely of overexaggerating selected traits to fulfill its own agenda and bear the weight of contemporary ideological values, perhaps just as medieval writers mostly did. When we critique the mis/uses made of the Arthurian world, we should recall that it was always a glamorous myth and an idealized, virtual reality, and that it too was in its very beginnings a vehicle for political and social commentary. Its appeal was to create a fantasy landscape fit for youthful, idealistic heroes, a theatre for staging symbolic conflicts, and a platform for the iteration of patterns and formulae.

The very first texts deplore the decline in moral standards and yearn nostalgically for a better model, a more romantic spirit, and a finer hero. How can we then critique modern expressions of the fictionalized feudal world on the grounds of inauthenticity? It is obvious that medieval imaginative fiction rehearsed the doubts and fears of an age, sought a comfortable dialectic of good and evil, and allowed the individual to triumph over adversity and achieve integration into a more just society, and those central concerns are as vibrant now as they were centuries ago. Celluloid replaces the manuscript (though the manuscript too has its visual glamour), but through it all, we can see the medieval as a kind of palimpsest. Here we are rubbing away the modern overlay to get at the old manuscript beneath. Simultaneously, we rub away the old in order to see what we are really saying about ourselves.

This trilogy of knights' tales, while they are for the multiplex rather than a cultural elite, demonstrates once more that the spirit of medievalism is alive and well in postmodern times, and that the need for eternal love triangles and elegant single combat has not waned. Today's knightly *bellatores* reflect the sensibility of the age. Time has not permitted them to become less clichéd since their medieval counterparts came into being, but their symbolic load has changed in character, and at best they can connect us in spirit with the energetic narrative drive of the medieval romance. In these films the Arthurian backdrop allows exploration of democracy and globalization, the politics of upward mobility, and even issues related to race and gender. The royal banquet may well have given way to Burger King, but there is still food for thought.

Notes

1. Sean Connery as Arthur in Jerry Zucker's *First Knight* (1995), Paul Bettany as Chaucer, with Mark Addy as Roland, in Brian Helgeland's *A Knight's Tale* (2001).

2. On this point Rebecca A. Umland and Samuel J. Umland come to the defense of *First Knight* in *The Use of Arthurian Legend in Hollywood Film* (Westport, CT: Greenland/ Contributions to the Study of Popular Culture 57, 1996), "Hollywood as Melodrama," pp. 73–103: "This problem [of the 'weight of tradition' in producing a legend] became intensified for film-makers because with the release of strong films like *Excalibur* we can detect not only an established literary tradition, but perhaps also an emerging cinematic one as well. One of three objections to *First Knight* exemplifies this response: It is not Malory, it is not *Camelot*, and it is not *Excalibur*. This criticism can and should be disregarded, since the film is in no way a remake of these earlier works" (p. 95). On the dismissive side, Robert J. Blach and Julian Wasserman, in their article "Fear of Flyting: The Absence of Internal Tension in *Sword of the* Valiant and *First Knight*" (*Arthuriana* 10.4 (2000): 15–32), see little redeeming value in *First Knight* on account of its refusal to generate any sense of real conflict. Shira Schwam-Baird, in her excellent "King Arthur in Hollywood: The Subversion of Tragedy in *First Knight*" (*Medieval Perspectives* 14 (1999): 202–13), highlights the "allergy to tragedy endemic in Hollywood" (p. 1) and, in the light of Aristotle and medieval commentators on tragedy, analyzes how it plays out in the recasting of the Lancelot-Arthur-Guinevere triangle. Of the results she concludes: "It remains in the memory as little more than a colorful melodrama, ultimately unsatisfying to anyone who ... craves a more layered cinematic experience" (p. 13).

3. Jacqueline Jenkins, "First Knights and Commen Men: Masculinity in Modern American Arthurian Film," in *King Arthur on Film: New Essays on Arthurian Cinema*, ed. Kevin J. Harty (Jefferson, NC: McFarland, 1999), pp. 81–95. Susan Aronstein and Nancy Coiner, "Twice Knightly: Democratizing the Middle Ages for Middle-Class America," in *Medievalism in North America*, ed. Kathleen Verduin (Cambridge, U.K.: D.S. Brewer/Studies in Medievalism 6, 1994). Aronstein and Coiner use Umberto Eco, "The Return of the Middle Ages," in *Travels in Hyperreality*, tr. William Weaver (San Diego: Harcourt Brace Jovanovich, 1986), as an enlightening point of departure for a road trip to Las Vegas's Excalibur and Disney World and reflection on the recontextualizing of the Middle Ages in the casino/theme-park setting.

4. See, for example, Susan Aronstein's excellent article "Not Exactly a Knight: Arthurian Narrative and Recuperative Politics in the Indiana Jones Trilogy," *Cinema Journal* 34.4 (Summer 1995): 3–30. A noticeable feature of U.S. rhetoric in the months spanning the war on terrorism has been the use of the Crusades as a way of valorizing the response to political events, clearly without the realization of how problematic it is to consider being Crusaders in that particular context.

5. Jay Carr, *Boston Globe*, July 7, 1995.

6. I am grateful to Mr. Nicholson for both faxes and an interview (Febru-

ary 21, 1996) concerning *First Knight*. References to his opinions on matters Arthurian are drawn from these sources.

7. Jenkins, pp. 84–5.

8. Aronstein and Coiner, p. 8.

9. Review of *First Knight* in the French journal *Positif* (416, October 1995: 38): "Projet sans ambition—ou constamment raboté par les exigences d'un commerce consensuel, mondialiste—qui veut rassembler tout le monde, mais qui finit par ne toucher personne à force de compromis et après élimination de toute originalité, *Lancelot* [the French title] sombre sans enchantement."

10. Janet Maslin, *New York Times*, July 7, 1995.

11. With no thought of adding period authenticity to this medieval film setting, Carter Burwell, who scored the film, sets a retro tone of a different kind that conveys a consonant gritty, flashy sense of bravado through use of stadium-style anthems and rock songs of the 70s. They are, in sequence: Queen, "We Will Rock You," 1977; War, "Low Rider," 1975; Bachman Turner Overdrive, "Taking Care of Business," 1974; David Bowie, "Golden Years," 1975; Eric Clapton, "Further on up the Road," 1975; Rare Earth, "Get Ready," 1969; Sly and the Family Stone, "I Want to Take You Higher," 1967; Thin Lizzy, "The Boys Are Back in Town," 1976; and Queen, "We Are the Champions," 1977, rere-corded with Robbie Williams for the film.

12. Web site production notes, p. 5.

13. Umland and Umland, p. 99.

14. I have tried to argue the strong medievalism of Tarantino's film in "Heroes and Heroin: From *True Romance* to *Pulp Fiction*," *Journal of Popular Culture* 33.4 (2000): 39–61.

15. The many versions of Twain's text are listed in Kevin J. Harty, *The Reel Middle Ages: American, Western, and Eastern European, Middle Eastern, and Asian Films about Medieval Europe* (Jefferson, NC: McFarland, 1999). See also Elizabeth Sklar, "Twain for Teens," in Harty, *King Arthur on Film*, pp. 97–108. This is not the first time a black comedian has entered Camelot, as there have been at least two other attempts in made-for-TV movies, the most notable starring Whoopi Goldberg as Dr. Vivien Morgan in Roger Young's *A Knight in Camelot* (Disney, 1998), propelled back to the sixth century, where she becomes Sir Boss during the course of her adventures and uses her technology and street smarts to save the day.

16. The other significant lyric is James Brown's "Get up Offa That Thing" (1976), which overlays the scenes in which the peasant rebels train to confront King Leo's soldiers.

Works Cited

Aronstein, Susan. "Not Exactly a Knight: Arthurian Narrative and Recuperative Politics in the Indiana Jones Trilogy," *Cinema Journal* 34.4 (Summer 1995): 3–30.

Aronstein, Susan, and Coiner, Nancy. "Twice Knightly: Democratizing the Middle Ages for Middle-Class America." In *Medievalism in North America*, ed. Kathleen Verduin. Cambridge, U.K.: D.S. Brewer/Studies in Medievalism 6, 1994.

Blach, Robert J., and Wasserman, Julian. "Fear of Flyting: The Absence of

Internal Tension in *Sword of the* Valiant and *First Knight,*" *Arthuriana* 10.4 (2000): 15–32.

Carr, Jay. "The Fantasy Lacks Fire in 'First Knight,'" *Boston Globe,* July 7, 1995.

Eco, Umberto. "The Return of the Middle Ages," in *Travels in Hyperreality,* tr. William Weaver. San Diego, CA: Harcourt Brace Jovanovich, 1986.

Harty, Kevin J. *The Reel Middle Ages: American, Western, and Eastern European, Middle Eastern, and Asian Films About Medieval Europe.* Jefferson, NC: McFarland, 1999.

Jenkins, Jacqueline. "First Knights and Commen Men: Masculinity in Modern American Arthurian Film," in *King Arthur on Film: New Essays on Arthurian Cinema,* ed. Kevin J. Harty. Jefferson, NC: McFarland, 1999, pp. 81–95.

Jewers, Caroline. "Heroes and Heroin: From *True Romance* to *Pulp Fiction,*" *Journal of Popular Culture* 33.4 (2000): 39–61.

Maslin, Janet. "The Tale of Camelot, Now Color Coordinated." *New York Times,* July 7, 1995.

Niogret, H. "*Lancelot,*" *Positif* 416 (October 1995): 38.

Schwam-Baird, Shira. "King Arthur in Hollywood: The Subversion of Tragedy in *First Knight,*" *Medieval Perspectives* 14 (1999): 202–13.

Sklar, Elizabeth. "Twain for Teens," in *King Arthur on Film: New Essays on Arthurian Cinema,* ed. Kevin J. Harty. Jefferson, NC: McFarland, 1999, pp. 97–108.

Umland, Rebecca A., and Umland, Samuel J. *The Use of Arthurian Legend in Hollywood Film.* Westport, CT: Greenland/Contributions to the Study of Popular Culture 57, 1996.

Web site www.aknightstale.com

Filmography

1938 *The Adventures of Robin Hood,* d. Michael Curtiz and William Keighley, with Errol Flynn. U.S.: Warner Bros.

1991 *Robin Hood: Prince of Thieves,* d. Kevin Reynolds, with Kevin Costner and Morgan Freeman. U.S.: Morgan Creek.

1995 *First Knight,* d. Jerry Zucker, with Richard Gere, Julia Ormond, Sean Connery. U.S.: Zucker Brothers, Columbia.

2001 *Black Knight,* d. Gil Junger, with Martin Lawrence. U.S.: 20th Century–Fox.
   A Knight's Tale, d. Brian Helgeland, with Heath Ledger. U.S.: Columbia, Escape Artists/Finestkind Prod.

V
"Stond and Delyver"
Teaching the Medieval Movie
Martha W. Driver

There are very few movies on medieval themes that hold a viewer's interest steadily all the way through or that are entirely instructive and appropriate to the classroom. Among the exceptions are *The Seventh Seal* (1957) and *The Return of Martin Guerre* (1982). But most of the films in this genre have wonderful scenes, some of which work very well in teaching the Middle Ages. If one were to compile a DVD with favorite clips of heroic speeches, for example, among them might be the speech to rouse the Merry Men given by Errol Flynn in *The Adventures of Robin Hood* (1938), perhaps compared and contrasted with parodic versions in *Robin Hood: Men in Tights* (1993) and in *Black Knight* (2001), then perhaps placed into the larger context of the Crispin Crispian speech in film versions of *Henry V*. A brief exercise of this sort could be used to explore historical reference and allusion, parody, and evolving ideas of the hero.

Other scenes that have proved useful for in-class discussion include, from *The 13th Warrior* (1999), the funeral scene drawn from Ibn Fadlan's chronicle and based on actual Norse practice, the unsanitary morning ablutions of the Norsemen (with Ibn Fadlan's and the viewer's revolted reaction to them), Ibn Fadlan's mastery of Anglo-Saxon, and Buliwyf's learning to write. The battle scenes in the film underscore the loneliness and isolation of Anglo-Saxon warriors as documented in Old English poems such as "The Battle of Maldon" and "The Wanderer." *A Knight's Tale* (2001), which becomes increasingly less interesting as the plot progresses, is, however, useful in the classroom for its witty introduction of Geoffrey Chaucer and the subsequent tournament and longsword scenes, which have some visual validity and can lead to discussions of actual practice. G.B. Shaw's *Saint Joan* may be effectively taught in conjunction with excerpts from the trial records and *Le Ditié de Jehanne d'Arc* by Christine de Pizan.[1] Showing clips from various films about Joan, which might include relevant scenes from *La Passion de Jeanne d'Arc* (1928), *Joan of Arc* (1948), and *Saint Joan* (1957), is perhaps the best way to introduce undergraduates to some of the complex issues surrounding the history of this determined and accomplished young woman who united France, then was burned at the stake, when she was about their own age. The story of Joan of Arc is one of the earliest to be produced cinematically, by Edison in 1895, but it is still waiting for a definitive representation on film, as Edward Benson points out.[2]

The best medieval movie remains the best perhaps because it is episodic. *Monty Python and the Holy Grail* (1975) is comprised of classic scenes which can be readily appreciated by the pedagogue, along with everyone else. We might begin with the opening credits. The subtitles in pseudo–Swedish pay homage to *The Seventh Seal*, Bergman's famous film, but also slyly refer to *Beowulf* and other early English epic literature which features battles between Norsemen (Danes and Swedes) rather than Englishmen. And, as medievalists know, the cry "Bring out your dead" was heard during the several outbreaks of plague, also known as the Black Death, that swept across Europe periodically. The Python's Plague Cart episode (a scene that is usually already well known to students in my classroom) is a humorous way in which to begin discussion of the major plagues that wiped out a large proportion of the European population in the fourteenth century. The scene can further introduce the graphic description of the effects of the plague in Florence found in the prologue to *The Decameron* by Giovanni Boccaccio. The prologue vividly presents the reader with details of mass burials, the carting of bodies, and the destruction of human life as well as of religious and moral values. In the Python sketch, the man pushing the death cart seems to be receiving a fee from the family member who is trying to get him to take away the old man, who, in fact, is not quite dead yet, as he keeps pointing out in statements like: "I feel happy," "I think I am going for a walk."

A related scene in *MPHG* shows the chant of the flagellants, hooded men dressed in monks' robes hitting themselves over the head with boards. This seems silly to students but could be profitably compared with a similar serious scene of crowd hysteria and flagellation in *The Seventh Seal*. From the twelfth century on, many groups of flagellants roamed the English and European country sides, particularly during times of famine or plague, though they are more usually described, in contemporary accounts, as whipping or scourging themselves.[3] We see further the nature of hysteria and the irrational action of crowds, which could become irrational and carried away by mob violence, in another scene in which the villagers bring a woman before their lord with the charge that she is a witch. This sort of non-thinking hysteria was most horribly observed in Nazi Germany in the modern period but also occurred in the witch trials that persisted from the later Middle Ages through the

The Pythons (Graham Chapman, Michael Palin, Terry Jones, and John Cleese) are instructed by God, from *Monty Python and the Holy Grail* (1975).

eighteenth century in America. When the lord (who turns out to be Sir Bedivere) asks his people: "how do you know she's a witch?" one peasant (John Cleese) replies, "She turned me into a newt!" When the lord looks carefully at the peasant, who does not seem the worse for wear, he lamely explains, "I got better." There is then a long conversation about how to determine whether or not the woman is a witch, and we get a good example of medieval logic (or rather non-logic): "If she weighs the same as a duck, she's made of wood and therefore a witch."

The hilarious episode in which King Arthur meets Dennis the peasant (and member of an "anarcho-syndicalist commune") points up the problematic relationship between peasants and nobles in the Middle Ages, while Arthur's scene with the Black Knight shows us the completely irrational bravery of the latter warrior, who is courageous but also stupid beyond belief. The scene is anti-idealization, an upending, of the supposed nobility of medieval battle, chivalry, and warfare. Another scene shows Lancelot relentlessly killing guards and wedding guests in order to rescue someone he thinks is a fair maiden in distress (who turns out to be Herbert, a stage-struck young man). In the Arthur legends, Lancelot has the reputation as a knight who slaughters violently without always knowing who his victims are (this is specifically recounted in Sir Thomas Malory's *Morte Darthur*, in which Lancelot kills the brothers of Gawain by mistake as he is rescuing Guinevere from being burnt at the stake). Lancelot is a well-trained athlete and a courageous knight who shows great prowess in swinging a variety of large steel weapons, but he is not the best guest, even uninvited, at a wedding as the Pythons demonstrate.

The scene in which Arthur and his knights encounter the French knights in the castle in England may be analyzed from a number of perspectives. First, there was an exchange of nobility in the French and English courts through the fourteenth century, French nobles mixing readily with English ones, without a clear definition of nationality. French was the language spoken in the English courts until Elizabeth I. During the 100 Years War in the fifteenth century, the English invaded France and held certain towns for a number of years, for example Calais, which became outposts of English culture. There was a long-standing enmity and competition between the French and the English. In the scene presented by the Pythons, the French knight taunts Arthur from the castle walls. Taunting, or exchange of formal insults, was a part of formal warfare in the Middle Ages, though it is very doubtful that the insults exchanged were quite like those imagined by Monty Python. The French knight says, among other things, "You English pig-dogs!" and "I blow my nose at you." His other insults include: "I fart in your general direction" and "Your mother was a hamster, and your father smelled of elderberries." The French knight also makes fun of the Middle English pronunciation of the word "knights," which would have originally been pronounced with the "k" sound: "You 'k-nig-hits!'"

These are just a few of the episodes that are worth a second and third look by students of the Middle Ages and their teachers. Aspects of medieval narrative and the playful use of language more generally, both in medieval stories and in this film, may be more fully explored in the scene of the "Knights Who Say Ni," for example, in which words are imbued with irrational power. The resourceful teacher might further use the knights' adventure in the cave of Caerbannog to discuss the composition of actual medieval texts. The monk deciphering the inscriptions made by Joseph of Arimathea on the wall of the cave says the Holy Grail is located in "the castle of Arrrghhh"; one of the knights then suggests that "perhaps he was dictating." The interruptions in the Python's narrative and the intermingling of stories are also typical of medieval tales as any student of *Perceval, Tristan and Isolt,* Malory or Chaucer will have noticed.

As a medium for teaching, as John Ganim points out in the final essay in this volume, film is accessible to a range of viewers, creating lively dialogues between students and their professors, as well as between source texts and images, the film-maker's vision, the screenplay, the interpretation by the actors, the cinematography, sound, and editing. When talking about the movies, every viewer becomes an expert, and everyone, a teacher. The movies can teach us history through what they show but also through what they omit. Literature, read first and then viewed in film interpretations, can be discussed and debated. Film further raises questions about the original performance of medieval works and also about perceptions of the Middle Ages, our own and those of previous eras. Though the idea of the hero remains elusive, shifting shape to fit time and place, the engaged dialogue with the past offered by the movies can instruct an astute learner about a range of subjects, for example, about observation, analysis, and reception, as well as about history, literature, and art.

Notes

1. *Bernard Shaw's Plays,* ed. Warren Sylvester Smith (New York: W. W. Norton & Co., 1970), includes excerpts from Joan's trials, pp. 435–446. A translation of *Le Ditié de Jehanne d'Arc* may be found in *The Selected Writings of Christine de Pizan,* tr. Renate Blumenfeld-Kosinski and Kevin Brownlee (New York: W. W. Norton & Co., 1997), pp. 252–262. This volume further includes a useful essay by K. Brownlee, "Structures of Authority in Christine de Pizan's *Ditié de Jehanne d'Arc,*" pp. 371–390.

2. For a history of Joan on film, see Robin Blaetz, *Visions of the Maid: Joan of Arc in American Film and Culture* (Charlottesville: University Press of Virginia, 2001); see also Carina Yervasi, "The Faces of Joan: Cinematic Representations of Joan of Arc," in *Film & History* 29.4 (1999): 8–19.

3. For more on the effects of mass hysteria in the Middle Ages see: Norman Cohn, *The Pursuit of the Millennium: Revolutionary Millenarians and Mystical Anarchists of the Middle Ages,* rev. ed. (London: Maurice Temple Smith, Ltd., 1970); Mark Pegg, *The Corruption of Angels: the Great Inquisition of 1245–1246*

(Princeton: Princeton University Press, 2001). The Children's Crusade was one specific example of a group engaged in a form of hysteria. This Crusade was undertaken by children in the thirteenth century, who, inflamed by stories of Christians battling the infidel (or Muslims) in the Holy Land, walked barefoot through the mountains spreading the word that Christ's cross and belief would help them to conquer the Holy Land. Thousands of children died before they arrived in Jerusalem.

Oh, What a Lovely War!
Joan of Arc on Screen

EDWARD BENSON

Feature films are often an effective way to get undergraduate students to think about the past; to the extent they claim ownership of cinema as an art form, they engage more willingly in discussion of the conflicts enacted on screen than those figured by the written word. Much of students' fondness for film comes from the immediacy and intensity of their reactions to what they see on screen, on the other hand, so they need help to recover a context for people and incidents distant from them in place or time. Nowhere is that more apparent than with the story of Joan of Arc. She has fascinated filmmakers since the invention of the cinema, so there ought to be feature films we can use to help our students understand her.[1] I shall review the four most readily available in the United States, although two of them are deeply flawed, and even the two more useful films fail to capture some of the contradictions enacted in her story; the best we can do is to select extracts from them and engage our students in discussion of why it has proved so difficult to film Joan's short and violent public life.

The flawed films are *The Passion of Joan of Arc* (1928/1985), directed by Carl Dreyer, written by Dreyer and Joseph Delteil, and starring Renée Falconetti as Joan, and *The Messenger: The Story of Joan of Arc* (1999), directed by Luc Besson, written (in English) by Besson and Andrew Birkin, with Milla Jovovich as Joan. Dreyer's *Passion* limits itself to showing Joan at the climactic trial for her life, but the historicizing effect of that choice has been undermined in the version we see today through the elimination of Delteil's intertitles, which included some of her most disruptive responses to her judges' relentless queries.[2] *The Messenger* was made during Besson's marriage to Jovovich and is typical of the "*cinéma du look*" for which he is known.[3] Despite exceptional performances by Tchéky Karyo as Dunois and John Malkovich as Charles VII, it works primarily as a psychological reconstruction of Joan, with lurid and counterfactual explanations for her behavior. In what follows I shall devote less attention to the *Messenger* or Dreyer's *Passion* than to *Joan of Arc* (1948/1950) directed by Victor Fleming, written by Andrew Solt and Maxwell Anderson, and starring Ingrid Bergman at the height of her fame,[4] and a four-hour *Joan the Maid* (1997) directed by Jacques Rivette and written (in French with English subtitles) by Christine Laurent and Pascal Bonitzer, with Sandrine Bonnaire as Joan. Excerpts from the latter two allow undergraduates to appreciate the breadth and depth of the revolution Joan helped unleash.

Let me start by sketching some of the contradictions in the historical record, then show how Joan's legend emerged with the birth of the absolutist state and continued to grow down to Le Pen's custom of holding the climactic Front National rally of each campaign at an equestrian statue of Joan at the head of the Rue de Rivoli. Finally, I shall rehearse some of what the surviving record tells us about her life, the better to help instructors choose excerpts from the 1948/1950 *Joan of Arc* and the 1997 *Joan the Maid* to tell her story.

Most of what we know about Joan comes from the four trials to which she was subjected in her short life, as well as the one held twenty-five years after her death to rehabilitate her and, more urgently, to discredit her judges and their supporters from the House of Lancaster. Joan's first trial was in the Bishop's Court in Toul for what we would now call breach of promise, her refusal to follow through with a marriage contracted by her parents.[5] The second was an inquiry, as soon as she arrived at the royal court at Chinon, on her character and her self-declared mission to the king. The third was another, fuller inquiry on the same subject conducted immediately thereafter by the supreme judicial court, the Parlement de Paris acting in exile in Poitiers.[6] The records do not survive from the latter two trials, the first of many instances we shall see of Joan's escaping our gaze even as we turn it on her.[7] Records of Joan's fourth trial, in Rouen in 1431 for heresy, apostasy, sorcery, and idolatry have survived, though, and they yield a picture of an extraordinarily articulate and independent young woman who succeeded for almost two months in resisting the relentless pressure of as many as sixty interrogators to recast her experience in their terms.[8]

Modern scholars are all but unanimous that Joan's voice comes through in the transcripts of the fourth trial; Ingrid Bergman gave voice to many of her most famous replies in the final twenty-five minutes of *Joan of Arc*. The judges pressed Joan hardest on epistemology: How could she be so sure that the divine guidance on which she relied was

Joan of Arc (Ingrid Bergman) at the stake, from *Joan of Arc* (1948).

divine and not diabolical in origin? In the course of their interrogation, they finally asked her if she was in a "state of Grace." She responded, "If I am not, may God place me there. If I am, may He keep me there." Several historians report that her judges were thunderstruck by the brilliance of this reply, and the trial record shifts at this point to recording her replies in indirect discourse, as if to silence her troublesome voice.[9]

Even the record of this trial is marred, however: it begins over a month after the judges first convened, and includes several erasures.[10] This is part of what I meant by the contradictions in the historical record, but only a part. Françoise Meltzer has argued persuasively that even more than her irreverent replies, Joan's refusals to answer were disruptive of her judges' efforts to defend their society of orders and the political system protecting both it and them.[11] Meltzer presents these judges as serving the inchoate nation-state formed when Henry V of England inherited the French throne as well, but that depends on seeing the Anglo-French monarchy as a viable forerunner to modern nations. I argue instead that it was a quintessentially feudal counterweight to the Holy Roman Empire; the only real alternative to the feudal political order was tighter organization of smaller units, such as was being practiced principally on both sides of the English Channel. I began this essay promising to "recover" the historical context for Joan's story as if it were simply waiting for us, but it is already clear that the context for her story is no less contentious than the narrative itself.

Let us begin to historicize this record with a summary chronology of the evolution of Joan's image. The first full-length chronicle devoted to her was published in 1612 by an author claiming to be descended from her family; by the middle of that century, she was claimed by the *ancien régime's* historians as the savior of the French royal house.[12] Voltaire took aim at this royalist historiography with his scabrous *Pucelle d'Orléans*, so, when Republicans sought to commemorate Voltaire during the centenary of the Revolution, their monarchist and Catholic opponents gravitated to the equestrian statue of Joan on the Rue de Rivoli.[13] There is room for astonishment that those defending the role of the Church in French life should appeal to the memory of a young woman it burned alive, or that fervent partisans of traditional social roles should evoke a young peasant woman known for having cross-dressed as a knight.[14]

Not only has Joan come to embody sharply differing sets of values but she has come to be seen as enacting the energy with which partisans hold to such values, in great part because their opponents often find their own values no less incarnated in her.[15] Canonized in 1920, Joan became the unofficial patron saint of the Maréchal Pétain; soon after the 1940 *débâcle*, Claude Vermorel wrote a play about her called *Jeanne avec nous* [Joan with us]. After the war, he recalled with understandable pride the thunderous silence of the audience at each daring allusion to the Occupation. The Nazis and their French allies had good reason to view Joan with special favor, since she was such a visible victim of the English, but "*Jeanne avec nous*" was a slogan used during the mid-thirties by demonstrators for the Popular Front, so it was inevitable that the play should be banned. Simone de Beauvoir recalled seeing it during its short life in

Paris—but she recalled outbursts of applause at references to the Occupation, which she also took as no less "unequivocal demonstrations against Nazi rule."[16]

Vermorel's and Beauvoir's recalling the few performances of the play in opposite ways shows how our eagerness to find preferred moral lessons in Joan's story takes precedence over our ability even to recall what we have read or heard. Much of what we think we know about Joan is false, moreover; for instance, she would not have recognized the name Jeanne d'Arc. She called herself *"la pucelle,"* or "the maid," during her abbreviated public life; apostrophes were not in common use then and, even if they had been, patronymics had not yet become standard, so she had no reason to adopt her father's name, Dars.[17] She is called "Pucelle" throughout Rivette's 1994 *Joan the Maid (Jeanne la Pucelle: Part One: Les Batailles, Part Two: Les Prisons)*, and that is how I shall refer to her as I review her public career.

The Maid has long been presented as a young peasant woman, the better to contrast her to the mature noblemen alongside whom she fought, but her family was among the wealthiest in her village and prominent enough that her father represented the village, Domrémy, in a dispute with a local lord named Robert de Saarbruck over some irregular levies he was trying to charge and again later in the court of Robert de Baudricourt, commander for Charles VII of the fortress of Vaucouleurs.[18] None of the films under review take proper account of the prominence of her family, but viewers of *Le Retour de Martin Guerre* (Daniel Vigne, 1982) can gain a rough understanding of the level of comfort in her life and the role played by her family in the village by looking at the Guerre household and its impact on the village of Artigat just over a century later.

There were two respects in which the area from which the Maid came was altogether exceptional for its time; first, Vaucouleurs was one of only four strongholds north of the Loire maintaining allegiance to Charles VII; second, the land to the west of the Meuse, including Domrémy, was allodial, held without owing feudal dues to an overlord.[19] Making these points clear in a feature film might require too much exposition, but if readers wish to use fiction films to acquaint their students with medieval culture, both points are worth emphasizing. The tiny number of northern strongholds holding out for the Valois helps us understand the impact of the Maid's intervention at Orléans, the largest city of the four, as well as her judges' fury at the dramatic shift in military and political momentum.[20] Charles VII was becoming derisively known as the "King of Bourges" before her arrival because his reign was increasingly confined to the southwestern corner of his kingdom, but none of the films I have reviewed makes this context clear.

Domrémy's allodial status is yet more interesting, for it may help explain the intensity of the Maid's devotion to her sovereign. The lands on the eastern side of the meandering course of the Meuse were part of an imperial fief whose lord, Saarbruck, was a vassal of the Duke of Burgundy, locked in a struggle to the death with Charles VII's house of Valois. When the Burgundians assassinated Charles's uncle Louis d'Orléans twenty years before, they had taken the precaution of chopping off his right hand to prevent his rising from the dead to cause them more mischief. Charles VII and Jean sans Peur, the duke of Burgundy, arranged an interview in the middle of a bridge at Montereau, but Charles had the duke assassinated before his eyes, and had his hand cut off in turn.[21] No peace was possible between these two families, and the dividing lines between their holdings traversed the Maid's village of Domrémy. Had Saarbruck defeated Baudricourt and taken the territory on the western side of the river, Dars and his fellow villagers would not have automatically lost their exemption from feudal rents, but those rights were obviously much easier to defend in the royal courts than they would have been in Saarbruck's. This is by no means to affirm that the Maid undertook her public and highly transgressive career in order to defend her family's material interests; there is ample evidence of her desire to separate herself from her parents' plans for her.[22] It is rather to suggest that she had a sharper appreciation than most of what they stood to lose if the Valois monarchy were replaced by one more eager to defend traditional feudal social organization.

The Maid began her public career by appearing in February of 1429 at Vaucouleurs, demanding an escort and support for travel to France in order to reach king Charles VII at Chinon before mid–Lent.[23] How was she able to convince Baudricourt to provide her with retainers and a horse so she could importune his king the way she had been importuning him? It would appear from the record of the posthumous rehabilitative trial that her first and probably most important victory was convincing Jean de Nouillopont (also known as Jean de Metz), a squire in Baudricourt's household, of the rightness of her cause.[24] Rivette's *Joan the Maid* conveys my own sense of the relentless display of willpower that so impressed her contemporaries, though it remains mute on her motivation for undertaking this adventure in the first place.

When we turn to the (partial and faulty) record of deliberations by the judges at the Maid's trial for her life, we find them focused more closely on that question than on how she could have succeeded; these great clerics had an easier time imagining how their enemies could have grasped at even such an unlikely straw as a young woman, and a commoner to boot, than understanding how she could have hatched such a scheme on her own. They worked above all to make her see her temerity at believing in her inspiration without consulting those responsible for the health of her soul. What allowed her to think she had been inspired to do God's bidding?

The Maid started, as she does in *Joan the Maid*, invoking the authority of God with no intermediary and little hesitation, in much the same way that, for instance, Teresa of Avila had done, but her judges pressed her for more than two months for specific signs of His favor.[25] Besson's *Messenger* presents the judges' questioning as duplicitous, and there is no gainsaying the anger they must have felt over the losses the Maid had inflicted on their cause, but the operative biases were deeper and more pervasive than their preference for Lancaster over Valois. The few medieval aristocrats who had occasion for close contact with peasant culture had long been uneasy with what they regarded as rank paganism, and their unease became ever more pronounced over the later Middle Ages.[26] I have argued elsewhere that judges' insistence that those appearing before them put their stories into a form they could understand ultimately hardened into the sixteenth-century witch hunt.[27]

The remarkable thing about the lengthy interrogations to which the Maid was subjected is not the judges' insistence that she recount her experience in a way congruent with the mental categories they had spent so much energy learning and elaborating, nor is it her determination to remain true to the way she perceived that experience.[28] What is most astonishing is the skill and persistence of her efforts to manipulate the legal system, apparently in order to force her judges to respect the form of her narrative. She repeatedly directed the judges not only to the verdict of the inquest conducted by the Parlement de Paris but also to the testimony recorded there,[29] and we see her appeal unsuccessfully to the Pope in Fleming's 1948/1950 *Joan of Arc*. The litigious character of her resistance is also unmistakable, for instance, in the record of her reply to questions about gloves lost at Charles's coronation in Reims. The Maid was aware enough of the judges' tactics that she promptly volunteered that she had never promised to find them—because one of the alleged occupations of late-medieval witches was finding lost articles.[30]

Even in the films I find most useful for helping students imagine her story, though, we see far more footage of the Maid entering the great hall at Chinon or storming the walls of the Tourelles than answering her judges, although most of what we know about her, including her feats of arms, comes from the record of her verbal sparring with her sixty interrogators. We do see Ingrid Bergman snapping at them at the end of *Joan of Arc*, but Rivette's *Joan the Maid* simply leaps from the failure to ransom her to her abjuration.[31] Even the surviving print of Dreyer's *Passion*, based as it was on the trial record, shows the Maid's suffering but none of her ingenious resistance.[32] This is of course what I meant to suggest by my facetious title: part of the reason there is no film we can simply adopt to show the Maid's story is that filmmakers have apparently become convinced that today's ever younger (and more often male) viewers are more likely to return for repeat screenings of battle scenes than for a courtroom drama, however freighted with the seeds of historical change.

For all her skill and determination, the Maid was ultimately unable to hew to her memory of her experience.[33] Forced to account for the strength of her inspiration to the satisfaction of her judges, she characterized it first as "voices," then as the saints Catherine, Margaret, and Michael, whom she finally claimed to see as surely as she was gazing on her interrogators.[34] In spite of the Maid's own testimony that she described the saints as she saw them painted in churches, her "voices" still dominate modern images of her inspiration and encourage us to discount her beliefs as superstitious.[35] Her piety was not only unusually intense, moreover; it was so uninflected by contemporary religious practices that her judges ended up complaining about her "thirst" for communion.[36] The emphasis on her voices in most films makes her seem medieval and safely distant from us, but her fifteenth-century judges found her piety utterly foreign to the religious practices they meant to encourage among the faithful.[37] Another reason we cannot use any single film to show young viewers what her story must have been like is that filmmakers have been unwilling or unable to show the elements of modern culture in it.

Persuading King Charles of the divinity of her mission was her second important success, and, in spite of the popularity and persistence of legends about it, it remains no more easily understandable than her success at winning over Nouillopont. She arrived dressed in somber male attire at court during mid–Lenten festivities, when 350 knights and courtiers engaged in "burlesque gaiety" awaited her.[38] It is difficult for readers raised in a culture that claims stridently to have moved beyond class to imagine how anomalous this commoner from the far edge of the kingdom must have felt[39] as she made her way through the throng of nobles, prelates, financiers, and ladies attendant on the king. We have already had an indication of her extraordinary independence and self-assurance in her willingness to persist in importuning Baudricourt; this scene ought to have been a clearer representation of the qualities and characteristics that allowed her to play such a central role in the formation of France. As a counterexample, let us consider Cate Blanchett in the Shekhar Kapur/Michael Hirst *Elizabeth* (1999), in Elizabeth's first scene at the court she meant to make hers. We see her terror (presumably due to her tender years, gender, and religion), then her exhilaration at having survived. I shall conclude with some suggestions as to why no one has been able to achieve this effect in the story of the Maid's arrival at court.

The trial records also show that, along with the two inquiries into her character, the Maid was physically examined no fewer than three times in the last year of her life to determine whether she was a virgin.[40] Colette Beaune has shown that virginity was a way for women to escape the submission to men figured in the marriage handoff from father to husband, but it was also widely held to endow virgins with charismatic power.[41] The attention to her virginity should alert us to the critical importance of gender to this story: she was finally executed for putting men's clothes back on after having agreed to dress as a woman.[42]

It may be hard for us to believe that cross-dressing could have been her most deadly offense, but her judges took it very seriously indeed.[43] Her hair may help us see some of the problems the Maid poses for modern filmmakers; the trial record shows that it offended the judges as much as her clothes did, because she shaved the hair over her ears, the better to look like "a fashionable boy."[44] There was nothing androgynous about it; her hair was shaved and shaped as if she were an early-fifteenth-century knight.[45] Most of the films under review show men in stylized coiffures; while the Maid's is hair shorter than that of the other women in the films, it is nonetheless very different from that of the other warriors. A final reason it has proven impossible to recover the context for her story is that filmmakers, facing the daunting task of luring adolescent male viewers to repeat showings of a film about a young woman, find themselves unable to represent her aggressively claiming male identity; they can show Milla Jovovich or Sandrine Bonnaire on horseback or in battle but not adopting the shaved hairstyle of her comrades-in-arms.

At the same time as the Maid was seeking a new identity as a fighting man, she always appeared in battle accompanied by an unmistakable banner. Her use to the Valois cause was her ability to rally those fighting alongside her, which depended on their being able to identify her in the heat of battle as the Maid who was fighting like a man but was not one.[46] It is hard to imagine a more radical challenge to her judges' society of orders, but the problems we are still having in viewing her story suggest that categories that were already hoary with tradition in the fifteenth century have persisted all but unchallenged into the twenty-first.[47]

University-trained intellectuals like the Maid's judges supported the Lancastrian claim to the French throne because they saw the creation of an Anglo-French kingdom as the culmination of the feudal tendency toward horizontal rather than vertical political organization. We have come over the last four hundred years to regard the nation-state as the natural to way organize our political allegiance, but these clerics saw the lack of sharp divisions between the various principalities of Europe as compensated for by a stable and uniform set of horizontal relationships between individual subjects.[48] The cross-border similarities between the status and duties of individual peasants, artisans, nobles, clerics—and ladies—allowed them all common citizenship in Christendom. The Maid, however, refused to be subsumed under these categories; we could even say that she embodied modern social as well as political organization and that her success at doing so at just the moment that the Anglo-French monarchy was on the point of assuring the feudal organization of Europe was the reason that she so infuriated her judges and captors.

The only prominent group to favor innovation in social relations and royal initiative in political ones were the king's lawyers, who worked from the fifteenth to the seventeenth centuries to recast North Atlantic culture. The Maid referred her interrogators to the Poitiers inquiry, conducted by the Parlement de Paris acting in exile, and sought to elude interrogation by appealing to the Pope. Neither expedient worked, but I find it remarkable that she tried, for it showed that peasants, even if wealthy and extraordinarily articulate ones, were ready to use late-medieval and early modern courts for their own purposes. Viewers of the *Retour de Martin Guerre* were astonished to see a (wealthy) peasant making such savvy use of *ancien régime* courts; we see the same thing here on the part of a younger (wealthy) peasant woman. The seventeenth century in France is widely seen as an arena for the struggle between the traditional aristocracy and a new one made up of the king's functionaries and bureaucrats, but I think we can see an early skirmish in the Maid's cool "I appeal to the Pope" in 1431.[49]

Régine Pernoud wrote at the end of a long life devoted in large part to study of the Maid that: "She defines the shaping significance of the subject in history."[50] This is a large claim, but I do not think it is overstated, providing we study the Maid's feelings of gender solidarity in their effect on the bases of fifteenth-century social organization. At the very moment she was bursting so flamboyantly on the scene of the exclusively male and aristocratic activity of armed combat, the Maid was also posing difficult questions, in a way that could be said to have altered politics itself, about the way military victory affected women in conquered towns.

Warfare was the normal state of "international" relations in Europe at the time; it was what the traditional nobility did to justify the dues and forfeits charged the peasantry.[51] Medieval French "armies" were primarily collections of knights who did not depend on their commanders for sustenance but lived off the land as best they could and looked to the plunder of conquered places and the ransom of captured knights for recompense, emotional as well as fiscal, for the risks of combat.[52] Into the stalemated conflict between Lancaster and Valois burst a young woman who refused to allow those fighting with her to loot places they conquered, apparently because of the nefarious effects on women in the captured towns.[53] Many commentators have remarked on the rapid shift in the fortunes of war as towns large and small across the North of France rushed to shift their allegiance to Charles VII; Deborah Fraioli has found a suggestion that they did so, at least in part, because of the Maid's stance against plunder.[54]

Her *modus pugnandi* threatened to change warfare from a speculative activity with rewards matching downside risks to little more than a potentially lethal obligation owed to the sovereign. Ransom payments for great nobles could reach immense sums, but the Maid was no more sympathetic to the quest for prize prisoners than she was to plunder; as far as she was concerned, battles were waged to gain towns and cities loyal to her king.[55] It is hard to overstate the import of the change she was demanding.[56] The fissures opened in the feudal military order by her impatience at Orléans did not became apparent until later in the fifteenth century. It may have been the Maid's passionately nationalistic and unabashedly utilitarian perspective on the inherently male, aristocratic activity of armed combat that helped open them in the first place.

The knights who fought alongside her noticed her curious mindset, and testified about it during the posthumous trial, but they described it somewhat differently. They noted her dislike of camp followers, a point well illustrated early in Fleming's *Joan of Arc*, and that she wished all those fighting with her to confess their sins before each battle.[57] They put the Maid's strangeness in terms of her fervent piety, in other words, rather than in anachronistic terms such as feminism. Several, on the other hand, testified that they had seen and admired her naked breasts and legs but that they had never felt desire for her, and Dunois, the commander of Valois forces in Orléans and one of the more articulate witnesses, even confessed to losing heterosexual desire altogether in her presence.[58] Beaune and Meltzer, in particular, have emphasized the importance of her virginity as obviating her customary submission to men; Dunois's memory of his reaction to the sight of her naked body shows the depth of his puzzlement over his extraordinary comrade-in-arms and therefore of her challenge to the sexually charged experience of late-medieval warfare. I urge viewing her refusal to allow plunder in association with her cutting her hair like a warrior's; the gender solidarity the Maid felt for the women in conquered towns bade her stop those fighting alongside her from giving vent to their sexual view of battle, and particularly of victory, at the same time as she claimed what they had always viewed as a quintessentially male role alongside them.[59] Because the new code of conduct she was demanding appeared to offer the possibility of outright victory, however, it attracted a surprising welcome from the hard-bitten veterans with whom she fought in the spring and summer of 1429. The films under review here suggest, again, that the combination is not much easier for modern filmmakers to understand than it was for late-medieval warriors or clerics.

I have also noted that her piety, while undeniably fervent, was unusually abstract; the Maid alarmed contemporary prelates by insisting that she enjoyed a direct relationship with God. Deborah Fraioli and Philippe Contamine have seen a modernist side to the Maid's single-minded pursuit of a separate French state instead of the pan–European monarchy pursued by the French intellectual elite, but I think her modernism goes farther than that.[60] She sought the creation of a warrior class in service to the sovereign and forced the warriors who fought alongside her to adopt many of the tactics and principles of organization that would eventually accompany such an innovation.[61] She adopted a religious practice fundamentally at odds with the one being put in place across the European countryside but which would prove more congenial to the direct experience of sanctity characteristic of Reformation and Counter-Reformation piety.

For all of these reasons, it is difficult to think of a more appropriate figure for a volume on the medieval hero in film than the Maid; indeed, she insisted on claiming heroic status for herself, even at the cost of her life. She never tired of advancing the cause of the nascent nation-state, perhaps because it seemed to offer a defense against the extension of feudal social relations to those who had so far escaped them. All three films that show us Charles VII encourage our bewilderment and anger at his refusal to follow up on the Maid's victories, but for him to do so he would have had to share her vision of a nation whose elites served the national—that is, his—interests above their own. She apparently imagined a new, direct relationship with her king as well as her God, but there is no evidence either that Charles VII shared her conception for very long or that he would have survived if he had.

I have already detailed my objections to Dreyer's famous *Passion* and Besson's hypercontemporary *Messenger*; there is little to be gained from rehearsing them here. Some of Fleming's *Joan of Arc* is unlikely to help contemporary undergraduates imagine this story; I cannot imagine their accepting the conventions necessary to filming epic dramas in the heyday of the Hollywood studio system.[62] The scenes of Ingrid Bergman convincing those fighting alongside her to adopt a new code of conduct are the most convincing currently available, however, and show more of the Maid answering her judges with her unique combination of stubbornness and tactical brilliance than any of the other films. *Joan of Arc*

Joan on the walls of the castle from *Joan of Arc* (1948).

hence gives us the best chance to glimpse the personal and historical resources she used to challenge the reigning politico-military ideology.

Rivette's *Joan the Maid* has the strength of Sandrine Bonnaire's brilliant characterization of the Maid's impatience and her imperious piety[63] but it also shows many scenes that do little to advance our understanding of the Maid's brief public career. Those seeking a way to help undergraduates imagine this episode would do best to pick scenes from this film such as the trial in Poitiers along with the camp-follower and trial scenes from *Joan of Arc*. Had she posed a less radical challenge to contemporary ways of ordering social relations, it would probably be easier to find films that help us see her as she must have been.

The Maid proposed nothing less than a radically new political settlement in which military power served the needs of the state (in the person of its sovereign) rather than the interests of those wielding it. Her view of gender was even more revolutionary, allowing her to claim a male role and female identity at the same time; the most astonishing thing about her public life may be that she survived two years.

The feature film that respects the specific anomalies and contradictions from which she sprang does not exist. I hope instructors will find the extracts identified here useful in helping their students appreciate the challenge posed by the Maid's short public life, but I fear we are still too deeply mired in the civilization she helped create to be able to make a film to meet that challenge. The best explanation for our inability is probably that our culture remains dependent on the one in which she grew up, particularly for its gender categories; it proved easier at least partly to dispossess a bellicose aristocracy in favor of a more bureaucratic one than it was—or is—to imagine egalitarian ways for men and women to relate to each other.

Notes

My thanks to Anne Berthelot, Susan Porter Benson, and Martha Driver for their perceptive comments on earlier drafts of this essay.

1. The hyperabundance of what has become known as the Jehannic literature has become a cliché. Three of the best introductions to the films about Joan are Robin Blaetz, *Visions of the Maid: Joan of Arc in American Film and Culture* (Charlottesville and London: University of Virginia Press, 2001); Kevin Harty, "Jeanne au cinéma," in *Fresh Verdicts on Joan of Arc*, ed. Bonnie Wheeler and Charles T. Wood (New York and London: Garland, 1996), pp. 237–264; and Nadia Margolis's bibliography on Joan with 1,500 items, fifty of them on film, Margolis, *Joan of Arc in History, Literature, and Film: A Select Annotated Bibliography* (NY: Garland, 1990).

2. The Gaumont 1985 version is restored from the copy recovered in 1981 and includes Richard Einhorn's *Voices of Light* on the soundtrack. Dreyer castigated the young Falconetti at the beginning of each day's shooting until he got the requisite expression of suffering on her face; see Blaetz, "'La Femme Vacante,' or the Rendering of Joan of Arc in the Cinema," *PostScript* 12.2 (1993): 63–78, 72, citing screenwriter Jean Hugo, *Le Regard de la mémoire* (Paris: Actes Sud, 1983), p. 258.

3. Indeed, Jovovich writes in publicity material released with the DVD that

that was why she and Besson decided to make the film: "It all started with a picture of me that Luc and I were looking at. It's one of my favorite pictures. It's sepia-toned and very crazy. The hair is really wild, and the make-up is very smoky, very strange. And I was looking at it, and I said to Luc, 'This is Joan. This is her.' That picture really made us want to make the movie."

4. The film was adapted from Maxwell Anderson's play, originally written in 1936, about playing Joan of Arc in a modern drama, but that aspect of the play was ignored in the 1948 version, and the film was cut from 145 minutes to 100 and realigned as well in 1950, in the version we see today (Blaetz, *Visions of the Maid*, pp. 127–35).

5. Joan's insistence on autonomy and self-definition started early: cf. Regine Pernoud and Marie Veronique Clin, *Joan of Arc, Her Story*, tr. and rev. Jeremy duQuesnay Adams, ed. Bonnie Wheeler (New York: St. Martin's, 1998), p. 119; Marina Warner, *Joan of Arc: The Image of Female Heroism* (Berkeley and Los Angeles: University of California Press, 1981), p. 153; Georges and Andrée Duby, *Les Procès de Jeanne d'Arc* (Paris: Gallimard, 1995), p. 91. Colette Beaune argues that the Church annulled the marriage planned by her parents, sparing her the perils of childbirth that had claimed her sister Catherine (*pace* Besson), in order to preserve her virginity, a state that became increasingly important to her during her public career; see Beaune, "Jehanne la Pucelle," *Perspectives médiévales* 27 (Dec., 2001): 21–35, 30.

6. The standard account is Pernoud and Clin, *Joan of Arc*.

7. See Charles T. Wood, "Joan of Arc's Mission and the Lost Record of her Interrogation at Poitiers," in *Fresh Verdicts*, pp. 19–29, esp. pp. 25–6 on why the Poitiers record, subsequently reviewed by the Pope (see note 43), went missing from all archives.

8. Specifically one cardinal, six bishops, thirty-two doctors of theology, sixteen bachelors of theology, seven doctors of medicine, and 103 associates (Blaetz, *Visions of the Maid*, p. 209).

9. The Dubys find her wish to be a standard feature of contemporary prayers (cf. pp. 22–4, 48, and Pernoud, p. 112).

10. Cf. H. Ansgar Kelly, "The Right to Remain Silent: Before and after Joan of Arc," *Speculum* 68 (October, 1993): 992–1026, 993; and Pernoud, p. 112.

11. See Meltzer, *For Fear of the Fire: Joan of Arc and the Limits of Subjectivity* (Chicago and London: University of Chicago Press, 2001), pp. 122–23.

12. With Jean Chapelain's overblown *La Pucelle* in 1656; see Marc Fumaroli, *The Poet and the King: Jean de la Fontaine and His Century* (Notre Dame, IN: University of Notre Dame Press, 2002), p. 80.

13. The 1874 inauguration of the equestrian statue on the Place des Pyramides was followed immediately by a "discussion" so virulent that the police were called to disperse it; see Rosemonde Sanson, "La 'Fête de Jeanne d'Arc' en 1894: Controverse et célébration," *Revue d'histoire moderne et contemporaine* 20 (July–Sept 1973): 444–63, 445; and Margolis, p. 267.

14. Her judges had pardoned her and declared her relapsed only when they once again found her in men's clothes (cf Warner, pp. 146–51; Blaetz, *Visions of the Maid*, p. 9; Meltzer, p. 202).

15. Jean-François Kahn traced the left-right division so crucial to French civic life over the past century to Joan herself; see Kahn, "L'Affaire Jeanne d'Arc," *L'Événement du jeudi* 392 (May 7–13, 1992), cited by Margolis, "The 'Joan Phenomenon' and the French Right," in *Fresh Verdicts*, pp. 265–87, p. 267.

16. Gabriel Jacobs, "The Role of Joan of Arc on the Stage of Occupied Paris,"

Vichy France and the Resistance: Culture and Ideology, ed. H. R. Kedward and Roger Austin (London: Croom Helm, 1985), pp. 106–122, p. 115, citing Beauvoir, *La Force de l'âge* (Paris: Gallimard, 1960), p. 470; and Vermorel, *Opéra* (December 19, 1945).

17. Her mother was known as "Romée" because she had made a pilgrimage (Pernoud, p. 36).

18. In 1423 and 1427, whereas the Maid's public career began early in 1429, see Duby, p. 31; Warner, p. 41; Kelly DeVries, "A Woman as Leader of Men: Joan of Arc's Military Career," *Fresh Verdicts*, pp. 3–18, p. 3.

19. Orléans, Mont Saint Michel, and Tournai were the other strongholds of Valois allegiance; see Duby, p. 31; and for Domrémy's allodial status, Warner, pp. 39–40.

20. The chief judge at her trial was Pierre Cauchon, Bishop of Beauvais and one of the most able and energetic intellectuals in the employ of the Dukes of Burgundy. He was driven precipitously from his diocese when the city shifted its allegiance to Charles VII in the aftermath of the Maid's victory at Orléans.

21. See Warner, pp. 97–98.

22. Relations in her family were far more fraught with tension than one would think from the films: her father told her brothers to drown her if she tried to run off; see Pernoud, p. 161; Duby, pp. 238–39; Warner p. 154, and Jean Fraikin, "Was Joan of Arc a 'Sign' of Charles VII's Innocence," *Fresh Verdicts,* pp. 61–72, p. 67, for earlier misunderstandings of his threat.

23. The Maid's description of "France" as her objective comes from the testimony of members of Baudricourt's household at the nullification trial; see Philippe Contamine, *De Jeanne d'Arc aux guerres d'Italie: Figures, images et problèmes du XVe siècle* (Orléans, Paradigme: 1994), pp. 31–5. It is worth noting that she saw France as an entity separate from her region.

24. See Pernoud, pp. 19–20; the transcripts of the 1431 trial and the 1455–1456 inquest to nullify it were edited by Jules Quicherat in the mid-nineteenth century and have been published in several modern editions—by Raymond Oursel for the 1431 trial, and Pierre Duparc for the later one; see Pernoud, pp. 286–87.

25. See Warner, pp. 121–23; Meltzer, pp. 216–17.

26. See my "Culture Wars Medieval and Modern in *Le Moine et la sorcière*," *Film & History*, 29.1–2 (1999): 56–70, for an early-thirteenth-century encounter.

27. This is the principal contention of the first half of my *Money and Magic in Montaigne: The Historicity of the Essais* (Geneva: Droz, 1995), esp. pp. 69–74.

28. See Karen Sullivan, *The Interrogation of Joan of Arc* (Minneapolis and London: University of Minnesota Press, 1999), p. xxiii, and her "'I Do Not Name to You the Voice of St. Michael': The Identification of Joan of Arc's Voices," *Fresh Verdicts*, pp. 85–111, p. 88.

29. See Warner, pp. 120–121.

30. Duby, p. 78. She made a similar denial, equally spontaneously, later in the same interrogation session (3 March); Duby, p. 81. While witchcraft was one of the original charges, she was finally condemned solely for cross-dressing.

31. It does use some of the replies from the later trial in its representation of the Poitiers inquest, permitting viewers to see the Maid's character at work.

32. The print of *La Passion de Jeanne d'Arc* currently available is very different from Delteil's screenplay, published in Carl Theodor Dreyer, *Four Screenplays*, tr. Oliver Stallybrass, intro. Ole Storm (Bloomington and London: Indiana University Press, 1970, also available in no. 100 of *L'Avant-Scène du Cinéma* [Feb., 1970]).

33. Karen Sullivan argues, as I did in *Money and Magic in Montaigne*, that the result of intensive judicial interrogation is finally to force the witness to recast her experience in terms familiar to the interrogators; see *Interrogation*, pp. xxiii, 83–4, 90–1, and 147.

34. Sullivan reports that eighty percent of the contemporary references to the Maid's inspiration were to God, her Lord, Messire, or the King of Heaven (*Fresh Verdicts*, pp. 90–7). Catherine of Alexandria and Margaret of Antioch were virgins who dressed as monks in order to preserve their virginity—and avoid their fathers' plans for their marriage, while Michael was patron of Mont Saint Michel, again another of the last Valois strongholds in the North. Catherine and Margaret were dropped from the calendar after the Council of Trent; see Warner, pp. 28, 131.

35. See Duby, p. 121. Jean Wirth has demonstrated convincingly that superstition is what others believe; see his "La naissance du concept de croyance (XIIe—XVIIe siècles)" *Bibliothèque d'Humanisme et Renaissance* XLV (1983): 7–58.

36. At a time when most believers took communion once a year, her taking communion before each military engagement, for instance, was heterodox enough to draw condemnation; see Beaune, p. 26.

37. Cf. Duby, p. 35; Deborah Fraioli, *Joan of Arc: The Early Debate* (Woodbridge, U.K.: Boydell, 2000), p. 17.

38. See Fraikin's description of the welcome Charles's courtiers gave the Maid in *Fresh Verdicts*, pp. 61–4.

39. The Meuse, which bifurcated her village and set the allodial lands apart from those owing dues to Saarbruck, was also the Eastern boundary of the kingdom.

40. See Pernoud, p. 31; Marie-Véronique Clin, "Joan of Arc and Her Doctors," in *Fresh Verdicts*, pp. 295–302, p. 300.

41. Beaune, pp. 21–27. She suggests that the Maid staked her claim to public attention self-consciously after the first such examination, during the inquiry by the Parlement de Paris in Poitiers (p. 22). Beaune concludes, moreover, that the Maid's claim was less to moral purity than to the charisma associated with virginity in popular and learned cultures alike (p. 27).

42. Gender was given insufficient scholarly emphasis until very recently and ignored or repressed in the films under review here, but the preoccupation with the Maid's virginity is central to Meltzer's reading of her life; see also Duby, p. 157; and Blaetz, *Visions of the Maid*, p. 9.

43. The Pope's only quarrel with the Parlement de Paris's exoneration of the Maid was her cross-dressing (Fraioli, p. 52).

44. In the words of the charge against her; see Sullivan, pp. 50–2; Warner, p. 211; Blaetz, p. 181.

45. Confronted with her hair after she agreed to resume women's dress, the best they could do was to shave her head; Duby, p. 171; Susan Schibanoff, "True Lies: Transvestism and Idolatry in the Trial of Joan of Arc," *Fresh Verdicts*, pp. 31–60, p. 37.

46. Unlike Catherine of Alexandria and Margaret of Antioch, who dressed as monks to avoid marriage (recall the suit for breach of promise) and whom she eventually identified as two of her voices, the Maid never sought to *pass* as male; see Sullivan, *Interrogation*, pp. xxiii, 83–4, 90–1, 147.

47. See Judith Bennett, "Introduction," in *Ale, Beer, and Brewsters in England: Women's Work in a Changing World* (New York: Oxford University Press, 1996);

and her *Medieval Women in Modern Perspective* (Washington, DC: American Historical Association, 2000).

48. One student of the Maid's story wrote of the "clear logic" of nationhood, even after the recent struggles over Bosnia and Kashmir call that logic into urgent question and as Europe seeks to leave it behind.

49. Enacted by Ingrid Bergman in *Joan of Arc*. One of the first plays that Shakespeare wrote was *King Henry VI, Part II*, about the aftermath of the Maid's intervention: his celebrated "First thing we do, let's kill all the lawyers" from that play (4.2) takes on a more partisan coloration in this context.

50. In a new foreword to Adams' translation, p. xi; cf. Blaetz, *Visions of the Maid*, p. 3: "The historic Joan of Arc serves the cultures in which she appears to the degree that her story can mask or resolve social conflict."

51. See M. H. Keen, *The Laws of War in the Late Middle Ages* (London: Routledge and Kegan Paul, 1965); and Georges Duby, *Les trois ordres: ou L'imaginaire du féodalisme* (Paris: Gallimard, 1978).

52. Ferdinand Lot identified the combatants as the knight himself, and two mounted archers; Lot, *Recherches sur les effectifs des armées françaises des Guerres d'Italie aux Guerres de Religion 1494–1562* (Paris: SEVPEN, 1962), pp. 15–16. They were sometimes accompanied by a *"coutillier,"* whose role was played by Panurge in Pantagruel's battle with the werewolf; see Rabelais, *Pantagruel* (Geneva: Droz, 1947), pp. 173–75; it was to finish off those unlucky enough to fall from their horses by "opening" their armor.

53. DeVries, p. 5. In Rivette's *Joan the Maid*, she asks La Hire if it is true that the grass no longer grows after he has passed through. He demurs but unsatisfied, she assures him that he is going to have to make war differently with her.

54. The suggestion comes from a contemporary treatise, *De quadam puella*; see Fraioli, p. 29.

55. The most famous captive may have been Richard Lionheart at the very end of the twelfth century, but Charles d'Orléans's ransom was so great that he spent twenty-five years, including the Maid's entire public life, incarcerated in England; see Contamine, p. 80.

56. Medieval knights had developed elaborate body armor and fortifications to minimize the risk of combat, but the middle years of the fifteenth century were dominated by the development of siege artillery and (barely) portable muskets that undid the advantages previously enjoyed by knights; see my unpublished dissertation, "'Engin mieulx vault que force:' Rabelais' Portrayal of Warfare in its Literary and Historical Contexts," Brown University, 1970, esp. Chap. 2.

57. See Georges and Andrée Duby, p. 264. She says to the other commanders, in Rivette's *Joan the Maid*: "If you want to win, be pure."

58. Schibanoff points out that this testimony would have confirmed Cauchon and his fellows in their condemnation of her, but the testimony was heard only in the nullification trial, twenty-five years later; pp. 51–2.

59. It is not difficult to feel sympathy for Dunois's bewilderment; again, Tchéky Karyo's portrayal of it is the strongest point of Besson's 1999 *Messenger*.

60. See Contamine, p. 35; and Fraioli, p. 78.

61. See Meltzer, p. 129: "Let us not forget that Joan's campaign had the effect of strengthening the monarchy at the expense of feudal lords, thus paving the way for the modern state."

62. Namely the elaborate painted backdrops of Vaucouleurs and Chinon.

63. It also shows such important details as the horrific treatment she probably suffered after her public abjuration stripped her of the aura of sanctity which

had prevented her guards from venting their spleen on her; see Warner, p. 105, and minutes 90–92 of the second disk. The film shows the gendered hostility of her guards and the terror it induced in her without claiming that they raped her.

Works Cited

Beaune, Colette. "Jeanne la pucelle." *Perspectives médiévales* 27 (December 2001): 21–35.

Benson, Edward. "Culture Wars Medieval & Modern in *Le Moine et la sorcière*." *Film & History*, 29.1-2 (1999): 56–70.

_____. *Money & Magic in Montaigne: The Historicity of the Essais*. Geneva: Droz [*Travaux d'Humanisme et Renaissance* ccxcv], 1995.

_____. unpublished dissertation. "'Engin mieulx vault que force:' Rabelais' Portrayal of Warfare in its Literary and Historical Contexts." (Brown University, 1970).

Bennett, Judith. *Ale, Beer, and Brewsters in England: Women's Work in a Changing World, 1300–1600*. New York: Oxford University Press, 1996.

_____. *Medieval Women in Modern Perspective*. Washington, DC: American Historical Association, 2000.

Blaetz, Robin. "'*La Femme Vacante*,' or the Rendering of Joan of Arc in the Cinema." *PostScript* 12.2 (1993): 63–78.

_____. *Visions of the Maid: Joan of Arc in American Film and Culture*. Charlottesville and London: University of Virginia Press, 2001.

Clin, Marie-Véronique. "Joan of Arc and her Doctors." In *Fresh Verdicts on Joan of Arc*, ed. Bonnie Wheeler and Charles T. Wood. New York and London: Garland, 1996, pp. 295–302.

Contamine, Philippe. *De Jeanne d'Arc aux guerres d'Italie: Figures, images et problèmes du xve siècle*. Orléans: Paradigme, 1994.

DeVries, Kelly. "A Woman as Leader of Men: Joan of Arc's Military Career," *Fresh Verdicts*, pp. 3–18.

Dreyer, Carl Theodor. *Four Screenplays*, tr. Oliver Stallybrass, intro. Ole Storm. Bloomington and London: Indiana University Press, 1970.

Duby, Georges and Andrée. *Les Procès de Jeanne d'Arc*. Paris: Gallimard, 1995.

Duby, Georges. *Les trois ordres: ou, L'imaginaire du féodalisme*. Paris : Gallimard, 1978.

Fraikin, Jean. "Was Joan of Arc a 'Sign' of Charles VII's Innocence?" In *Fresh Verdicts*, pp. 61–72.

Fraioli, Deborah. *Joan of Arc: The Early Debate*. Woodbridge, U.K.: Boydell, 2000.

Fumaroli, Marc. *The Poet and the King: Jean de la Fontaine and his Century*, tr. Jane Marie Todd. Notre Dame, IN : University of Notre Dame Press, 2002.

Harty, Kevin. "Jeanne au cinema." In *Fresh Verdicts*, pp. 237–264.

Jacobs, Gabriel. "The Role of Joan of Arc on the Stage of Occupied Paris." In *Vichy France and the Resistance: Culture and Ideology*, ed. H. R. Kedward and Roger Austin. London: Croom Helm, 1985, pp. 106–122

Keen, M.H. *The Laws of War in the Late Middle Ages*. London: Routledge and Kegan Paul, 1965.

Kelly, H. Ansgar. "The Right to Remain Silent: Before and after Joan of Arc." *Speculum* 68 (October 1993): 992–1026.

Lot, Ferdinand. *Recherches sur les effectifs des armées françaises des Guerres d'Italie aux Guerres de Religion 1494–1562*. Paris: SEVPEN, 1962.

Margolis, Nadia. *Joan of Arc in History, Literature, and Film: A Select Annotated Bibliography.* New York: Garland, 1990.

Meltzer, Françoise. *For Fear of the Fire:* Joan of Arc *and the Limits of Subjectivity.* Chicago and London: University of Chicago Press, 2001.

Pernoud, Régine, and Marie Véronique Clin. *Joan of Arc, Her Story,* tr. and rev. Jeremy duQuesnay Adams, ed. Bonnie Wheeler. New York: St Martin's Press, 1998.

Rabelais, François. *Pantagruel,* ed. Verdun Saulnier. Geneva: Droz, 1947 [1532].

Sanson, Rosemonde. "La 'Fête de Jeanne d'Arc' en 1894: Controverse et celebration." *Revue d'histoire moderne et contemporaine* 20 (July-Sept. 1973): 444–63.

Schibanoff, Susan. "True Lies: Transvestism and Idolatry in the Trial of Joan of Arc." In *Fresh Verdicts*, pp. 31–60.

Sullivan, Karen. *The Interrogation of Joan of Arc.* Minneapolis and London: University of Minnesota Press, 1999.

_____. "'I Do Not Name to You the Voice of St. Michael': The Identification of Joan of Arc's Voices." In *Fresh Verdicts*, pp. 85–111.

Warner, Marina. *Joan of Arc: The Image of Female Heroism.* Berkeley and Los Angeles: University of California Press, 1981.

Wheeler, Bonnie, and Charles T. Woods, eds. *Fresh Verdicts on Joan of Arc.* New York and London: Garland, 1996.

Wirth, Jean. "La naissance du concept de croyance (XIIe—XVIIe siècles)." *Bibliothèque d'Humanisme et Renaissance* 45 (1983): 7–58.

Wood, Charles T. "Joan of Arc's Mission and the Lost Record of her Interrogation at Poitiers." In *Fresh Verdicts*, pp. 19–29.

Filmography

1928 *La Passion de Jeanne d'Arc (The Passion of Joan of Arc)*, d. Carl Theodor Dreyer, with Renée Falconetti, Antonin Artaud. France: Société Générale des Films.

1948 *Joan of Arc*, d. Victor Fleming, with Ingrid Bergman. U.S.: RKO, Sierra.

1997 *Jeanne la Pucelle: Part One: Les Batailles, Part Two: Les Prisons (Joan the Maid)*, d. Jacques Rivette, with Sandrine Bonnaire. France: Pierre Grise Productions, La Sept Cinéma, France 3 Cinéma, Canal Plus, Centre National de la Cinématographie.

1999 *The Messenger: The Story of Joan of Arc*, d. Luc Besson, with Milla Jovovich, John Malkovich. France: Gaumont.

The Hero
in the Classroom

JOHN M. GANIM

From my students I have learned that teaching the medieval film hero is both an easy and difficult task, the reasons for which are, in fact, the theses for this essay. The medieval film often owes as much to other cinematic genres as it does to medieval texts. Among these genres and sub-genres are Westerns, Hollywood and cinecitta costume dramas, and science fiction and fantasy films. The result is that students' reactions to the medieval hero on the screen are mediated by their other expectations of medieval heroism or heroism in general. One aspect of these hero-isms is the generally ironic treatment of heroism in modern populist cinema; an equal and opposite aspect is the often mythic treatment of the medieval hero on film. These smaller-than-life and larger-than-life qual-ities (often coexisting) in the medieval cinematic hero often have ana-logues in medieval texts, where conflicting sources and conflicting political and religious agendas produce similar effects. The challenge in teaching the medieval hero on screen, then, is to make students aware of this largely analogous and homologous quality.

Behind these difficulties and pleasures is the recognition of a larger issue involving medievalism. The Middle Ages no longer offers the crit-ical political and ethical challenge to the modern world that it offered in nineteenth-century and turn-of-the-twentieth-century medievalism from Thomas Carlyle to John Ruskin, William Morris to Henry Adams. Instead, it is medievalism itself, the self-conscious interpretation and reformulation of medieval themes, often ludic and performative, that has become the subject of apparently "medieval" forms in the modern world, resulting in a sometimes self-deluding and sometimes revelatory argument with modernity. The present range of medievalisms (some of them wonderfully catalogued in Umberto Eco's essential article, "Dreaming of the Middle Ages," with its list of ten little Middle Ages) has more to do with other medievalisms than with any positivist Middle Ages.[1] Because of the special status of film in relation to modernity, this argument is often more clearly expressed than in other cultural productions.

Nowhere is this intertextualized medievalism more obvious than in the representation of the medieval hero, and nowhere are the connections to what might be considered hidden medievalisms more obvious. Over the past few years, the number of courses on medieval literature and film, on medieval history and film, and on medieval film as a subspecies of the genre of historical films has mushroomed. This is the result partly of the convenience of new teaching technologies but also of the rise of the study of medievalism, the postmedieval adaptation of medieval themes and representations of the Middle Ages, as a subject of both teaching and research.

The course that I have taught began with close reading of selected Arthurian texts, including Chrétien's romances, *Sir Gawain and the Green Knight*, and Malory's *Morte Darthur*. We then screened and discussed a few key medieval films, including John Boorman's *Excalibur*, Eric Rohmer's *Perceval le Gallois*, and Robert Bresson's *Lancelot du Lac*. Students were responsible for viewing the entire film, either on their own or at scheduled screenings. Class consisted of viewing clips and discussion, with questions provided as guides. This took nearly half of a ten-week term. The next phase of the course consisted of student reports. Students were formed into teams of two to four members. They chose from a list of films I provided, with the possibility of choosing one not on their list after consulting with me. The student teams then presented their reports, which could cover a number of areas, such as the relation of script to sources, the visual reproduction of the medieval setting, the idea of the Middle Ages represented in the film, and the relation between this film and other films, medieval, historical, or not.

A number of problems related to the teaching of film in this context quickly or eventually emerged. I had not realized how much of an influence the instant movie reviews on television news would have on my students. The result was a sometimes uncanny sense of public presentation but relatively superficial analysis on their part. In addition, the tremendous amount of information on the Internet on individual films, many with several Web sites devoted to them, and the expanded background offered on DVD versions of popular films meant that the reports were tilted towards production process. Because of these sources, students were also more likely to emphasize the intentions of directors and screenwriters in their reports. I had to revise my guidelines for the reports to encourage students to become more analytical and to allow themselves to be critical of the stated intentions of screenwriters and directors, at least as represented in publicity materials.

Where I ascribed my assignment of medieval texts in the beginning of the course to professorial traditionalism (at least they would learn something of permanent and non-postmodern value!), in fact the immersion in medieval texts, which continued through the reports, turned out to be both interesting and revelatory. Students were asked to distribute copies, when relevant, of "source" texts. Again, except for their own sacred texts, such as Tolkien, they turned out to be highly sophisticated about both the context and meaning of the medieval works. Students also understood the complex relation between screen and script and between script and source. As a result, we had interesting discussions of Blind Harry's *Wallace* and Barbour's *Bruce* and the changes in historical and literary sources made by Mel Gibson's *Braveheart*. The text that inspired the screenplay for Ingmar Bergman's *The Virgin Spring*, the (possibly) fourteenth-century ballad, "The Daughter of Töre in Vänge," led to an interesting discussion on literary and cinematic genres. I was disappointed by the disjunction between the "literary" opening of the course and the "cinematic" body and ending of it, but my students actually liked it and seemed to see a logical transition that still escapes me.

A paradox also became evident from the student reports. As a literature professor, I had to repress the desire for fidelity to the text, for a literary authenticity. In teaching a course on film, I also had to make students aware of the independent aesthetic of a film, of its own requirements as an art form. But I turned out to be more troubled by this than my students were. They were comfortable with pastiche and with what seemed to me jarring conglomerations of film style. This was because most of them had their cinematic coming-of-age in the 1990s, when commercial film had become so dominant that "art" film could exist only by knowingly and ironically alluding to dominant commercial forms. For the same reason, they were also much more visually knowing of the successes and failures of special effects than I was. My own cinematic coming-of-age was in the early 1960s, dominated by French New Wave and post-neorealist Italian cinema, including the now enshrined pantheon of the last great wave of auteur directors around the world (Fellini, Antonioni, Bergman, Godard, Truffaut, and many others). I also had a somewhat more unusual immersion in "underground" and experimental film as a result of organizing a college film society in the days before film became a widely taught academic subject. While acknowledging the provincialism of my own dated sophistication, however, I was equally taken aback at the literalism of my students when their sacred texts were at stake: they could not judge movies such as Peter Jackson's *The Lord of the Rings: The Fellowship of the Ring* by any standards other than fidelity to Tolkien's text.

These generational differences also accounted for some interesting perspectives on the nature of heroism. From the 1960s through the early 1970s, representations of heroism had taken an increasingly ironic turn on the typical hero of, say, Westerns or war movies. The postwar disillusion reflected in cinema noir, the redefinition of heroism as refusal in the civil rights and antiwar movements, the demilitarization of military heroism as a result of the Vietnam War, wherein survival or witness became as heroic as action, all these had extended the life of the existential hero through the early 1970s, after which many of my students were born. At about that time, traditional heroism was given a new twist by means of vehicles connected to medieval themes directly or indirectly. One of these was *Excalibur* itself, which, whatever groans it may elicit from professional medievalists, has an iconic status even today among younger enthusiasts of medievalist popular culture. Another was George Lucas's *Star Wars*, with its debt to medieval romance, on the one hand, and its quotation of World War II flyboy heroics on the other. Although not a medievalist theme, the enormously popular *Rambo* series rewrote heroism as both obedience to and defiance of authority, as a kind of tortured exorcism and reenactment of the right-wing theme, from Algeria to Vietnam, of betrayal of the military by politicians. In this reinvention, it is not heroism itself that is revised, as it was in the previous existentialist phase, but the contexts and services of heroism. This was an important change, for it portended yet another change in the nature of the cinematic hero, one that is surprisingly reconnected with medieval themes.

For by the late 1980s and through the present, the medieval haunts technology and is represented through it. The earliest computer games were variations on chess, itself a medievalist (as well as medieval) pursuit in its earliest history. With the advent of more power and visual capacity, computer games quickly adapted the motifs of such popular obsessions as "Dungeons and Dragons" and converted them into a panoply of Gothic fantasies. Drawing on the fascination with a westernized idea of "Oriental" heroism that equates the samurai with the medieval knight and drawing on the worldwide popularity of even poorly made kung fu movies, the medieval was fused with the oriental in a cultural appropriation that is familiar from the Romantic period (as in Raymond Schwab's book, *Oriental Renaissance*, with its account of the Romantic "discovery" of the Orient as equivalent to the Renaissance rediscovery of classical antiquity) but which has an even prior history. However fascinating these cultural lineages may be, their narrative and visual cinematic expression tended towards disturbing formulae: a stylized violence and a gamelike emphasis on repetition and recursion.

In this new Middle Ages, violence is removed from a moral context. It is framed or condemned or justified only by magical intervention, by leading to bad luck or a wrong turn. The gamelike mapping of the action hero's plot allows tests to happen again and again, allows the hero to stand up, dust off, and try again. The result is a suspension of moral judgment on the part of the viewer. The hero may or may not be on the right side; it is not that he consciously chooses evil, but that good and bad sides keep shifting valences, or, as in that archetypal medieval romance, *The X-Files*, all sides may be equally untrustworthy. Scholars who have been pointing to the centrality of the Grail myth to modern art and literature have a point: twenty-first-century heroism's starting point feels and looks like that of the Grail continuations, designed to question the chivalric heroism of high Arthurian romance, emphasizing the wastefulness and anarchic cycle of violence, which it must describe at length, and narrating a well-nigh impossible quest, which requires constant renarration and repetition. It is a world where, as in the subgenre of action hero movies, heroism devolves into an alternating cycle of masochism and sadism, of sacrifice as much as resistance.

Partly as a result of this shift, it becomes culturally possible to toggle the gender of the new medieval hero, who can just as easily now, and perhaps more easily, be a heroine, as long as the plot allows a passive subheroine somewhere else in the story as a retainer of traditional cultural values. None of this will seem new to traditional medieval and early modern scholars, who will be able to cite parallels from Chrétien through *The Faerie Queene*. Indeed, what the redefinition of heroism in contemporary cinema, partly enabled by medieval themes, teaches us, is that heroism is always being redefined in ironic ways because of its accidental and sacrificial nature, which the viewer can never be fully prepared for.

But the medieval film itself, while it alludes to the medievalism of the action hero, seems to the viewer and to my students to retrieve traditional heroism. *Braveheart* is a good example, partly for its intentions and partly for reasons of local culture. I teach at a campus which, when it was founded in the 1950s, chose the "Highlanders" as its logo and name, for reasons lost to history, given a semiarid climate and a research origin in citrus agriculture. For many years its symbolic mascot was a teddy bear dressed in a kilt. A few years ago this image was deemed too meek, and a New York consulting firm was brought in, the result of which was that the little bear was put on steroids, given a rabid face that would allow the park service to shoot on sight, and, of course, painted with *Braveheart*-style blue war paint. In fact, my present students remain as puzzled by these connections as I. But what my students did do was to Americanize the plot, to take it out of the frame of Scottish history and contemporary British politics and to read its heroism in American terms, as an individual rising to an occasion, throwing off an oppressor and sacrificing himself for a patriotic cause.

Mel Gibson's revision downward of Wallace's class background contributed to this. Gibson himself was born in the United States and went on to make *The Patriot*, which moves the scene of heroism to Revolutionary America, with a decidedly Jeffersonian narrative, so they may not have been far off. American students studying in Scotland at the same time, however, reported the adoption of *Braveheart* as the symbol of Scottish patriotism, which had to redefine itself in the context of a united Europe. The film's appearance coincided with the rise of local nationalisms against weakening European nation-states, as well as with the long tradition of Scottish separatism, which had been co-opted by a new regional autonomy. It became a commonplace to pair *Braveheart* and Danny Boyle's *Trainspotting* as national myth as opposed to national reality. I tried to suggest that *Braveheart* also reflected Gibson's Australian experience and described some of the remarkable Australian movies of the 1970s and 1980s, with their heroes pessimistically and resentfully opposing colonial and class slights, tyrannies and betrayals. But in general, my students' interpretation of the heroism of *Braveheart* fell into an Americanized narrative of self-motivation and self-creation, in which tragedy consists of the interruption of autonomy by fate.

One surprise in teaching the course was the interest on the part of students in what might be called spiritual heroism and their seriousness in approaching the religious dimensions of medieval movies. In fact, it dawned on me, again perhaps belatedly, that except for genre films explicitly on biblical themes, which more often mined the setting and characters rather than the theology, commercial cinema has never been able to deal in a full and complex way with religion. The great exception, however, is the medieval film. From Carl Theodor Dreyer's *The Passion of Joan of Arc* through Bergman's *Seventh Seal* through Roberto Rossellini's *The Flowers of St. Francis* through Suzanne Schiffman's *The Sorceress* and Chris Newby's *The Anchoress*, the Middle Ages becomes a setting in which spiritual states can be explored in a relatively uncontroversial arena. This neutrality contrasts strongly with the vitriolic reactions to, say, Pier Paolo Pasolini's or Martin Scorsese's lives of Christ or the controversy surrounding Jean-Luc Godard's *Je Vous Salve, Marie*, set in modern times. Time and again in my student reports, students observed that, for instance, the protagonists of Andrei Tarkovsky's *Andrei Rublev* or Dreyer's *Joan of Arc* were heroes or heroines through their spiritual travails. They were equally attuned to the anticlerical themes in, for instance, Sergei Eisenstein's *Alexander Nevsky* or the emphasis on action rather than contemplation in Luc Besson's *The Messenger: The Story of Joan of Arc*.

The nature of spiritual experience as represented on screen led to some interesting discussions. I had not planned on assigning the classic 1970s and 1980s texts which concerned the revival of interest in female spiritual experience, such as Julia Kristeva's essay on the language of the female mystics and Carolyn Walker Bynum's *Holy Feast and Holy Fast* and *Jesus as Mother*, but there was so much interest as the result of a brief discussion that I quickly put them on reserve.[2] Female students especially were interested in whether heroism could be defined in some way other than male activity, political, martial or aggressive, and could be understood as inward, passive (in the positive sense of the term), and transforming by example. But other students objected that this redefinition came close to essentializing femininity and celebrating a secondary role. These students noted, for instance, that a number of films set in the Middle Ages that we had reports on, such as Bergman's *The Virgin Spring* and Akira Kurosawa's *Rashomon*, depended on rape for the motivation of their plots.

The Kurosawa film also raised questions of racial and cultural difference, which I was not prepared to answer as fully as I would have liked, especially given the rich ethnic mix of my own campus, where nearly 40 percent of the students are of Asian descent and nearly a third are Latino. The concept of Japanese "feudalism," after all, depends on analogies with Western economy and society. What did the Middle Ages mean in Japanese historiography? And what about such "medieval" films as *Seven Samurai*? Of course, these films also partly derive from the very Westerns and other genres that they in turn influenced in the 1960s, but the question of cultural nostalgia and cultural origin became an important one, especially when we also considered Eisenstein's *Alexander Nevsky* (and *Ivan the Terrible*, which we did not screen or report on). I realized that I had understood these films in terms of their politics (postwar Japan and the symbolic place of the Meiji restoration, Stalinist Soviet Union) and not in terms of their national traditions. That is, I had understood these films as always already postmodern, but my students were interested in how they addressed historical tradition.

On the other hand, the interjection of cultural others in such films as Kevin Costner's *Robin Hood: Prince of Thieves* and the Beowulfian variations of John McTiernan's *The 13th Warrior* seemed hardly to require comment on the part of my students, whereas I thought of them as critical to postmodern orientalism and to the relation of heroism to advanced and refined civilization, in these cases represented by the Saracen other. Both films introduce appropriately aristocratic Saracen characters into their Western European medieval settings. Antonio Banderas takes the role in *The 13th Warrior* and Morgan Freeman in *Robin Hood: Prince of Thieves*.

From the left: King Arthur (Graham Chapman) with his knights (Eric Idle, Michael Palin, Terry Jones, and John Cleese; Terry Gilliam- in front) in *Monty Python and the Holy Grail* (1975).

What is interesting about these themes and my students' reaction to them is that in the 1970s, when popular medievalism first articulated itself, it had about it an air of white nostalgia, an attempt to escape to a fundamental European past, which in North America could comfortably include Celtic medievalism as part and parcel of whiteness. My present students did not register this at all and in fact were puzzled as to why I thought that Gil Junger's *Black Knight* was such an interesting concept and had been disappointed that it had not worked, largely because, I thought, the critical relation between past and present that informs the best Connecticut Yankee genre of movies was missing.

Once removed from the world of the medieval film's action, however, students can become perceptively critical of movies that attempt medieval nostalgia. Their perspective is shaped by an unlikely mirror: *Monty Python and the Holy Grail.* Almost as ubiquitous as *Excalibur* in the students' frame of reference, Terry Jones's film allows them simultaneously to enjoy and to jeer at the pretensions of medieval nostalgia. This is no accident—Jones's fiercely antiaristocratic demolition in his book, *Chaucer's Knight: Portrait of a Mercenary,* in fact underlies the com-

Ibn Fadlan (Antonio Banderas) armed for battle in *The 13th Warrior* (1999).

edy of *Monty Python and the Holy Grail.*[3] Again, American students are frequently at something of a loss to decode a humor based on class, region, and a claim to tradition, but they instinctively understand the film's anarchic attack on social illusions. Indeed, as with *Braveheart*, they tend to Americanize its Middle Ages, reading the film as an update of *A Connecticut Yankee in King Arthur's Court*, which they also paradoxically enjoy for both its medievalism and its antimedievalism.

My professorial conservatism was stronger when I began the course than when it ended, and I learned from my students that important conclusions could be drawn from what I had dismissed as slight material. Television programming was one good example. This was a generation that had grown up on *Xena: Warrior Princess*. They loved—but knew to be a fabrication—the conglomeration of prehistoric, classical, and medieval and characters, scenes, references, and settings in the series. That is, in the same way that the structure of the computer game inculcated a suspension of moral belief, the television show inculcated a willing suspension of historical belief. While the series consciously alluded to (as did Roland Emmerich's *Stargate*, which in its film version distributed publicity about the scientific accuracy of its linguistic codes) New Age mystification of certain historical periods and the possibility of the permeability of time, my students had grown up recently enough to regard such beliefs as a trifle dated and comical. That is, although students felt themselves possessed of some arcane trivia as a result of these series (which spent a surprising amount of development time on historical research), they were sufficiently aware of the distinction between a postmodern pastiche of historical moments on the one hand and a philologically and archaeologically correct Middle Ages on the other.

What does such a broad course on the medieval hero on film teach, finally, about the nature of heroism? Despite my emphasis on the unique vision of individual directors, the surveylike nature of such a course leads to a certain stereotyping of heroism, in the sense of a catalogue or cookbook or taxonomy of heroism. Yet such stereotyping can be read in very different ways. My students implicitly (if not explicitly) understood the heavily Jungian bias of many medieval heroic films, many of them influenced by Joseph Campbell's *The Hero with a Thousand Faces*. The similar sequences of so many heroic narratives set in the Middle Ages reinforced, for my students, a profoundly essentialist notion of heroism.

As someone who has lived through the postmodern intellectual revolution, I inevitably assume that heroism is constructed in certain ways and shaped towards certain ends: heroism is a rhetoric and the medievalism that surrounds heroism is part of that rhetoric, inventing an authorizing tradition for a very historically specific notion of what a hero is. The 1960s rewrote heroism as a form of witness and refusal as much as a form of action and rescue, and while the screen action hero and the screen medieval hero of the past three decades have accommodated that new awareness, they do so only as part of a narrative that inevitably retrieves an older form of heroism, one that postwar reactions, such as that of the Lost Generation after World War I, cinema noir after World War II, and the redefinition of masculinity after the Vietnam War had framed as futile, absurd, or contradictory. The appeal of the medieval heroic film depends, finally, on nostalgia for a transhistorical heroism purged of the compromises of modernity even as it builds those compromises into the Middle Ages it purports to recreate. Students respond instinctively to the idealism of the medieval film hero. They react more slowly to a critique of that idealism, and leading them to an awareness of that critique is ultimately the challenge of teaching the medieval heroic film.

Notes

1. Umberto Eco, "Dreaming of the Middle Ages," in *Travels in Hyperreality*, tr. William Weaver (San Diego, CA: Harcourt Brace Jovanovich, 1986).
2. Carolyn Walker Bynum, *Holy Feast and Holy Fast: The Religious Significance of Food to Medieval Women* (Berkeley, CA: University of California Press, 1987)

and *Jesus as Mother: Studies in the Spirituality of the High Middle Ages* (Berkeley, CA: University of California Press, 1982).

   3. Terry Jones, *Chaucer's Knight: Portrait of a Mercenary* (Baton Rouge, LA: Louisiana State University Press, 1980).

Works Cited

Barbour, John. *Barbour's Bruce*, ed. Matthew P. McDiarmid and James A.C. Stevenson. Edinburgh: Scottish Text Society, 1980.

Biddick, Kathleen. *The Shock of Medievalism*. Durham, NC: Duke University Press, 1998.

Bloch, R. Howard and Stephen Nichols, eds. *Medievalism and the Modernist Temper*. Baltimore: Johns Hopkins University Press, 1996.

Burns, E. Jane. "Nostalgia Isn't What It Used to Be: The Middle Ages in Literature and Film." In: *Shadows of the Magic Lamp, Fantasy and Science Fiction in Film*, ed. George Slusser and Eric S. Rabkin. Carbondale: Southern Illinois University Press, 1985.

Bynum, Carolyn Walker, *Holy Feast and Holy Fast: The Religious Significance of Food to Medieval Women*. Berkeley, CA: University of California Press, 1987.

_____. *Jesus as Mother: Studies in the Spirituality of the High Middle Ages*. Berkeley, CA: University of California Press, 1982.

Campbell, Joseph. *The Hero with a Thousand Faces*. New York: Pantheon, 1953.

Chandler, Alice. *A Dream of Order*. Lincoln: University of Nebraska Press, 1970.

Chrétien de Troyes. *Arthurian Romances*, tr. W.W. Comfort. London: Dent, 1968.

Dakyns, Janine. *The Middle Ages in French Literature 1851–1900*. London: Oxford University Press, 1973.

Dinshaw, Carolyn. *Getting Medieval*. Durham, NC: Duke University Press, 1999.

Eco, Umberto. *Travels in Hyperreality*, tr. William Weaver. New York: Harcourt Brace, 1986.

Ellis, Steve. *Chaucer at Large: The Poet in the Modern Imagination*. Minneapolis, MN: University of Minnesota Press, 2000.

Emery, Elizabeth. *Romancing the Cathedral: Gothic Architecture in Fin-de-Siècle French Culture*. Albany: State University of New York Press, 2001.

Frantzen, Allen. *The Desire for Origins*. New Brunswick, NJ: Rutgers University Press, 1990.

Harty, Kevin J. *King Arthur on Film: New Essays on Arthurian Cinema*. Jefferson, NC: McFarland, 1999.

_____. *The Reel Middle Ages: American, Western and Eastern European, Middle Eastern and Asian Films about Medieval Europe*. Jefferson, NC: McFarland, 1999.

Isaksson, Ulla. *The Virgin Spring*, tr. Lars Malmstrom and David Kushner. New York: Ballantine, 1960.

Jones, Terry. *Chaucer's Knight: Portrait of a Mercenary*. Baton Rouge, LA: Louisiana State University Press, 1980.

Kristeva, Julia and Catherine Clément. *The Feminine and the Sacred*, tr. Jane Mane Todd. New York: Columbia University Press, 2001.

Lindley, Arthur. "The Ahistoricism of Medieval film." Available at http://www.latrobe.edu.au/www/screeningthepast/firstrelease/fir598/ALfr3a.htm.

Malory, Thomas. *The Works of Sir Thomas Malory*, ed. Eugene Vinaver. Oxford: Clarendon, 1948.

Matthews, David. *The Making of Middle English*. Minneapolis: University of Minnesota Press, 1999.

Moir, James, ed. *The actis and deidis of the illustere and vaiłðeand campioun Schir William Wallace, Knicht of Ellerslie, by Henry the Minstrel, commonly known as blind Harry*. Scottish Text Society Publications, nos. 6, 7, 17. Edinburgh: Blackwood, 1889.

Peacock, Richard Beck. *The Art of Moviemaking: Script to Screen*. Upper Saddle River, NJ: Prentice Hall, 2001.

Rubey, Dan. "Star Wars: "Not So Long Ago, Not So Far Away." In: *Jump Cut: Hollywood, Politics, and Counter-Cinema*, ed. Peter Steven. New York: Praeger Special Studies, 1985, pp. 83–10.

Schwab, Raymond. *The Oriental Renaissance: Europe's Rediscovery of India and the East, 1680–1880*, tr. Gene Patterson-Black and Victor Reinking. New York: Columbia University Press, 1984.

Simmons, Clare A. *Reversing the Conquest : History and Myth in Nineteenth-Century British Literature*. New Brunswick, NJ: Rutgers University Press, 1990.

Trigg, Stephanie. *Congenial Souls: Reading Chaucer from Medieval to Postmodern*. Minneapolis: University of Minnesota Press, 2002.

Umland, Rebecca A., and Samuel J. Umland. *The Use of Arthurian Legend in Hollywood Film*. Westport, CT: Greenwood/Contributions to the Study of Popular Culture 57, 1996.

Williams, David John. "Looking at the Middle Ages in the Cinema: An Overview." *Film and History* 29.1-2 (1999): 8–19.

Williams, Linda. "Eric Rohmer and the Holy Grail," *Literature/Film Quarterly*: 11 (April 1983): 71–82.

Filmography

1928 *La Passion de Jeanne d'Arc (The Passion of Joan of Arc)*, d. Carl Theodor Dreyer, with Renée Falconetti, Antonin Artaud. France: Société Générale des Films.

1938 *Alexander Nevsky*, d. Sergei Eisenstein, with Nikolai Cherkasov. USSR: Mosfilm.

1943 *Ivan the Terrible, Part One*, d. Sergei Eisenstein, with Nikolai Cherkasov. USSR: Mosfilm.

1946 *Ivan the Terrible, Part Two*, d. Sergei Eisenstein, with Nikolai Cherkasov. USSR: Mosfilm.

1950 *The Flowers of Saint Francis*. d. Roberto Rosellini, with Aldo Fabrizi, Monks of Nocere Inferiore. Italy: Cineriz.

Rashomon, d. Akira Kurosawa, with Toshiro Mifune. Japan: Daiei Motion Picture Co.

1954 *Seven Samurai*, d. Akira Kurosawa, with Toshiro Mifune. Japan: Toho.

1957 *The Seventh Seal*, d. Ingmar Bergman, with Max Von Sydow. Sweden: Svensk Filmindustri.

1960 *The Virgin Spring*, d. Ingmar Bergman, with Max Von Sydow, Brigitta Valberg. Sweden: Svensk Filmindustri.

1966 *Andrei Rublev*, d. Andrei Tarkovsky, with Anatoli Solonitsyn. USSR: Mosfilm.
1974 *Lancelot du Lac*, d. Robert Bresson, with Luc Simon, Laura Duke Condominas. France: Compagnie Française de Distribution Cinématographique (CFDC).
1975 *Monty Python and the Holy Grail*, d. Terry Gilliam and Terry Jones, with Terry Jones, Terry Gilliam, Graham Chapman, John Cleese, Eric Idle, Michael Palin. U.K.: Python (Monty) Pictures Limited.
1977 *Star Wars*, d. George Lucas, with Mark Hamill, Harrison Ford, Carrie Fisher. U.S.: 20th Century–Fox.
1978 *Perceval le Gallois*, d. Eric Rohmer, with Fabrice Lucchini. France: Gaumont.
1981 *Excalibur*, d. John Boorman, with Nichol Williamson. U.S.: Orion.
1982 *First Blood*, d. Ted Kotcheff, with Sylvester Stallone. U.S.: Caralco Pictures.
1985 *Je Vous Salve, Marie*. d. Jean-Luc Godard, with Myriem Roussel. U.K.: Channel Four Films.
1987 *The Sorceress*, d. Suzanne Schiffman, with Christine Boisson. France: Bleu Productions.
1991 *Robin Hood: Prince of Thieves*, d. Kevin Reynolds, with Kevin Costner, Morgan Freeman. U.S.: Warner Bros.
1993 *The Anchoress*, d. Chris Newby, with Natalie Morse. U.K.: British Film Institute.
1994 *Stargate*, d. Roland Emmerich, with James Spader. U.S./France: Centropolis Entertainment.
1995 *Braveheart*, d. Mel Gibson, with Mel Gibson. U.S.: Icon Productions, Ladd, 20th Century–Fox.
1996 *Trainspotting*, d. Danny Boyle, with Ewan McGregor. U.K.: Channel Four Films.
1999 *The 13th Warrior*, d. John McTiernan, with Antonio Banderas. U.S.: Touchstone Pictures.
The Messenger: The Story of Joan of Arc, d. Luc Besson, with Milla Jovovich, John Malkovich. France: Gaumont.
2000 *The Patriot*, d. Roland Emmerich, with Mel Gibson. U.S.: Centropolis Entertainment.
2001 *Black Knight*, d. Gil Junger, with Martin Lawrence. U.S.: 20th Century–Fox.
The Lord of the Rings: The Fellowship of the Ring, d. Peter Jackson, with Elijah Wood, Ian McKellen, Viggo Mortensen, Cate Blanchett. New Zealand/U.S.: New Line Cinema.

Notes on Contributors

Edward Benson teaches French and film at the University of Connecticut at Storrs. He is the author of *Money and Magic in Montaigne: The Historicity of the Essais* (Droz, 1995). He has also written a series of articles on the representation of history on film in such journals as *Film & History*, *Film Criticism*, *Literature/Film Quarterly*, and the *Radical History Review*.

Anke Bernau, a lecturer in medieval literature and culture at the University of Manchester (UK), specializes in medieval sexualities and foundation myths. She has been a speaker at various international conferences including the International Medieval Congress and has published articles in several collections on medieval women. She recently co-edited a collection of essays entitled *Medieval Virginities* with Ruth Evans and Sarah Salih (University of Wales Press, 2003).

Martha W. Driver is distinguished professor of English at Pace University in New York. In addition to publishing many articles, she has edited ten journals in seven years, including two numbers of *Film & History: Medieval Period in Film*, and with Deborah McGrady, a special issue of *Literary & Linguistic Computing*, "Teaching the Middle Ages with Technology" (1999). Her book *The Image in Print* about fifteenth-century English text and illustration is forthcoming from British Library Publications in fall 2004.

John M. Ganim is professor of English at the University of California, Riverside. He is the author of *Chaucerian Theatricality* (Princeton University Press, 1990) and *Style and Consciousness in Middle English Literature* (Princeton University Press, 1982) as well as many articles. His present research, for which he received a Guggenheim fellowship, is on the connections between medievalism and orientalism.

Carl James Grindley is assistant professor of English at the City University of New York. He has presented papers at over a dozen interna-

251

tional conferences and has just completed a book on Kurt Vonnegut. His on-video analysis of the uneasy relationship between Hollywood, text literacy and old books is titled "The Big Bad Book" and has been shown at Western Michigan University and at Pace University.

Kevin J. Harty, professor and chair of English at La Salle University in Philadelphia, has published extensively on cinematic representations of the medieval. He is the author or editor of ten books, including most recently *Cinema Arthuriana: Twenty Essays* (McFarland, 2002). His next book, *Joan of Arc and Robin Hood on Screen: Reel Lives, Hidden Agendas*, will be published by McFarland in 2004.

Tom Henthorne teaches English and women's and gender studies at Pace University in New York. He is currently working on a book-length study of Joseph Conrad. His recent work has appeared in *Conradiana*, *Studies in Popular Culture*, and *The Midwest Quarterly*.

Caroline Jewers is associate professor of French at the University of Kansas in Lawrence. She is the author of *Chivalric Fiction and the History of the Novel* (University of Florida Press, 2000). She has published articles in *The Journal of Popular Culture*, *Speculum*, *Arthuriana*, *Tenso*, *Exemplaria*, and *Neophilologus*. She is a self-confessed film fanatic.

Sid Ray is associate professor of English at Pace University in New York. She has published articles in *Shakespeare Quarterly*, *Film & History*, and in several collections on gender in the early modern period. Her book *Holy Estates: Marriage and Monarchy in Shakespeare and His Contemporaries* is forthcoming from Susquehanna University Press in 2004.

Jonathan Rosenbaum is the film critic for the *Chicago Reader* and author of *Moving Places* (1980), *Film: The Front Line* (1983), *Greed* (1993), *Placing Movies* (1995), *Movies as Politics* (1997), *Dead Man* (2000), *Movie Wars* (2000), and *Essential Cinema* (2004), and the coauthor of *Midnight Movies* (with J. Hoberman, 1983) and *Abbas Kiarostami* (with Mehrnaz Saeed-Vafa, 2003). He is also the editor of *This Is Orson Welles* (1993) and the coeditor of *Movie Mutations* (with Adrian Martin, 2003).

Susan Butvin Sainato recently completed her Ph.D. at Kent State University, where she is currently assistant professor. She has published several articles, including "The Final Encyclopedia: Gordon R. Dickson's Creative Universe" in *Extrapolation: A Journal of Science Fiction and Fantasy*.

David Salo is a graduate student in linguistics at the University of Wisconsin–Madison and an expert in Quenya and Sindarin, languages created by J.R.R. Tolkien. He has served as linguistic advisor to the recent *Lord of the Rings* films.

Diana E. Slampyak is a lecturer at the University of New Mexico. She recently completed her Ph.D. on memory and translation in medieval English romances. In addition to hosting a weekly radio program, she writes music and film reviews for on-line magazines and acts and directs theater or film whenever she can.

Michael A. Torregrossa is a graduate student in English at the University of Connecticut at Storrs. His published work includes essays on both Arthurian film and Arthurian comics, a filmography on Merlin, a bibliography of Arthurian comic books, and entries in recent supplements to the *New Arthurian Encyclopedia*. He has presented papers on the Arthurian tradition at regional, national, and international conferences.

William F. Woods is professor of English at Wichita State University, where he teaches classical and medieval literature. His most recent publications have appeared in *The Chaucer Review* and in *Studies in Medieval and Renaissance Teaching*.

Index

Numbers in *italics* indicate photographs.